From my heart
to yours!

 Heather Meadows

D1418014

An Inspiring Story of Changing Painful to Powerful

Transforming
Tragedy

Heather Meadows

Copyright ©2018 by Heather Meadows

All rights reserved. For use of any part of this publication, whether reproduced, transmitted in any form or by any means, electronic, mechanical, photocopying, recording, or otherwise, or stored in a retrieval system, without the prior consent of the publisher, is an infringement of copyright law and is forbidden.

The author shall have neither liability nor responsibility to any person or entity with respect to loss, damage, or injury caused or alleged to be caused directly or indirectly by the information contained in this book. The information presented herein is in no way intended as a substitute for counseling and other forms of professional guidance.

For further information about speaking engagements, special bulk pricing, or other related inquiries, see the author's website at www.heathermeadows.com.

Scripture quotations marked (NKJV) are taken from the New King James Version®. Copyright © 1982 by Thomas Nelson. Used by permission. All rights reserved.

Scripture quotations marked (NIV) are taken from the Holy Bible, New International Version®, NIV®. Copyright © 1973, 1978, 1984, 2011 by Biblica, Inc.™ Used by permission of Zondervan. All rights reserved worldwide. www.zondervan.com. The "NIV" and "New International Version" are trademarks registered in the United States Patent and Trademark Office by Biblica, Inc.™

Scripture quotations marked (ESV) are from The ESV® Bible (The Holy Bible, English Standard Version®), copyright © 2001 by Crossway, a publishing ministry of Good News Publishers. Used by permission. All rights reserved.

Scripture quotations marked (NLT) are taken from the Holy Bible, New Living Translation, copyright ©1996, 2004, 2015 by Tyndale House Foundation. Used by permission of Tyndale House Publishers, Inc., Carol Stream, Illinois 60188. All rights reserved.

Cover Photo: Mallory Billups
Cover and Interior Design: Sara Mankin
Editor: Kim Foster

Print ISBN: 978-1-7326349-2-3

First Printing 2018
Printed in the United States of America
Published by Heather Meadows LLC

To Jon—

Thank you for taking me on all your

greatest adventures and grandest journeys.

Until I see you again, I'll forever carry you along in mine.

Contents

Welcome

"Heather, you have forgotten," Mom said as I styled her hair.

Mom never cared too much about the feminine intricacies of makeup, wardrobe, or tidy hairdos. She held to the quick-and-easy approach, which is why she kept it short. However, Mom wanted to look her best when she left that day for New York City. So she called asking if I'd fix her hair. It didn't present any type of inconvenience, considering she lived less than a quarter mile down the road.

"What do you mean I've forgotten?" I asked.

"I mean you have forgotten. I've listened to you speak for years now. At first, I thought you were just leaving out pieces of the story, but over time I realized you really have forgotten."

I guess I'll find out. If I were going to forget something, I figured I would've worked to forget details of the accident that happened five weeks to the day after my seventh birthday. Perhaps I would have shut down the recollections of my body burning and being pulled out of the fire. It would have been nice to forget the excruciating bandage changes or being braced in a hospital bed, unable to move and speak. There is so much I *have* remembered. How could there possibly be more?

Sure enough, I soon discovered Mom was right. Despite how much I had recalled, I had blocked out dark details of my life's story. She was trying to warn me. Trying to prepare me for the pain and turmoil I had apparently stuffed in a compartment, closed the lid, and locked. Mom's words were the key. The key to unlocking images my mind had closed its eye to seeing. They weren't specifics I intended to forget. I didn't have to work at *not* remembering. I simply just *hadn't* remembered. Not until I read Mom's memories—the memories I asked her to write for me so I could tell my story.

Because this book is a memoir, it certainly suggests I wrote it for me. But I didn't. Although that's what many have assumed, saying it'd be healing or cathartic.

It wasn't.

Unpacking what I would have rather kept inside the compartment I had securely locked was a brutally painful process. Writing this for me alone would not have been enough. I had to write this for someone, for someone needing to see a real-life illustration of a heart-wrenching tragedy transformed into something good. I had to write this book for those individuals struggling to believe the heartache they are confronting could possibly get better.

However, let's just put it out there. No one cares about a normal run-of-the-mill girl living out in a pasture on family land in Oklahoma; a girl who hasn't established a name, an importance or a fan base; a girl who hasn't roped in accomplishments, such as founding a stellar nonprofit or developing a groundbreaking business strategy.

The only reason anyone would consider picking up this book is because, while we know it's not right, we *do* judge books by their covers. Maybe this one caught your eye, or perhaps the title sparked some interest. The fact of the matter is people don't care about my journey as much as they care about how it's going to relate to their journey. Which is why *this* is the book for you!

This memoir doesn't merely contain the story of my life but a *message* for yours—a message of persevering through life's painful places and overcoming life's darkest moments. It's a message for imperfect families hurting from hang-ups, for empty marriages reevaluating commitments, for tired health-care workers questioning contributions. It's a message for survivors redefining beauty, for unsettled individuals exploring new possibilities; it's for insecure teens seeking approval and the bullied student finding courage. It's a message the world needs of hope, encouragement, optimism, strength, faith, perseverance and victory.

We're drawn to hard stories with happy endings. Stories that prove there is hope beyond today. This is my story of hope. Hope to not merely *live* but to one day live *alive* again, with no chance of life ever being the same. Hope to confront the desperate wish to change one moment from ever happening. Hope to embrace the tragedy of what took place and accept the scars that serve as its lifelong reminder.

Hope helped me let go of longing to be restored to how I was before the accident. Hope helped me reach for new goals and open my hand to grasp for what life could be beyond the accident.

Those big challenges early in life established the foundation of strength that has carried me through my life. I gained assurance for brighter tomorrows in the midst of life's lowest places. The fight of adversity developed valuable lessons, insurmountable strength, and persevering optimism.

The path established a realization that my attitude had a greater influence on determining my life than what actually happened in life. Life wasn't fair, pleasant or kind, but employing a positive reaction created a spark igniting positive thoughts, events, and outcomes from even the hardest challenges. What happened to me wouldn't determine who I would be. That part was within my control. The difficulties were a catalyst creating extraordinary results.

Every individual knows the darkness of challenging circumstances. It could be despair from a dream never fulfilled; grief from broken relationships or lost loved ones; depression from a diagnosis, disappointment or layoff. The scenery changes on the pages of each life. Every person encounters hardship and pain. What we all want to know is how we'll get through it.

While you read through the pages of my journey, I aim for you to be so connected with my words you feel as if you're having a cup of coffee at my kitchen table or a glass of wine on my back patio. I'm inviting you in to see the hardest places of tragedy—the raw wounds of a body, soul, and family learning to live again. Allow me to unpack the pieces of how we got through it, and how we came out changed, transformed, and stronger on the other side.

1

Country Beginnings

Oklahoma. Where you can find a classic musical and every element of a good country song, like pickup trucks, football, and family. Memories made at the lake range from boating and competitive fishing to family fish-fries. Deer, ducks and doves are hunted; tornadoes are expected in the spring; and farming involves either crops or cattle or both. A good steak isn't hard to find. And oil and gas are hot topics of the state's economy. However, the people are the crown of Oklahoma. Friendliness and strength are attributes of its culture.

My roots are deep in Oklahoma.

The Second World War brought together an Oklahoma guy and a British girl. Eighteen months after my dad's birth, when the war was over, he set sail with his mother on the Queen Mary to join his father and grow his roots in Oklahoma.

My Oklahoma heritage was even stronger on my mom's side. Mom's paternal grandma, whom we called Little Grandma Ward because of her four-foot-five stature, came to Oklahoma shortly after statehood in 1908. Her family brought her and her twelve siblings across the plains in a covered wagon.

In 1951, my mom's maternal grandparents, Lonnie and Minnie Creekmore, illustrated the spirit of hard work and vision as they purchased their own land to farm when they were fifty-four years old. Lonnie was like many children of his time, completing his education only through the fifth grade in order that he could work, contributing to the needs of his family. He married Minnie Edwards in 1919 and began a family shortly thereafter. The one hundred and sixty acres they purchased, farmed and made home would be the place my grandma called home and the place my mom and dad would build a home to raise a family.

Oklahoma historian Bob Blackburn shared his thoughts regarding the original spirit of Oklahomans from the 1889 Land Run in the documentary, *The Boom, The Bust, and The Bomb:* "One of the benefits of immigration in any community is those kids have to fight a little harder than anybody in their generation. By the time they get to production, they're battle tested, they're ready to go fight and they're not going to be put down by a couple of defeats 'cause they've been defeated so often they're gonna keep trying."[1]

This land and the legacy it carries cultivated pride in where I came from, strength from my roots, and a sense of inherited resiliency. They were essential components in the days to come.

• • • • • • •

Susan Ward and Mike Cochrane didn't have much in common back in 1973. Nothing more than the business communications class they were taking at Northeastern State University (NSU).

My dad sat in the back of the class with several guys who, like him, were older students attending college on the GI Bill. The bill was signed into law as the Serviceman's Readjustment Act in the spring of 1944 by President Franklin D. Roosevelt and was extended several times over, providing benefits for returning veterans—funding for college being one.[2]

Dad had nearly finished his senior year of high school when he determined there were other options for his life that would be better than living in the volatile environment he had with his father. Dad was seventeen years old when he dropped out and signed up for the Navy. He lied about his age the day he entered the recruitment office; however, by the time documents were required, he had turned eighteen and was off serving in the military during the Vietnam War. He was stationed in San Diego and Guam over his years of service from 1962 to 1965, never having to encounter the war zone so many of his generation faced.

An officer took compassionately to my dad, being one of the first people who acknowledged his potential, his intellect and his drive. Frank conversations with this leader motivated Dad to pursue an education after the Navy.

Upon honorable discharge after completing his three years of service, Dad returned home, took a job and attended school to complete his final credits for his high school diploma.

In 1970, he began his journey toward a college degree and was admitted to Oklahoma Military Academy. OMA, referred to as "The West Point of the Southwest," contributes an interesting piece to Oklahoma's history. The state-sponsored military school opened in the fall of 1919 in Claremore, just about thirty minutes outside of Tulsa. By 1923, cadets could attend four years of high school and two years of college. Despite the academy's attributes, enrollment by the 1960s declined as anti-Vietnam War sentiment grew, leading legislators to close the school in 1971. The campus began offering classes the next month as Claremore Community College, changing to Rogers State College in 1982, and later becoming Rogers State University.[3]

Dad completed his associate's degree at the newly named Claremore Community College before transferring to NSU in Tahlequah, Oklahoma. He wasn't the typical college student on campus—twenty-nine years old; divorced from his first wife with whom he shared his three-year-old son, Barry; working full time at night and making the two-hour round-trip commute from Tulsa to Tahlequah for classes. His life looked quite different from that of the twenty-one-year-old girl coming in late to the business communications class that fall of 1973.

My mom was as typical a college student as my dad wasn't. She lived in the dorms on campus, funded her education through student loans and a work-study program, and maintained an active social life attending parties and visiting a bar near campus cleverly named *The Library*. Parents calling to speak to their children imagined their kids studying hard when they were told, "Oh, she's not here. She's at the library."

While Mom soaked up the college social experiences, she balanced it with her commitment to class. She wasn't normally late, but a visit to the infirmary for an injury to her broken ring finger she had sustained playing flag football the night before took longer than expected. When she arrived to class, the seat she normally chose was already occupied, forcing her to migrate to the back of the room.

"That's a nice blouse," my dad said to her as she took a seat near him.

It was the seventies and even though there wasn't much difference in length between some shirts and the short dresses, Mom corrected him in a smirky tone: "It's not a blouse. It's a dress."

One would think it wouldn't have been a good start, or even considered a start at all. Nevertheless, it was. By the end of the next year on New Year's Eve 1974, Mom and Dad were married in a cozy ceremony with a few of their friends and family.

Dad walked across stage for the graduation ceremony in the spring of 1975 having achieved his goal of completing his bachelor of science in business administration. A move to Wichita, Kansas followed where they enjoyed the first years of their marriage, working and making friendships. However, after a return visit to Oklahoma for Grandpa Creekmore's funeral in 1978, Mom made a decision to move back.

Without considering whether he would agree with her decision, she stated, "I'm moving back to Oklahoma." Amusingly, she recalled Dad's response: "Well, can I come with you?" Within a month, they had left their jobs in Wichita and made a move to a place neither of them had ever lived in their lives.

The country.

Being in a rural area was new for both of them, who had grown up in neighborhoods, but they loved it. Even though they were living in a run-down trailer that leaked every time it rained, they appropriately described the joyous time as "hog heaven." And yes, I'm pretty sure their pun was intended!

Two years later in 1980, they moved into the home they had built on the exact spot where Grandpa Creekmore's barn once stood. Even more fitting, they built their two-story home in the shape of a barn. It was especially picture-perfect for their expanding family—one room for Barry, who lived with them part of the time, and one as a nursery for their thirteen-month-old baby boy, Jon.

• • • • • • •

The spring of 1981 wasn't so picture-perfect. Mom tells me I was the only good thing during that season. Both sides of my family were enduring difficult trials at the time. One of them had to do with our next-door neighbor.

My mom's mom, whom I simply called Grandma, lived right next door in the farmhouse her parents had lived in. Grandma was the most practical and frugal person I knew. And hard working. I watched her stand on her feet for hours on end in her beauty shop, intentional to save every dollar she could.

Grandma was the poster child for recycling. It was her method of operation long before public service announcements of *Reduce. Reuse. Recycle.* She embodied the slogan. The economical challenges at the time of her birth in 1922, coupled with her divorce from my grandfather in 1961 during a time when people didn't get divorced, created a mindset in her to save, save, save. She was quiet yet feisty, content yet determined, passive and yet strong.

Grandma was so frugal she didn't even have an automatic garage-door opener, leading to her unfortunate decision one day to stand in a wheelbarrow to close the door. The situation ended with her falling and breaking her hip, resulting in not one total hip replacement but two! An infection developed from the hardware, requiring it to be replaced. Grandma's wheelbarrow choice landed herself a setup for recovery in my parents' dining room. In consideration of other current events, it was not the best place to be.

After one failure-to-progress labor for my brother, Jon, twenty-six months earlier, my mom's physician decided my birth should be a scheduled repeat cesarean section. It was down for a Monday morning, March 23, 1981. And it was hardly a day of celebration. No one really had time. Dad worked in sales, and while it provided beautifully for our family financially, it required much travel. He was there for my birth and gone the next day.

Katherine, Mom's best friend and neighbor down the road, brought us home later in the week. Before Mom and I were discharged from the hospital, Jon was scheduled to have a myringotomy—a procedure for draining fluid from the eardrum.

Chronic ear infections had resulted in him having a 90-percent reduction in hearing. When the audiologist reported the information to Mom, he included a date for surgery. The doctor emphasized the procedure could not be delayed despite her schedule to have her baby the same date. So Mom, as she did, made it work by enlisting her aunts to take Jon.

Cancer also had a presence at the time. Dad's mom, my tall, red-headed British grandmother, whom I called Grandma Cochrane, was diagnosed with breast cancer and scheduled for a total mastectomy. And my Aunt Donna, Mom's sister, lost her husband a week later after his battle with leukemia.

There was much difficulty, challenge, sorrow and pain in the midst of my arrival. It's almost as if these were welcoming me, considering there was even more in store for my future.

• • • • • • •

It was a world of our own, growing up in the country. Grandma lived right next door, and on a whim I'd ask if I could stay the night with her. I'd grab my blanket (as I never ever left home without it), Mom would stand at our door and Grandma would stand at hers, both watching as I walked the ten yards between.

It took the most courage I could find to cross that driveway.

Even though my parents never allowed us to watch scary movies, I feared the coyotes I heard howling would snatch me up and eat me on that very short journey. Oh, the imaginations of children!

As much imagination as we had within us, we had in land around us. Jon and I would spend hours at the creek in our make-believe world, pretending our work moving sticks and rocks was noteworthy and valuable. We gave names to our projects and recruited others when they'd come to visit. We made mud pies, and like any typical older brother, Jon demanded I take a bite. We spent summers swimming in the pool in our backyard. We went on grand adventures climbing up into the tree house Dad built in Grandma's bald cypress. We dissected frogs, we played dress up, we sang, and we rode motorcycles.

Motorcycles were part of our world. I can't recall a memory before them.

I believe I was three when I got my first three-wheeler. It was yellow, and while I felt special as if it were just for me, it was actually a hand-me-down because Jon was moving up to the big leagues with a two-wheeler. His was blue. Even though I had my own, I rarely rode it. My spot was on the back of Jon's seat, my arms around his waist, with him in his big-brother manner deciding the way.

We rode that blue motorbike all over our family land, singing songs like

"She'll Be Coming 'Round the Mountain" or "I've Been Working on the Railroad." The world felt so big in the vast openness where we rode. It was the truest feeling of freedom and the closest sensation to flying, the wind blowing through our hair, riding where our imaginations could lead us.

Getting on our motorcycle was as normal to us as sitting down for dinner. It wasn't unusual for us to get off the bus, do our homework and chores, and then go ride. It was something we had done countless days before, but April 27, 1988, would be different.

2

The Dirt Road

Like many Americans, the television in our home was tuned in to see eighteen-month-old Baby Jessica pulled from the oil well in Midland, Texas. I remember watching. My six-year-old self could process enough to know it was a bad situation, but it felt far, far away. I sat on the stairs, carpeted with a popular eighties brown shag, looking at the television. Mom sat on the edge of the couch viewing with the intense sympathy of a mother. Somberly I thought, *I'm glad bad things don't happen here.* Six months later I would remember that very thought with an entirely different perspective.

Springtime in Oklahoma can be beautiful. Trees are blossoming, like the Bradford Pears bearing a pretty white bloom and the Oklahoma Redbuds producing rosy-purple flowers. The annual Azalea Festival attracts both locals and travelers to enjoy over thirty thousand azaleas.

As beautiful as Oklahoma may be, the weather can be equally as devastating. Severe thunderstorms, flooding, hail and tornadoes are common conditions anticipated in the spring. Homeowners invest in safe rooms and storm shelters for lifesaving protection, and tornado drills are practiced in every school for preparation.

The sun was shining on April 27th. The high was about seventy-five degrees. The winds were low. Hardly a breeze to rustle the leaves.

I sat beside my best friend, Sarah, in the front of the bus on the ride home after school. Jon always sat in the back with the big kids. No matter how close our relationship was at home, he wouldn't have sat with his little sister for a million bucks. There were images to maintain, even for kids. Plus, I didn't have the best reputation as a seat buddy. My struggle with motion sickness in the mornings deterred anyone from sitting with me on the trip to school.

Most mornings I threw up. It happened so frequently that the bus driver carried kitty litter to pour over it. Why we couldn't have carried a bucket is beyond me. Understandably, the kids didn't want to take any chances, but my best friend Sarah knew it was only a morning occurrence. Considering we were the third drop-off, she'd sit with me on the route home.

Jon and I got off the bus like any other day. Mom typically was home from work within the hour. We had our chores and homework to keep us busy, and Grandma was right next door. The list on the fridge reminded us what needed to be done.

Jon:

1. Feed and water pigmy goats and rabbits.
2. Do your homework.
3. Read 1 book.
4. Pick up your bedroom and make bed.

Heather:

1. Feed and water:
   a. Dogs
   b. Cats
   c. Tweedy Bird
2. Do your homework and read tomorrow's story.
3. Read 1 book.
4. Pick up your bedroom and make bed.

However, there had been a recent reduction to my list. In our mind, every creature would cohabit in the most peaceful environment. In reality... not so much. And I learned this early one morning.

Jon was first to see the yellow feathers scattered on the floor. Mom was trying her best to clean up the evidence while formulating the best way to tell me. When Jon discovered that our cat had indeed got Tweedy Bird, he quickly headed off to inform me.

Mom stopped him in his tracks. "Jon, I will tell her. Understand? Don't say anything. You let me tell her."

He was disappointed but agreed that he wouldn't *say* anything...

As soon as I walked downstairs, Jon grabbed my attention, took me into the kitchen facing the fridge where our chore chart hung. With a red pen in hand, he asked, "Heather, do you see this?"—pointing to *Tweedy Bird* written out under *feed and water.* "Well," he said as he put pen to paper marking it out, "you won't have to do this anymore!"

Oh, he was in trouble. So much trouble! But for him, like so many times before, it was totally worth it.

The chore charts were still relatively balanced, and we marked each item off rather quickly this April 27th, because we had plans.

It was expected for us to change out of our school clothes into play clothes when we got home. Mom knew how we played. School clothes wouldn't be in shape for school if we wore them for our typical outside-after-school activities. But even my desire to be outside with Jon was accompanied by a certain sense of fashion. Jelly shoes were all the rage in 1988, and I treasured every different-colored pair I had. Shorts, a T-shirt, my purple jelly shoes, and I was set to head out.

I'm not sure how the plan unfolded. Did Sarah and I get the idea rolling because we wanted to play after school? Or was Jon in the back of the bus talking about his motorcycle, setting a plan into motion to drive it over for his friends to see? However the idea came about, we both had every intention of doing something we had never done before—driving on the road and visiting friends a couple miles away.

The driveway beside our house wrapped around the back of Grandma's house, making a pull-through drive. Directly behind her house sat a small, yellow, barn-shaped shed. There were steps leading up to the shed and beside it, steps leading down to an underground storm shelter. The shed was no ordinary shed. Although it held common items like Weed-eater string, oil and gasoline, it was another area for our imaginations to roam. I'd sit on the steps reading to our goats, disappointed they were more interested in eating the pages of my book than hearing the stories I shared. Jon made it feel like a clubhouse by assembling a wooden sign to hang with the words written in red Sharpie marker: "Jon's Clubhouse." He made it feel like a privilege to be included, even though my name didn't make it on the sign.

I was *in* the club this particular day. Outside the small, yellow shed, I stood near as Jon lifted a can of gasoline to fill the motorcycle's tank for our adventure.

We ran our plan by Grandma, knowing she'd let us go. Grandma almost never said no. But she did this day. We raised the level of request to begging, pleading, and whining. We wore her down. She reluctantly agreed.

The feeling of independence was monumental. We weren't on the family land. We were driving on the road! We were going to see friends! For country kids who didn't have neighborhood kids to play with, the realization that we were going to our friends' houses was exhilarating.

We traveled down the road, took a left at the section line and journeyed around the curves crossing over the bridge of the turnpike. I felt apprehensive taking those bends in the road. I couldn't see around them. There was no way to know what was on the other side. Jon drove confidently, and I calmed myself knowing he was in control. I aimed to dismiss anxiety. It was familiar to me.

All my growing up I feared being injured in a car wreck. My mom driving up on hills I couldn't see over would scare me. I'd hear, "Heather, you're all right." None of my concerns ever manifested into what I was most afraid of; therefore, I pushed it to the back of my mind on our journey to see our friends that day.

Jon dropped me off at Sarah's house. Just past her house was the house of Jay and Angela, a brother and sister who rode our bus. Angela was in Mrs. Cox's second-grade class with Jon. He went down to their house for a visit, or rather, to show off his motorcycle. They went for rides around the yard. Before long, he came back to get me. I didn't want to leave. It seemed we had just got there. I wanted to play. Jon said it was time to go, but I wouldn't come. He went home, frustrated with my resistance to comply.

Mom heard the news of our travels when she arrived home from work. Grandma informed her Jon and I had gone up the road to visit a friend. Mom's heart sank. She didn't want us riding out on the road.

Before long, the front door opened. Jon yelled, "Mom!" The sound of his voice was a relief. *Thank God they're home*, she thought. She went outside to find him refilling the bike's tank.

"Heather wouldn't come home," he informed with much exasperation. "I told her it was time to go, but she wanted to stay."

Grandma had stepped outside to see what the commotion was all about.

"Put down the can. I will go in and call," Mom instructed.

It's a memory my mind suppressed. The phone call. It's understandable why I'd so naturally bury it. My opposition to oblige my big brother was an element in the magnitude and weight of what followed.

The phone rang at my friend's house. The call was for me.

Mom was on the other end of the line telling me it was time to leave, and to be ready and waiting, because she would be there to get me right away. However, as soon as she hung up the phone, Jon was on the motorcycle heading down the road, leaving to fulfill his mission of bringing me home. To no avail, Mom yelled for him to stop. But he never heard her voice over the roar of the motor. Grandma tried to offer some assurance, reminding Mom how my oldest brother, Barry, had been riding these dirt roads since he was Jon's age.

The road had just been graded. It was common for country dirt roads to be graded with a long blade, creating a flat surface in efforts to control the flow of water and fill in the ruts and potholes.

The weather was warm and the air was still. No hint of a breeze. The dust that stirred stood like fog on a humid summer morning. Without any wind to dissipate it, the particles of earth held together like thick clouds.

Jon passed our friends and neighbors on his drive back to get me.

Katherine, with her kids, Brad and Mary, was headed home at the end of the day from the store. She and her husband Mike owned a bait and tackle shop and gas station located on the highway at the end of 385th. Of course, back then roads didn't have signs, so their store was a landmark often referenced when giving directions. The house where I was playing was on that same road.

Katherine didn't recognize Jon when they passed. His hair was blown back from the speed of his journey. He was also farther from home than one would expect to see him. Brad, who was Jon's age, told his mom it was Jon they had just passed.

Jon arrived. Just as I had been instructed, I was ready and waiting to leave. I swung my legs over the bike as I had done numerous times before. I wrapped my arms around Jon's waist, and we headed back.

While we never experienced much traffic in the country, our ride did coincide with motorists returning home from work for the day. There was more traffic on that dirt road than there had been earlier.

We pulled out behind a small, red pickup truck. There was such an urgency to get home. We followed closely behind in the cloud of dust created by the truck. It was impossible to see. The dust burned our eyes.

Jon kept swerving to the left and the right to avoid the dust. I laid my left cheek against his back, trying to shield my eyes. On Jon's last swerve to the left, we were met with an oncoming truck. Worlds collided on that dirt road, marking devastation and tragedy in our lives.

Our bodies flew. A fire ignited.

3

Living a Nightmare

I was a thumb sucker. It was probably somewhat convenient for my parents. But more than seeing it as a convenience, they were truly grateful for the blessing of a baby with the ability to self-soothe in the middle of the night, during car rides or at family gatherings. Especially after having a baby just two years earlier who battled colic. After Jon, I was considered a very low-maintenance baby. So much so that Katherine's husband, Mike, jokingly questioned if my family really did have a baby. Mom said I was asleep every time he came down to see me. All I needed was my thumb and what we called my *rag*. I believe it had been a blanket at one time, but the cloth was so tattered and torn it wasn't anything more than a rag when I took to it.

Those habits are kind of cute for babies, and even toddlers. But not so much for seven-year-old little girls. By that time in my life, it was a bad habit.

Habits are hard to break. As much as I didn't want to suck my thumb, it was an automatic response.

When I started school, I made a conscious effort to refrain from thumb sucking in front of the other students. Even kindergarteners know it's babyish. But when I started riding the bus to school in first grade, I would huddle up close to the window and discreetly suck my thumb. I suppose it wasn't discreet enough, because Jon would let me know how embarrassing it was for him that I did it. Waking up in the morning was so hard. I still felt sleepy, and the motion of the bus made me nauseous. What was a girl to do?

I grew up on April 27th. Never again would I suck my thumb.

There I was within the flame, and I could see the blur from the waves of heat. My face felt so very hot. I never remember feeling like my body was on fire, but I do remember feeling the intense heat on my face.

The driver of the truck was my first hero. With unusual composure and calmness, I asked him, "Put out the fire. Please put out the fire." Using a blanket from his truck, he smothered the flames on my burning body.

Today's modern technology of cell phones was not a part of that era. The driver of the red truck in front of us continued driving, unaware of what was taking place in his dust. The only ones on the road were the driver who hit us, Jon and me. All alone, the man had to run to phone for help.

Adrian had nearly reached home before we collided. His driveway was approximately two hundred yards from the accident. He ran inside yelling to his brother, Jason, "I just hit two kids on a motorcycle. One of them is dead. Call an ambulance."

Jason instinctively felt he could be of more help having had some first responder training through his school's 4-H program. He was sixteen years old, running out to a setting most people live a lifetime without encountering.

As he ran upon the scene, he saw Jon's body covered with a blanket, and he came to me.

Confused, I asked, "Why did you run into us?" I had had my cheek against

Jon's back, trying to avoid the dust stinging my eyes. I knew we were swerving but didn't know we entered the wrong lane going the wrong direction. We both came out of nowhere. Adrian to us and us to him.

"I don't know, sweetie. I don't know what happened," Jason replied, holding my hand. He wasn't even certain who I was. At first, he thought I was a little boy who lived down the road from him.

My hair had burned just above my ears, and apart from scraps of cloth, I had no clothes to identify me other than what he noticed to be a small bit of my panty, the only indication as to who I was. Even the jelly shoes had melted to my feet.

At this point, a man driving a late sixties green Ford truck pulled up to the scene and rushed to help.

The fire was fierce.

Jon had just filled up the motorcycle's tank. And in the most unfavorable of circumstances, Adrian had also put gas in his truck, a dual-tank 1976 Ford. There was an abundance of fuel for this tragedy.

As the fire raged, Jason and the man moved me away from it. The memory has stayed with me of being grabbed under my arms and pulled away from the fire. Along with it is the comforting memory of someone holding my hand. I have lived my life not knowing the man's name but recalling the feeling of that hand with me.

Jason told the man he knew who we were and needed to get our mom. Jason had never driven a clutch; however, the inexperience didn't cross his mind as he jumped in to get Mom.

• • • • • • •

It was 5:20 p.m. I was supposed to be going to softball practice that Wednesday evening. Mom was making fried chicken for dinner, a meal she never prepared again.

She knew something was coming. As bizarre as it sounds, she knew something was going to happen, influenced by a conversation she and Jon had had just a few months earlier.

"I am not long for this world," Jon told her.

"What, Jon?" Mom asked.

He repeated his statement.

Was it something he heard or possibly read that he was merely repeating? Mom didn't think so. Still, she redirected him, saying, "Jon, you're going to live for a long time. For a long time." But she felt in her spirit God was preparing her for something. It seemed He had already prepared Jon.

Jason pulled in the driveway and honked his horn, petitioning Mom outside. As she walked to the door, she felt something say, *This is it.* Instinctively she grabbed her purse but refused to commit to the possibility of it being serious enough for shoes. She walked out the door in her house slippers.

Jason was instructing her, "Get in! There's been an accident!"

Mom could feel her heart pounding in her head. As they pulled away from our house, she started yelling, "It's not my kids!"

Jason would not answer. She continued yelling and yelling, "It's not my kids! It's not my kids!"

In the most desperate desire to avoid her inquiry but unable to do so, this sixteen-year-old young man was forced to answer, "Yes."

Making a fist, beating the dashboard, she pleaded to God, "Please let them be all right! Please, please let them be all right! *Please* let them be all right!"

They drove east down the road from our house, and when they turned north she could see smoke in the sky. Once more she begged, "Tell me if my kids are okay!"

He looked at her and said, "Your son is not alive."

Unable to comprehend the information, she thought, *This is a nightmare. This isn't really happening.*

At that moment, Jason said, "But your daughter is."

Mom's eyes beheld the horror of the scene. A white tarp draped over Jon, only his high-top Converse shoes showing. Falling to the ground she screamed out, "No, Jon! No, Jon!" To God she screamed, "No! This can't be happening!"

A state trooper's arm wrapped around her, lending his strength to walk her to his vehicle. Mom asked, "Where is my daughter?"

The paramedics hovering around my body obstructed Mom's view of me, but the trooper pointed in the direction, saying, "They're working on her."

He attempted to gather information, but Mom could not respond. She couldn't move and found it increasingly difficult to breathe.

I'll wake up soon and this will be over, she thought.

Mom received a supernatural touch in that inconceivable moment of tragedy. She recalled, "I felt God speak, 'It is done. Heather will be all right. She needs you.' At that moment I felt breath come through my body. No longer was I numb. God was right there. I could feel His presence and was able to begin responding to the trooper's questions."

• • • • • • •

Katherine was home, overhearing sirens in the background during her phone call with her husband, Mike. He was still at the store. The sound was unusual for country living. Their conversation finished quickly, and she made her next call. While she was speaking to her friend who lived down the road from their store, she heard those sirens again and asked about it. Her friend said there was a fire, and Katherine knew something was wrong.

Immediately she got in the car, leaving Brad and Mary at home. As she pulled up to the scene, she was met with a deputy trying to stop her. Katherine barreled through, not out of defiance but in a fog, almost unable to understand what they were saying to her. She had only one thought—*I have to get to my friend.*

Katherine approached Mom. Jon's body was covered. Steam rose from the tarp as they periodically hosed the area still hot with embers.

"How am I going to do it?" Mom asked.

"I don't know," Katherine replied, "but you're going to do it."

"Not that it really matters, but I think I left the stove on. Would you go check, and check on Mama?"

State trooper Gary Fears was the lead officer, orchestrating the team of emergency workers. He remembers loading me in the helicopter. Nearly three decades later, he recalled those moments: "I was amazed, actually, how calm you were. You weren't hysterical. You actually didn't even hardly cry. When we picked you up and put you on the sheet to put you on the gurney, you just kinda whined a little bit. To this day, I can feel that feeling when I picked you up, of your skin sliding from the burns in my hands."

Mom was instructed to ride with one of the state troopers to the hospital but felt God's favor at work as she was allowed to ride in the helicopter with me.

As she was getting ready to board, she looked behind one last time at Jon. Her body was weak, and she began to fall with her thought, *I can't leave Jon!* With what would be the start of countless interventions, the Holy Spirit spoke to her heart, "Look up!"

She looked up inside the helicopter and saw my hand reaching out to her. On our flight, Mom never let go of my hand.

"I want to go home," I said.

What was happening was scary, and in my childhood innocence, I simply thought that if I could just go home, then everything would be okay.

"We will," she answered. "But first we're going to the hospital and then we'll go home."

Mom apologized to the transport workers, knowing she was in their way. My color was starting to turn yellow, and Mom could tell they were doing everything to keep me alive. They reassured her with such kindness and gentleness, telling her she was fine and instructing her to keep talking to me. She did. Although I was displaying signs of hypovolemic shock, in and out of consciousness, Mom continued to talk and sing one of our familiar Sunday school songs, "Jesus Loves the Little Children."

Katherine went back to our house as Mom requested, and upon entering was hardly able to recall what to do when facing a potential grease fire. She was barely able to remember where anything was located in a kitchen she had known so well. She realized, *A lid, yes, a lid,* grabbing one to set over the black, cast-iron skillet, turning off the heat and using towels to carry it outside. She opened the windows to air out the house and then went next door to check on Grandma.

She joined Grandma in a programmed routine of folding towels, while they both attempted to grasp the tragedy happening. They occupied their hands in the face of the inconceivable.

They prayed.

They folded.

They prayed.

They began making phone calls to family with the tragic news. "Jon and Heather had an accident . . ."

4

A Battle Begins

Jon and I went to speech therapy twice a week for a portion of our school day.

Maybe I didn't know any better, but I counted it a privilege to have the school's speech therapist come to my class and call me out for my session. Felt like VIP treatment to me!

Jon had a speech impediment, or speech impairment. His was a type of communication disorder related to a speech sound disorder. *R* to be exact. He had experienced significant hearing impairment during a time when babies and toddlers are formulating language and speech skills. Jon misarticulated sounds because he couldn't fully hear them. His myringotomy and placement of tubes when I was born was the first step toward complete hearing restoration; however, as young as he was, he had already established his approach to communication. Something that would take a little more work to correct.

I, on the other hand, could hear fine. Perfectly fine. A completely irrelevant fact, because apparently the influence of language pattern modeled by those in my family who correctly pronounced and articulated sounds—Mom, Dad, Grandma and Barry—didn't matter. I patterned my speech after Jon. Even though I didn't have the slightest problem hearing the correct way to articulate sound, I instinctively articulated his.

So, we worked to learn the proper way together. We were healthy competition for each other, standing up on Grandma's couch to look in the large wall mirror, arguing over who pronounced their *R* better.

We did everything together. E-v-e-r-y-t-h-i-n-g.

Except this.

I was strolled into the burn center without him. I had no idea we were not facing *this* journey together.

• • • • • • •

A back hallway. Two doors with small windows at the top. A sign reading, "Do Not Enter. Staff Only."

Mom was instructed to go to the waiting room and wait for family to arrive. Within minutes a hurried doctor walked past. She started walking with him, asking if he had been called in for the case that came on Life Flight. He didn't acknowledge or respond but continued walking.

"That's my little girl back there."

He looked at her, nodded his head and proceeded through those do-not-enter doors. Mom was standing there looking through the window of those doors when a social worker came to ask her again to please sit down.

Sit? She couldn't sit. She proceeded back to the waiting room and was pacing the area when Dad turned the corner from getting off the elevator. Their eyes met, and they walked toward one another in the hallway.

"Where have you been?" Mom asked. It hadn't even been an hour since the accident happened, but time was moving so slowly. To Mom it felt like an eternity.

Dad was already in Tulsa where he worked at American Technical Institute when he received the call informing him of the accident. His brother, my Uncle Stoney, had a job at the same place, so they left together for the hospital. Only they didn't know which hospital we were at.

Mom worked in accounting at Saint Francis. Aunt Margie, Uncle Stoney's wife, also worked at Saint Francis in information services, and Grandma Cochrane, my dad's mom, worked there as a clinical secretary in the cardiac care unit. It's easy to see why when someone said "hospital," they all naturally thought Saint Francis.

But Saint Francis didn't have a burn center. The Alexander Burn Center at Hillcrest was the only burn center in our region and was the first in the state when it opened in 1968.

Dad and Uncle Stoney were rerouted, and upon arriving, Mom updated Dad.

"Why did they come here?" Dad asked.

"Because Heather has some burns, and this is the only burn center. She is in the back and the doctor is with her, but they're not allowing anyone in."

"Where's Jon?" he asked.

Not until that moment did Mom realize Dad did not know. Not until that moment did she have to state the horror of the nightmare they were living.

"He didn't make it." Mom herself could hardly understand the words she was speaking.

"What do you mean he didn't make it?"

"Jon is dead."

As the words fell from her mouth, she and Dad fell into one another's arms.

Ordinary places are often the settings for unimaginable moments. And sometimes, the most private pain has to be shown in public places. Mom and Dad opened the nearest door to escape the foot traffic of those coming off the elevator into the hallway. My five-foot-one mother and six-foot-four father held each other, sharing the weakest moment they had ever known, in the public men's restroom of the burn center.

It didn't take long for the waiting room to fill with our family and friends. Love and support poured out from that room. Our pastor, Dan Beller, and his wife, Marie, were two of those there on that dark night. Pastor Beller officiated my parents' wedding, just over thirteen years earlier. Now he would be the one to officiate their son's funeral.

Pastor Beller prayed for a miraculous intervention. He asked for peace and understanding. He requested God's hand to be upon our family and upon me. A decade later he used his experience from that night to illustrate his Mother's Day message. Mom's faith and declaration of "Heather will not die" were words he would never forget.

While she was resolved in her faith, her nature was drawing her to be with her child. Mom went back to those doors again. She was turned away again.

A moment later, unable to stand the separation, she returned once more.

"If we let you see your daughter, will you then step away from the door and go back with your family?" asked the social worker.

"Yes!" Mom answered. "Let me get my husband."

"No," replied the social worker, "only you."

Mom looked in each room as she walked down the hallway, hoping to find me. She and the social worker came upon a room full of doctors and nurses. As she entered, they all stepped away from the table where I was lying.

Mom gently rubbed my forehead and lifted my hand to her lips. "Everything is going to be okay. I can't stay, but we are just outside this room."

Then I asked my most important question. "Where's Jon?"

"He's in the next room."

"Is he okay?"

"Yes," she assured.

• • • • • • •

It was before shift change when we arrived at the hospital. All hands were involved as night shift came in and day shift was still working.

It was determined I had a third-degree burn injury covering 87 percent of my fifty-six-pound, seven-year-old body.

Third-degree burns are also known as full-thickness burns because the tissue is injured beneath the dermis. To visualize, it helps to think about skin in layers. The top layer is the epidermis, underneath is the dermis and under the dermis is subcutaneous tissue getting down into arteries, veins, nerves and muscle. Third-degree burns cause injury to the deepest part of the tissue.

Considering skin is the body's largest organ, many risks are presented when it is injured. The obvious being infection, since skin protects the body from foreign pathogens like bacteria. However, there are many more complications. Skin holds in necessary fluid. Burn injuries immediately cause excessive fluid loss leading to hypovolemia, decreased perfusion and metabolic acidosis.[1]

Hypovolemia means there is not enough blood circulating through the body, causing a decrease in the amount of blood being delivered to the patient's arms, hands, legs and feet. If the extremities are not getting enough blood (known as decreased perfusion) then organs may not be either. When the kidneys don't get enough blood, they don't work properly to rid the body of acid, so the body will become more acidic, known as metabolic acidosis.

But the burns were not the only threat.

A day shift nurse, Vicki, saw the image of the chest X-ray. "Her mediastinum looks large for a pediatric patient," she commented. She was right. The chest X-ray indicated internal injury from the image, reporting "fluid in the left pleural cavity, widening of the mediastinum, obliteration of the aortic arch and descending aorta."

A CT scan was obtained with consistent findings, stating, "Large left hemothorax, hemomediastinum with deviation of the ventricular to the right side and poorly defined aortic arch and descending aorta. Finding consistent with rupture of the aorta. Thoracic aortogram is recommended."

The last piece of information provided from the arteriogram confirmed that the efforts to save my life would require open-heart surgery. "Acute rupture of the intimal of the aortic arch just distal to the left subclavian artery where dissection is extending to the mid thoracic aorta."

Dr. George Cohlmia was the cardiovascular surgeon assigned the task of repairing the injury. His operative report captured the magnitude of the situation: "This patient has a traumatic transection of the descending thoracic aorta, and without surgery her chances of death are 85% to 95% or greater. With surgery her risk is increased because of the situation."

One doesn't need an anatomy lesson to gather the severity of the situation. It was critical. Those numbers, "85% to 95%" chance of death, were factored in with my chance of dying from the burn injury: 140%.

That was the figure reported to my parents.

That was the number they were praying against.

"She will not die." The faith of my mom was speaking in the face of medical diagnoses.

My parents, like many people, did not know how blood flows through the heart. The information wasn't relevant until that night. Nevertheless, whatever explanation offered could not pervade their wall of complete emotional shock.

They knew I was dying, and they wanted anything to save me. The risk of death was apparent. The risk of paraplegia was too because of decreased peripheral perfusion. If blood can't make it to an area of the body delivering the nutrient of oxygen and removing the waste of carbon dioxide, then tissue dies. The descending aorta is the road blood takes to get to those extremities.

Blood flow travels a path through the heart, like taking the same road to work, then taking a different route home but still repeating the same path every single day. Roads marked "artery" start with an "a" for *away*. This helps one to remember that all arteries carry blood away from the heart, so the blood can go work in the body. Therefore, the name of the road bringing blood back home to the heart is called "veins."

This journey starts when blood from our body enters our heart through our inferior and superior vena cava. From there blood is dumped into the right atrium flowing through the tricuspid valve into the right ventricle. Then the blood heads through the pulmonary arteries on its way to the lungs. After the blood has picked up oxygen in the lungs, it comes back home to the heart through the pulmonary veins and pours into the left atrium. Then it flows through the mitral valve into the left ventricle. It leaves the left ventricle through the aortic valve arriving in the aorta. The aorta is the largest artery in the body and has three sections—the ascending, descending and abdominal—carrying blood to major organs and the lower extremities.[2] My aorta was severed and death loomed.

Time was of the essence. There was none to spare.

Lois, one of the night shift nurses, was required to administer blood without a cross match. Blood typing is performed to determine whether the patient's blood is O, A, B, or AB, and whether the blood is positive with the Rh factor. Cross matching is another step performed before administering a blood transfusion. This is accomplished by mixing a little of the patient's blood with blood from the donor to verify compatibility.[3] When a patient's body receives blood that is not compatible, it produces antibodies to destroy the donor blood cells, called hemolytic transfusion reaction. Acute kidney failure, anemia, pulmonary edema and shock are complications associated with blood transfusion reactions.[4]

In this trauma situation, there was no other option, and realistically, there was nothing to lose. I was dying. If an incompatible transfusion wouldn't kill me, waiting for it surely would. Dr. Cohlmia ordered Lois to go to the blood bank and get two units of O negative, because O negative blood can be administered to any blood type. He said, "Tell the lab we will fill out the forms later—this is life or death!"

Mom, Dad, and Aunt Donna were allowed to see me before I was taken to surgery. Aunt Donna, my mom's only sister, was instructed how to answer should I ask questions regarding Jon. She was anything but prepared. Just moments before, she had been wallpapering her church's nursery. Now she was walking a hallway to see me, potentially for the last time.

"You're going to be okay," she assured me. "You're so brave." But my eyes revealed how scared I was. No one could hold me. No one could stay. I laid on a bed in a room full of strangers working over my body, and as much as my family wanted to comfort me, I was facing this alone. And I knew it.

I was in surgery for approximately six hours that night.

Two procedures back-to-back. Open-heart surgery with Dr. Cohlmia, immediately followed by Dr. Hans Norberg performing his first of many escharotomies and fasciotomies to relieve pressure and improve blood supply to my extremities.

The dead tissue from the burn causes eschar. It is tough, rigid and inelastic. When eschar is combined with fluid leaking from the injured vessels, pressure increases over the area of burn injury.[5] This causes constraint, even restricting chest expansion for breathing. Eschar can also lead to compression of the veins, arteries and nerves in the limbs. Such increase in pressure is called compartment syndrome.[6] When this happens, an incision is made down into the fascia, the tissue that surrounds muscle bundles, nerves and blood vessels.[7]

In the less than twelve hours since sustaining the injury, Dr. Norberg used a no. 15 blade to make incisions down my trunk, lower abdomen, anterior lateral compartments of my thighs, as well as the posterior and anterior compartments of my lower legs. The damaged blood vessels were then cauterized to stop the bleeding, wounds were packed and a sterile dressing was applied.

I would have innumerable operations to cut dead tissue and restore perfusion. But only once would my chest cavity be opened to mend my injured heart.

Dr. Cohlmia made a left posterior lateral thoracotomy incision, removed my left fourth rib and found 800 milliliters of blood after entering the thoracic cavity and retracting my lung. The operative report stated, "The descending thoracic aorta was [found to be] completely transected." A 10-millimeter interposition Dacron velour graft was used to perform the repair.

"Completely transected" meant it was like taking a sharp blade and completely slicing the aorta. Like running water through a water hose and then using a knife to cut that water hose. Water will no longer make it to the end destination of wherever that hose has been placed. This was the very reason why there was concern my lower extremities were not receiving blood supply for a period of time from the force of impact when Jon and I hit the truck.

It would be days before I would hear those words, "force of impact." The hematoma on my mid-forehead, the teeth marks in my lower lip, and the slice of my aorta were evidence of the force of impact. Eventually, I would discover it was a force impacting me for the rest of my life.

"Heather will fight," Mom told Katherine. Even at my young age, my family identified my headstrong nature, and they were believing it would be a tool in getting me through the night.

Mom and Dad, along with all the waiting room, prayed for a miracle. Make it to tomorrow.

Tomorrow.

April 28th.

Grandma's sixty-sixth birthday.

5

The Sting of Death

Every single day begins dark, when one day ends and the next one begins. Hours pass before the light of the sun ever shines in that brand-new day.

I came out from surgery in the early morning hours of April 28th. It was the middle of the night, but the beginning of a new day. Mom, Dad, Grandma and Aunt Donna were able to see me briefly, then told to leave and get some rest.

Rest. How does one rest?

They left together as daylight started breaking, heading east on the highway home with the sun coming up before them.

Despite the rising sun, my brother Barry was experiencing the same darkness as his day began in Houston. He had moved back with his mom the August before for his senior year of high school. It wasn't that he necessarily wanted to move. He had lived with us for his ninth-, tenth- and eleventh-grade years. But our home was not a very happy one. I realized that even as a little girl; however, not as greatly as my big brothers did—especially Barry.

Our childhood contributes to the person we become. What we do with it determines who we are.

My dad hadn't done much with his childhood at that point. And his choices didn't indicate much promise for change. He worked a lot. More than a lot, actually. Enough to classify him as a workaholic, which was okay for us. We didn't enjoy him being home. The house felt edgy when Dad was there because Dad was, well, edgy. Mom would continually tell us to "be quiet" and "keep it down."

Some say life was different in my dad's generation and the generation of his parents. Dad was born in England in 1944 and raised in Oklahoma. Back then fathers didn't interact much with their kids. At least that's the way it was for Dad. His father didn't interact much with him, but in all fairness, he was more of a father to my dad than what he had ever experienced. This grandpa I never knew spent a portion of his own childhood in the Tulsa Boy's Home. Even though he was present in my dad's life, the absence of a relationship with his father was a missing key element.

Fathers were the providers.

I guess that was the philosophy because while my dad never got on the floor to play with us or anything of the sort, he was the definition of a strong provider. But the issues of faithfulness and commitment to a family lifestyle kept Mom and Dad in a volatile cycle. A cycle Mom was ready to end the exact day of our accident. Dad had been out again the night before—what no one could have known would be Jon's last night on earth.

Mom's mind was preoccupied with arrangements for filing for divorce. Everyone wanted Dad to leave, but Barry had taken action months before by moving to Houston with his mom.

Although Barry was our seventeen-year-old half-brother and five hundred miles away, he maintained a close connection with Jon and me. His new job prevented him from being with us for Christmas, but he was coming to spend spring break with us. We couldn't wait!

However, a rear-end collision a week before spring break demolished more than the front of his car—it destroyed his transportation home. I still remember the night he called to tell us he wasn't going to be able to make it. Jon and I raced each other to the phone, trying to talk to Barry first. A celebrity couldn't have been more celebrated or admired.

And yet there he was on this April 28, 1988, sitting in the office of the assistant principal with his mom. "He may not be back," his mom informed the administrator through tears of emotion. "There will be one funeral, and from what we know, possibly two."

Such reality hit Barry as he walked into patient room 5424 later that afternoon.

• • • • • • •

There were seven beds in the intensive care unit (ICU) of the Alexander Burn Center. The nurses' station was located in the center of the square area with patient rooms straight across and a few patient rooms directly behind the desk.

Chairs are not often utilized by nurses, particularly in an ICU, but when the opportunity was taken to sit down for charting, the back of the seats were to my room. While I could not see the station, my nurse entered the small room through the door located just past the foot of my bed on my right.

There was limited space in that tiny room, but more space on my right than my left. Most everyone who came in the door did not walk past my feet to come to my left side. Instead, they entered the doorway, taking an immediate turn to their left for a direct path to my right side.

It's where Mom was sitting when Barry walked in.

Large amounts of fluids had been administered to my body in the hours since the accident. Two hundred milliliters of lactated ringers were given just on transport from the scene to the hospital.

The next day I had received a total of 7,250 milliliters of intravenous fluid and Plasmanate combined. However, my urine output was calculated to be 1.8 milliliters per kilogram per hour, resulting in a figure less than 600 milliliters. Considering over 7,000 had been administered and less than 600 had been excreted, the areas of body without burn injury were severely edematous. Meaning I was swollen beyond recognition, even beyond Barry's recognition.

He had barely walked through the door when he saw the figure lying in the large bed. The image was obscene and only such words came to his mind. He uttered expletives and turned to leave the room. Mom went after him and stopped him in the hall.

"Is she going to die?" Barry asked.

"That's what they keep telling us," Mom began, "but we don't think she will."

The ability to locate or quote a verse isn't necessary for God's Word to be at work in one's life. My mom's statement was evidence of that. We were a typical Bible-belt family who attended church, more routinely at some seasons than others; however, we weren't devoted to God's Word. We never read the Bible outside church, nor did we commit Scripture to memory. Nevertheless, Mom was demonstrating the very definition of faith: "Now faith is confidence in what we hope for and assurance about what we do not see."[1]

Nothing she could see indicated I would make it. None of the information given to her supported the chance I would pull through. Yet she was confident in what she hoped for. She was sure of what she could not see.

That April 28th day, my Grandma's birthday, I had surgery to cauterize the areas on my abdomen still bleeding from the escharotomy the night before and place a chest tube to drain the fluid in my right chest cavity.

That April 28th day, my Grandma's birthday, I was taken into surgery again in the evening for additional fasciotomies "carried out medially and laterally on the right thigh and right leg extending onto the dorsum of the right foot." The operative report concluded with the outcome of the procedure stating, "There was improvement in the appearance of the right foot slightly."

That April 28th day, my Grandma's birthday, my family gathered together at the funeral home, seeing Jon for the first time since the accident.

• • • • • • •

A few words handwritten on Jon's death certificate explained the immediate cause of his death: "massive head, neck, chest trauma." Nowhere on the official record did it indicate Jon's body sustained burns. Decades passed before I would learn the difficult specifics.

In his death, he protected me from mine. Both our bodies sustained the force of impact, yet his cushioned the amount I absorbed. Jon received force to the front and back of his body—oncoming from the truck and behind from me. A dent on the hood of the truck, looking as if a telephone pole had fallen on it, was made from his body. He landed face down on the road. The entire posterior of his body was burned.

The mortician who prepared his body was specially trained in reconstructing the face and used Jon's school picture to aid in the process, but our family's opinion was it didn't look like Jon. His chest was wrapped in cardboard to provide the appearance of a normal skeletal structure. The cuticles of his fingernails had a black residue. His eyebrows and lashes were singed.

Jon lay in his casket with one of his newsboy-style cabbie caps. He had a collection of them and rarely was seen without one on. His personality was expressed through the many bright prints and patterns.

"I just want time alone," Mom expressed to Dad on their drive to the funeral home that evening. She didn't really need to communicate it. He understood what she meant and what she needed. So did the small group of family who were there.

But someone Mom did not consider seeing was Michelle, one of Jon's classmates. The young second-grade student was walking toward the funeral home with her mom and sister when Mom and Dad pulled into the parking lot. They had sympathetic exchanges with one another as Mom knelt down to talk with Jon's friend.

Michelle saw from her porch the tower of black smoke rising in the sky the evening before. Later that night, her dad informed her a boy had been killed and his sister badly hurt in a vehicle accident. However, Michelle's dad never mentioned any names. She had no idea how closely that cloud of smoke would touch her life and memory.

It wasn't until the next day on April 28th, when Michelle walked into her classroom of crying students and teachers, did she learn Jon was the one killed in the very accident her father spoke of. The very accident that created the smoke.

"I looked over to his desk, hoping that it was not true," she recalled. "I looked around the room at all the faces of the kids, thinking, *The next face I'll see is Jon's face.* I looked for him all that day. We went to lunch and I looked for him. We went to recess and I looked for him, just hoping that maybe everyone had been wrong and that he was coming back." Michelle's broken hope of finding Jon at school was met with peace when she saw him in a casket that day.

The reach of the tragedy's impact was vast, touching lives both young and old.

While our family and friends were gathered together at the funeral home that evening, I was in the tiny burn center room off the nurses' station unaware of the loss my life had sustained. I longed to know where Jon was, but I couldn't ask. The tube pressing against my vocal cords providing the mechanical ventilation for my lungs restricted my ability to produce sound. I could not ask the one question I needed to know. *Where is Jon?*

Although I couldn't ask questions, I responded as I could to those asked of me. Doctors and nurses would instruct me to wiggle my fingers and toes. My eyelids were so swollen they could not be separated to assess my retina, but I was able to slightly move my eyelids and wiggle my fingers on request.

By the morning of Friday, April 29th, there had been notable change in the color of my right foot, and loss of pulses. Dr. Cohlmia reported, "It was felt there was a thrombotic occlusion of the right common femoral artery at the site where the arteriogram was placed and the catheter left in." In other words, a blood clot had formed where the catheter was placed to conduct the arteriogram performed the night of the accident for diagnosing the transection of my aorta.

My nurse, Vicki, taking care of me that Friday recalled Dr. Cohlmia proceeding with emergency exploration at the bedside. "I can't let this little girl lose her leg."

The operative report informed, "[The] right common femoral artery was found to be totally occluded by fresh and organized thrombus. 2cc of clot was removed from the right common femoral artery and right superficial femoral artery." The procedure restored blood flow in my leg, giving me a fighting chance to keep it.

In addition to the emergent bedside removal of the blood clot that day was the need to start administering nutrition. The only nutrients provided for quite some time were given by way of an IV, called parenteral nutrition. Due to limited access for IV sites and the long-term need for parenteral nutrition, Dr. Park placed a percutaneous triple lumen subclavian catheter.

Within forty-eight hours after the accident, my seventh operative report indicated the first performance for countless grafts. A hot knife was used to cut the tops of both my feet and lower legs, completely around both of my upper thighs, my abdomen and my left chest. My body was covered with the skin do-

53

nated from another. The very first skin graft provided because one life chose to give in their death.

"Donor skin was meshed to a ratio of 1.5 to 1 and laid over the wound, anchored in position using skin staples." The operative report continued, "Approximately 44% total body surface area was involved and 4 square feet of cadaver skin used before meshing."

Strangers gave me a fighting chance. I don't know their names. I don't know their stories. I don't know their faces or their families, but their blood flowed in my veins and their skin blanketed my body. Their choice to give life gave me the chance to fight for mine.

It was a battle my family prayed I would win, because as I was fighting for my life, my family was remembering Jon's.

●　●　●　●　●　●　●

Rain was forecasted for the day of Jon's memorial service.

Dirt roads become mud bogs after a decent rain. Which meant one had to be very careful getting out of a vehicle. The car would be filthy, and Mom didn't want anyone spending the day with mud-covered pant legs. In addition to producing severely dirty vehicles, cars and trucks commonly were stuck in the road's large ruts. When tires would sink into the soft surface, dirty clothes were the least of a driver's problems.

Our neighbor Mac had placed a call to the county road commissioner's office requesting fresh gravel be spread on the road where we lived. The county not only brought gravel, but they were so reverently quiet in doing so. Had the front door been closed, no one would have even known the road workers were out there. But Mom and Dad could see them through the glass screen door. While it appeared as a simple task of road maintenance, for Mom and Dad, it was a meaningful gesture of sympathy and support.

It never rained that April 29, 1988. The day was partly sunny.

"I'm not going," Mom said nonchalantly to Dad that morning.

54

"You're not gonna go?" Dad asked. He heard what she said and knew what she meant.

"No, I'm going to go back to the hospital. You go on," she instructed.

It was one of the first times Dad didn't know what to do with her. She just said she wasn't going to go to Jon's funeral, but he knew she had to. He had no idea how to tell her, so he went downstairs and called Katherine.

Katherine came immediately. She found Mom in bed, crying.

"I just can't," Mom began explaining to her. "I just can't do this. And I don't have to do this. I'm going to the hospital. That's where I belong. I don't have to do this."

Mom borrowed the strength of her friend that morning. Katherine would have taken the steps for her if she could have. Only seven years earlier, she had brought Mom home from the hospital with a brand-new baby girl, and she would walk with her through this day, the day Mom buried her baby boy.

"Now let's see what you are going to wear," Katherine said, opening the closet door, carrying Mom through the first step in facing the worst day of her life.

There was family in the living room when Mom came downstairs. Family and flowers. Lots and lots of flowers. A beautiful arrangement was brought to Mom's attention. "Susan, this is from the school," someone pointed out. More specifically, they were from Jon's class. Mom didn't realize it until she started reading the enclosed notes aloud—each one written by a student in his class. Even though she was in her own home, it was her first moment to publicly break in the presence of a group. She ran away, up the stairs, to be alone. Only moments would pass before the comfort of friends was offered again. Katherine returned to Mom's room with our dear neighbor Shirley.

Love and support poured in from countless so eager to give it, as evidenced by those gathered for the 2:30 afternoon memorial service honoring Jon's life at the First Baptist Church.

Even though we weren't faithful attendees, our home church was Evangelistic Temple. ET, as it was called, was a nondenominational church with a full-gospel message and atmosphere. The church was in west Tulsa, about half an hour from our house. Because of the distance, Mom and Dad felt it would be more appropriate having the service closer to home so Jon's classmates could attend. Jon's Cub Scouts met at the First Baptist Church in Porter, and it seemed the most fitting place to remember his life.

Our extended family, our school friends and teachers, Mom's coworkers from Saint Francis, and friends of Mom and Dad's, even some of their friends from Wichita, attended. There were more people than the small church could hold. Many stood outside.

Jon's Cub Scout Pack 635, Den Number 2, came dressed in uniform and sat together after carrying in the flags for the service. Their little lives paid tribute to their fellow member. A custom no one could imagine a young Cub Scout ever experiencing.

The pastor of the church had a son who was in Jon's Scout group and second-grade class. The boy had become a good friend to him. In fact, when it came time to go through Jon's things, Mom and Dad decided to give the boy Jon's BB gun. This pastor had a chance to know Jon and delivered the eulogy for his funeral.

Our family pastor, Dan Beller, brought the message, his wife, Marie, played the piano and Mom's cousin sang "Jesus Loves Me."

The service concluded with the traditional open casket, but many chose not to see Jon for that one last chance. He was swollen. His face looked somewhat plastic, like a doll. However, the most compelling feature that was not like him was the absence of his smile. Those who saw him all concluded, "It didn't look like Jon."

There were some still who needed to see him—Grandma being one. She stood and stood at his casket. For a very long time she stayed, looking and crying. Her thoughts, her burden and pain indicated by her inability to walk away.

Barry was the last to say his goodbyes. He needed time, too. He had a few moments before Dad said, "Okay. Come on now. Let's go." Barry just wasn't ready.

There was such sensitivity from everyone, especially the funeral director. Unfortunately, even for goodbyes, there is only so much time, so Dad nudged Barry along. Barry batted at his arm in response. Emotionally empty and physically weak, it was the first moment since his arrival after the accident he was embraced by our father. Dad didn't give many hugs back then. Even to the child being carried out in the casket. It would be the most painful regret of his life.

The burial was nearly thirty miles from the church. Yet the funeral procession was an indication of the tragedy's reach. The cars' headlights made for a long line of love, those hurting hearts looking for and offering comfort and healing to one another.

It was a long day that ended in the burn center.

It was another day I lived, having no idea Jon was gone.

6

A Little Girl's Loss

There is one activity that occupies a large amount of time during the spring and summer months in Oklahoma.

Mowing.

The chore can even extend into the early fall when we have what Grandma called an Indian summer, meaning we'd have warm, summer-like weather into the autumn season. It was first recorded in 1778 as a "spell of warm, dry, hazy weather after the first frost," but it's unknown whether the term came about because it was first reported by Native Americans to Europeans, or if it was first observed in regions occupied by Native Americans.[1] Nevertheless, I grew up knowing what an Indian summer meant. It meant Mom would be doing some more mowing.

Mom was always very particular about the yard. She wanted it done a certain way. Her way. So we rarely saw anyone other than Mom on the mower.

Jon and I ran after her, sometimes yelling over the roar of the motor, trying to tattle on one another, other times just playing. Which is what we were doing the day I got a bee sting.

I had stepped on a bee while running through the yard—barefoot, of course. Jon flagged Mom down, and she took a break to apply a paste made from mixing baking soda with water. She set me up in the house with what became one of my life's most favorite movies, *The Wizard of Oz.* At five years old, I could sing every single song on cue. It seemed I'd be set for my follow-the-yellow-brick-road sing-a-long from the comfy living room chair.

Moments later Jon flagged Mom down again with a report. "Mom, there's something wrong with Heather," he stated.

"What's wrong?" Mom asked.

"Her face is getting big."

With that information, Mom came inside with Jon following closely behind. When she saw my swollen face, she nearly started singing instructions as to avoid creating any sense of panic.

"Okay. Let's get up here. We're gonna run to the hospital real quick," she said with a sort of melody to her words. My face was swollen. My eyelids were starting to shut.

We drove thirty miles to Saint Francis, the hospital where Mom worked, in record time.

I received treatment from the discovery of my bee sting allergy. While we were in the emergency room, one of the sisters at Saint Francis came to the bay the gurney had been rolled into. She took note of my hair, commenting how blond and curly it was and paying the sweetest compliment to Mom: "She looks like a little angel."

It wasn't the first time I had heard someone say something so positive about my hair. I had gathered a feeling my long, blond, curly hair was special. But oh my, did it ever hurt to comb out.

My head was so sensitive, although my cousin Krista offered much practice for toughening up my tender head. She was seven years older than I and would say, "Pain is beauty," motivating me while she fixed my hair in a variety of styles. Even though it was fun having Krista play with my hair and pose me for pictures like a little model, what wasn't fun about my head of hair was how untamed it could be. It was difficult for me to fix on my own.

Mom had gone back to work by the time I started kindergarten, so she wasn't home to send me off to school. Therefore, she'd fix my hair the night before. After washing my hair, she'd comb it out and perform one of two styles: a single, braided ponytail or braided pigtails. Those were the options. And she braided it tightly enough to keep it together while I slept. It was so tight, in fact, I would stretch my face by opening my mouth and eyes as wide as they'd go in an effort to loosen it just a smidge. The benefit was avoiding a lengthy getting-ready routine, because as all my family could confirm, I was a little girl who loved to sleep!

On occasion when Mom wasn't able to arrange my hair into braids, due to time or my resistance, I would find myself faced with the challenge of combing it out. Let me say, No More Tangles was my go-to for my hair. But apparently, I plowed through the detangling spray rather quickly. No wonder, considering I would spray enough to practically wash my hair in it! The brush would slide through the soaked mane after I got finished.

One particular day, Dad was assigned the task of getting me ready to go to my afternoon kindergarten class. We were fresh out of No More Tangles, and I was fresh out of a plan to fix my hair. Dad didn't know what to do with my hair, and I didn't even plan to ask. Instead, I came up with another solution.

Being the six-year-old problem solver that I was, I discreetly retrieved a pair of scissors and escaped to the bathroom. I climbed up on the basin, propped myself up in front of the mirror and began cutting the culprit of each tangle out. Problem solved.

My idea wasn't as celebrated as I imagined. Grandma cut my hair short after that, and Mom decided to keep it that way. It was intended to be a better option for me. I could at least brush it. But I looked ridiculous. My head was now this poofy fluff resembling somewhat of a mop. The only perk of this new do came when wrestling with the boys.

The baby of every family wants to do what the big kids are doing. I wasn't any different. I wanted to join in when Jon and Barry began wrestling around on the floor. And I did. They let me play, but honestly, what boys want their baby sister involved in a wrestling match? Perhaps they did, but I often pulled out crying to Mom because "someone pulled my hair!" Never again would my hair get pulled while wrestling on the floor.

I was soon to find out Jon was gone. And shortly after, so was the hair he pulled during those impromptu wrestling matches.

● ● ● ● ● ●

Sunday, May 1st, was the first day I didn't have a surgery. I had been extubated so there wasn't a breathing tube restricting my ability to speak. Mom and Dad were to my right. Mom was in a chair. Dad was standing.

There in room 5424, they told me Jon had died.

I don't even remember the conversation. The words I don't remember. The feeling I do. I was confused. I didn't think it was possible. I now faced the emptiness they had been trying to process for the last four days.

I would never see Jon again. Never.

But hadn't I seen him? I thought I had. I just knew he had come to my bedside like so many of my family. He was alone though. No one came with him. And he stood, like everyone else, on my right side. He didn't speak. He just came. So how? How could this be happening? How could he be gone?

"He was killed on impact," one of my parents said. I had no idea what "killed on impact" meant.

I wanted to know if he hurt. I was hurting, and even my seven-year-old mind deeply desired he didn't have to know this pain.

"No, he didn't," they told me.

He never came to the hospital. We left the dirt road, but he stayed because he was already gone.

But he had come to the hospital. Someone told me he did. Someone told me he was in the room next to me, and someone told me he was in the waiting room with everyone else. He couldn't be gone.

He was gone. He was gone and buried.

Buried. It was another concept I didn't understand. What happened at a funeral? I had never been to one. No one in my life had ever died—not a grandparent, aunt or uncle, not even our dog.

I began to understand that our family and friends all gathered together at the church where they had a casket with Jon's body in it, and then they went to the cemetery and they laid his casket in the ground and covered it. I began to understand Mom, Dad, Barry, Grandma, Aunt Donna, Aunt Margie and Uncle Stoney, my cousins Krista and Slade, our teachers and friends, Mike, Katherine and Brad—everyone went to say goodbye to Jon and remember his life.

I didn't understand betrayal. I didn't even know the word. But I felt robbed— robbed of being able to say goodbye—and betrayed that so many people had lied to me.

It's for that very reason Howard, the child psychologist involved in my care, pressed Mom and Dad to tell me. "It's imperative she trust us," he told them. The charade was necessary to keep me fighting, but the battle was going to be a long one. The things the staff, and eventually my family, would have to do to my body required me to have the strongest sense of security and trust.

Sitting at my bedside, Mom and Dad held a stack of note cards, reading each message the students in Jon's second-grade class had written about him.

"Jon, you were the best friend I had. I loved the way you wrote your name and the way you told your jokes. You brought your radio every day. And your joke book too. We wished he could be here. Hope Heather is fine. Wish her luck."

"Jon was a sweet person. He was the smartest one in the classroom and he let us borrow paper when we didn't have any. He was a good boy too."

"I liked Jon very much. I had lots of fun with Jon. I laughed at his jokes. I wish he never wrecked. I hope Heather is ok. I hope you Mr. and Mrs. Cochrane have a good time and Heather too. He let me have money."

"Jon was a good friend. He colored with me and helped me. Hope Heather gets well. Sorry that Jon died."

"We all like Jon very much. We want him to be here a bunch. We all loved Jon a lot. I wish he could be here today with us."

"Jon was a good friend. He gave me paper and a pencil. I hope Heather gets better. I laughed at Jon's jokes. He wrote the best and helped me with my work."

The dedication page in the school yearbook featured more specific memories. Students wrote, "He was fun to be with. One day I went to his house and he filled cans with water and we shot BBs at them." "He never picked fights. He always liked people. He had a good attitude." "I liked Jon because he was always nice. Whatever he had, he would always share."

His teacher wrote, "Jon was a good student with an inquiring mind. He was always eager to try new things. Each of us has our own memories of Jon that make him special and unforgettable. He will be missed by his classmates because he was a good friend. He had a kind and generous nature. His willingness to help his classmates, whether it was to lend paper and pencil to assist with their work, will long be remembered by us all. As for myself, I will remember his sweet nature, infectious smile, and the hugs we shared."[2]

Jon had connected and built friendships in the few short years of his early education. His death created an empty space in the classroom, but his life left them with memories they would cherish forever.

My life, however, did not exist without him. I had no memory apart from him. I did not know a life without his presence. The strongest bond I had made in my family was with Jon. Who was I without him?

He was my big brother, yes, but he was also my best friend, not just a part of my biggest life moments, rather the major player of making those moments happen.

Like riding my bike. I couldn't manage riding without my training wheels. Or more accurately, I just didn't *want* to manage without my training wheels. I was completely content to leave them. They made me feel safe. But Jon was determined to get them off so I could ride with him.

There was a very small incline in the ground behind Grandma's house, just outside the window over her kitchen sink. Jon would position me on my bike at the top of the incline and give me a nudge. I fell more times than I could possibly remember; however, the memory of staying up after he sent me is one I'll carry forever. He was ecstatic.

"Mom!" he ran off yelling. "It's a miracle! It's a miracle! Heather's riding her bike!"

Only Jon could convince me to try, and the feeling of accomplishment he experienced from teaching me surpassed whatever joy I felt from learning. My moment wasn't made from riding my bike. My moment was made in pleasing my brother.

There was a similar feeling I remember when learning to tie my shoes. Jon taught me that skill, too. Mom and Grandma tried, and I think our neighbor Brad did too, but Jon made sense of it for me. He made sense of a lot of things for me.

So how did life make sense without him? I couldn't imagine it.

And I couldn't even begin to, because everything I was experiencing was strange and confusing. I didn't understand this life, but getting better and going home was a comforting thought. Everyone who came in to see me would say those words, "when you get better and go home."

"We can go camping when you get better and go home."

"We'll get a new puppy when you get better and go home."

Promises were pouring over my hospital bed with the attached words, "when you get better and go home." It's the place I had asked to go ever since they loaded me on the helicopter to come to the hospital. I just wanted to go home. Surely things would make more sense if I could just go home.

In the meantime, discussions took place regarding whether or not I would be transported even farther away from home. Within the week, the Shriners approached my parents about transporting me to their hospital in Galveston, Texas, stating that it was where I could receive "the best care."

"We want the best for her," Mom and Dad told Dr. Norberg in a meeting considering the matter. Conversations had been straightforward from the moment they met just days earlier. In addition to the respect they showed one another, they had trust in him, building a rapport very early.

"You don't have to go to Texas. You have the best right here." He began to explain, listing all the reasons I would be staying. Then he concluded the inquiry with, "And besides, she'll never make the trip."

Staying in Tulsa would not just be my best hope but the only option.

The following Sunday, May 8th, Mom spent her Mother's Day there with me in room 5424. I only laid there. The large, air-filled bed nearly swallowed my seven-year-old body. She couldn't hold me. We couldn't hug. She just sat holding my hand, the only option for embracing we could share. My body was wrapped from head to toe. Only pieces of my blond, curly, poofy hair protruded out from the edges of gauze enveloping it.

The next day, I went in for my fourteenth surgery where my own donor skin was obtained off the top of my right foot, my left forearm, my upper chest and my scalp.

My blond curly hair was gone.

7

Brave

The yellow, plastic bathtub Mom used when we were babies was kept in the upstairs hall closet. Jon frequently found creative ways to play with common household items. His imagination turned the ordinary into extraordinary.

He retrieved the tub from the closet and confidently walked me through his idea. Standing at the top of the stairs, he said, "Heather, get in and I'll push you down." Even though I was around four years old, it didn't seem safe to me. I declined. He persuaded. I eventually obliged and went sailing down the stairs in the yellow, plastic baby bathtub.

I was his test sample, or as Mom described, I was Jon's guinea pig. After using me to assess the risk, he decided it was his turn.

Within a year I was becoming more assertive, not following his lead so seamlessly. It was frustrating for him. But perhaps what was even more frustrating was my increasingly bossy nature. Jon would petition Mom, saying, "Tell her she's not my mother!"

Despite his aggravation with me, we continued leaning on one another. The dynamic of our relationship shifted a bit as our individual personalities started blooming. I was becoming quite sociable and Jon wasn't so much. I would instinctively mingle at social gatherings; he would stick close with me until he had warmed up and felt more comfortable. Regardless of the transition, there was no question he was the big brother in my eyes as I was beginning to express my own unique individuality.

It all started with kindergarten. And oh, how I loved kindergarten.

I was in the afternoon class, which meant avoiding my least favorite part of the day—morning. It was awfully difficult to get me going in the morning. My middle name should have been *Hurry* because that's what I consistently heard. "Heather, hurry!"

No hurrying was necessary for afternoon kindergarten. Often, I spent the night with Grandma. I would wake up in the most relaxing laid-back, slow-paced atmosphere anyone could imagine. To make it even more ideal, Grandma made whatever I wanted to eat for breakfast. I consistently requested pancakes every single morning. Every. Single. Morning. By the time I graduated kindergarten, I didn't have the slightest desire for pancakes. I had had my fill and never asked for another one.

Yes, I loved my kindergarten routine. Moreover, I loved the culture of the school system. There were just so many friends to make—a bit of a problem for my teacher, Mrs. Matthews. Even though my assigned seat was routinely reassigned, I was unaware it was a problem. I just thought I moved a lot.

Mom and Dad were made aware of the challenge at the first parent/teacher conference of the year. They walked into the classroom containing four to five little tables with chairs for the students. Mrs. Matthews practically constructed a compliment as she relayed her dilemma.

"In all my years of teaching, Heather is the first student I have had to make it to all the tables in the first nine weeks of school," she shared.

It wasn't ideal for me either. She once strategically placed me in between two stinky boys. I often thought, *I have to sit by them?* I didn't necessarily want to talk to them, but they were all I had. So while I wasn't thrilled about my situation, I made the most of it and visited with them too.

My gift of gab had been discovered, and the instinct to communicate accompanied me right on into the first grade, which I didn't enjoy nearly as much as kindergarten. The students were mostly those from Mrs. Matthews' class, so no new kids to be afraid of, and my teacher, Mrs. Smith, was as sweet as she was beautiful. However, the early rising, coupled with the morning bus ride, was brutal.

First grade was when I learned I was highly sensitive to motion. Even though I could feel it coming, I would try my best to have mind over matter. I would look out the window to focus on something. As my mouth watered and my stomach churned, I would swallow, and swallow, and swallow the increased production of saliva in my mouth. Mom and Dad even had me take some medication to treat the symptom, but nothing made much of a difference. Sometimes we would nearly make it to the school before it overcame me. Jon was humiliated—his barfing sister.

I determined it would be better to go back to kindergarten. The set-up certainly suited me more. Therefore, I informed Mrs. Smith that *that* was what was going to happen.

Apparently, I was quite convincing, because she sent a note home requesting a meeting. Mom and Dad both took off work to meet with Mrs. Smith regarding her concerns. Eventually the confusion was cleared by the fact Mom and Dad had no intention at all of returning me for an additional year of kindergarten. I would be staying in the first grade.

My consistent chatting continued to be a challenge. The habit hadn't resolved and ended up landing me in the quiet corner, a secluded area of the classroom separated by a bookcase. I thought my life was over as I stood with my nose in the corner. It was certainly embarrassing, but more so, I knew I had disappointed my teacher. That realization was punishment enough. There was an innate sense in me to please others.

What was a challenge for the culture of the classroom was a blessing in the hospital. My desire to connect, my drive to communicate in combination with my desire to please were the components that created the bond I needed to form with my nurses, my doctors, and everyone else who would become a newfound family to me—the people who saved my life and comforted me in the process.

• • • • • • •

In the first week after the accident, one of the top things I began to dread most about surgery was waking up with the mechanical ventilation tube in my throat. There wasn't anything more imprisoning to me than not being able to communicate. I was practically a born communicator. Thankfully, the quality surpassed the simple act of talking; I had the gift of connecting. It was the most beneficial blessing.

My nurses could read me. They studied my eyes and facial expressions. Lois had a curious knack for understanding me. Her presence brought much comfort. I didn't have the stressful anxiety of wondering if someone could figure out what I needed when she was there.

Everyone was very upfront with me about what to expect. Somehow, I didn't hold it against anyone for lying to me about Jon. I could discern their desire to help me and felt they were doing everything within their ability to make me better.

They gained my trust through their straightforwardness, and in doing so created a sense of security for me, developing my deepest confidence in them. I needed to feel safe. Even though my family was with me as much as possible, more often, I was alone in the hospital room. And no one was ever with me when the most painful procedures were performed. The journey was forming an entirely new family for me.

"You are so brave," they constantly said to me. I knew they realized I was terrified, but I believed them. I believed there was something in me that might just be brave.

Brave was what I tried to be when they told me my head was going to be shaved.

"We need to take some of your healthy skin and put it on your hurt skin," they said.

I pictured it just as they explained it to me. A machine was going to shave a very thin layer of skin off my head. The healthy skin would be put through a different machine that would poke holes in it to make it stretch out to be bigger. Then the last part would be the doctor placing the hole-poked-skin-from-my-scalp on the burned skin. I was told they would staple the healthy skin to the hurt skin. It was like planting a seed of good skin so the injured part could heal.

I was learning a lot about skin grafts. The donor site was the skin taken from a good part of my body. The graft was where the doctor would put the skin. I also learned the difference between split-thickness and full-thickness skin grafts. Split-thickness meant the donor skin taken would be a thin slice. Full-thickness meant the donor skin taken would be cut thicker. I knew it meant pain. And I tried to be brave.

"It will grow back" is what I was told about my hair. So when I woke up feeling the difference in how snug the bandages were wrapped around my head, I reminded myself of what they said and focused on being brave.

Three days later on Thursday, May 12th, Ed Kramer was eager to leave for some rest after being at the hospital for an entire week's span. The burn unit was his very first rotation during his fourth year of medical school. He wasn't a typical med student, having already passed the age of forty with a wife and children at home.

Dr. Kramer met me the day after my admission, assisting Dr. Norberg and Dr. Park in my care. He was nearly out the door, standing at the exit, when he felt a need to check on me one last time. He discovered my belly was rigid with no discernable bowel sounds.

In addition to my abdomen being tense and tender with rebound, it was documented my blood pressure was low, my potassium level had deteriorated, my white count was elevated, my temperature was "quite elevated," I had a rapid pulse and respirations, and I was "writhing in pain complaining of severe intra-abdominal pain."

An X-ray revealed "air fluid levels in the bowel in a variegated pattern. There was a consistent ground-glass haziness to the abdomen, right upper lobe pneumonia consistent with aspiration."

Dr. Kramer accompanied Dr. Norberg and Dr. Park into the OR for my emergency surgery. My parents gathered once more in the waiting area and contacted people to pray. Mom wrote an important message on the notepad sitting beside the waiting room phone for anyone who may read it: "Pray for Heather."

Pastor Beller was on a return trip home with a group from the church who had been touring the Holy Land. Mom's aunt and uncle were a part of the group. They stayed over in London to sightsee for a few days. It's where they were when they got word of my condition. There on the streets of London, a few members of their church family gathered together to intercede for a miracle. Pastor Beller encouraged Mom and Dad, reporting, "Prayer is holding her feet to the ground."

I had a life-threatening condition called pseudomonas peritonitis. The peritoneum is the tissue lining the inner wall of the abdomen. It covers and supports organs in the abdominal cavity. Peritonitis can occur from infection causing the peritoneum to become inflamed.[1] Pseudomonas, a common bacteria found in hospitals, was the cause of peritonitis in my case. Patients on mechanical ventilation, or those who have catheters (such as urinary catheters or central lines for IV fluid) or have wounds from surgery or burns are at an increased risk of contracting pseudomonas.[2] Considering my heightened risk, my health-care team knew to continually assess for such factors.

It was a long night performing four itemized procedures listed on the operative report.

A new central venous catheter was placed for nutrition and fluid administration along with a right radial arterial line placed to monitor my blood pressure. A surgical incision called a laparotomy was made to my abdominal cavity to assess the area of peritonitis. After evaluating my abdominal cavity that identified "blood from some subclinical upper GI bleed"; culturing a "cloudy sanguineous fluid"; and assessing the bowel, liver, spleen, stomach, pylorus, gallbladder, uterus, tubes, ovaries and bladder; closure was performed, leaving the subcutaneous and skin packed open.

To finish, the burn dressings were changed, which included the debridement of dead tissue, removal of the previous skin graft and application of new skin grafts. Sixty percent of my total body surface area was scraped with sharp and blunt means to remove the nonviable tissue. "Thirty-two carriers of homograft meshed 1.5:1 material were used" in providing fresh healthy skin for healing.

When Mom and Dad made it home in the early hours of that Friday the thirteenth morning, Dad was nearly broken. He had so often complained about Jon and me leaving our bicycles by the door. It was practically an obstacle course getting into the house. For two weeks now, the front porch had been clear.

"What I wouldn't give for there to be some bikes in front of this door," he said to Mom. They each had their moments of feeling hopeless but never at the same time. At least one of them was always carrying some hope for me to live. When Mom ran out, Dad continued believing. When Dad lost heart, Mom continued believing.

By the following Tuesday, May 17th, there was enough improvement in my condition to be moved to a new room. Room 5417.

I was still in the ICU but directly across from the nurses' station. It provided me with an awareness to life around me. Even through the fog of sedation, I would frequently hear people talking to one another and could turn my head to see patient rooms on my left and right.

There was a small window to the outside on my left at the head of my bed. I always preferred for the blinds to be drawn because the light agitated me. The stimulation it provided caused me to hurt even more. Mom couldn't understand how light could be negative. She always felt having natural light created a positive effect; therefore, she consistently aimed to open the blinds. I consistently protested, and she typically obliged despite her perspective.

My bed faced the nurses' station, and there was a television hanging on the wall over to my right toward the foot of my bed. I liked having the television on. Hearing the sound of shows we watched at home provided some much-needed familiarity and normalcy to my hospital environment. My family would come in to see me with their gowns, gloves and masks on. I couldn't see their smiles or feel the touch of their skin, but I would absorb the sight of their eyes, and I would try to be brave.

When the drugs sedating me periodically wore off, I would wake up in my dimly lit hospital room, my arms braced out in a ninety-degree angle, strapped down to the bed and unable to speak from the breathing tube in my throat, hearing the voices of the nurses just feet away at the nurses' station. I would feel anxious and scared as if I were forgotten and abandoned. But I tried to be brave.

I tried to be brave when they routinely rolled in the large, red heat lamp over my ICU hospital bed for bandage changes. The medical student involved in my care, Dr. Kramer, stood to my left holding my hand telling me how brave I was as bandages were peeled off my raw, bleeding body.

I tried to be brave for every assessment when my nurse would simply raise the white hospital sheet and ask, "Heather, can you wiggle your toes for me?" I focused so intently, trying my best to move them. After a few moments' pause, the sheet would be released and laid back over my feet. I never knew if I had accomplished the request or not.

I wasn't brave at all. I was terrified. The moments were horrific and so were the memories. But when something is continually spoken into the spirit, the message begins soaking into the heart until the mind starts believing it just might be true. And for me, I wanted so deeply to be what everyone needed me to be.

Lying in the hospital room, unable to move and unable to speak, I had many thoughts flow through my mind. I remembered Baby Jessica and how, only months earlier, I had thought bad things didn't happen here. Now I knew a different reality: *I guess bad things do happen here.*

• • • • • • •

Sucking my thumb had been my method of self-soothing since infancy. However, my arms braced and strapped down meant I couldn't utilize that piece of personal comfort anymore. Mom tried to make it better by removing her glove and offering her thumb to me. She would have taken my place if she could have. Her thumb just wasn't the same. Nothing was the same. And nothing would ever be the same again. I didn't know what it would be, but I had to be brave in whatever it was.

In my childlike thinking, "getting better" meant returning to how I was before the accident. More specifically, it meant *looking* like I did before the accident. My skin resembled something like raw hamburger meat. It was red, ugly and oftentimes smelly. My body was detestable. I knew that reality even in my seven-year-old mind. Nevertheless, I was going to get better and everything would be okay.

It wasn't until a burn survivor visited me in the ICU that I began piecing together the fact my body would never be the same. He came in and stood on my left side. He was soft spoken and kind, with the most gentle nature. Nevertheless, I did not like him. While I never said anything of the sort, those were my simple thoughts. I didn't like him because he was showing me his scars as if they looked good. He spoke of how they had healed and how soft they were.

Scars.

Permanent scars.

Evidence forever of what had happened and what was happening.

None of that sounded like getting better to me. It sounded like I was fighting to live a life I had already lost. I would never see Jon again, and I would never be like I was before the accident. Never.

But I tried to be brave. And lying in my hospital bed I tried to be polite to this man, as I knew was the proper way to behave.

I was part of a new community whether I understood it or not—the burn community. It was a group that surviving patients were fortunate to join, because as I was learning, not everyone did.

Mavis was in the room to my left. I would turn my head to see her through the glass dividing our rooms. She was an older woman with three grown daughters. Their Church of Christ upbringing brought the most beautiful harmonies to the ICU. My little life was blessed to listen as they sang for their mama.

Mavis went on to Heaven. Her room to my left became empty.

I was learning more and more about death. And I continued my quest to be brave in the midst of it.

8

Face of a Fighter

The words used in illustrating what takes place in an operation allude to something anticipated from a special ticketed event. Surgeries are *performed*, taking place in an operating *theater*, and patients are prepped and draped in a sterile *fashion*.

At my young age, I had quite a feeling for fashion, and for performing.

My growing repertoire of musicals was quite inspiring to the aspiring entertainer within me. *Annie* and *The Wizard of Oz* were two of the first on my developing list of favorites. Popular songs from those movies were covers I performed for my first live audience. It was mostly a dinner show routine. By *live audience*, I mean the cows on the other side of the fence of our backyard. By *dinner show*, I mean they were always chewing their cud during the performance. Sure, they looked a bit puzzled when I belted out "Somewhere over the Rainbow," but they were a gracious group.

Sometimes I had the opportunity for a different kind of live audience. Jon and I performed countless shows singing and dancing on the small area of tiled floor in front of our living room fireplace. We really felt like an official duet after Jon got his first guitar. I would bring my microphone, he would bring his guitar, and we performed for anyone who would listen.

Fashion, on the other hand, could be summed up in one word—shoes.

Shoes went missing around our house all the time. Mom's friends would take off their shoes at some point during their visit, providing me with the perfect opportunity to try them on. And wear them. The fact they were multiple sizes too big was no concern of mine. When I saw a cute pair of shoes, I was drawn to put them on. Not that I didn't have an array of my own collection. The only girl in the family certainly had a decent assortment of appropriately sized cute shoes.

I loved my tall, knee-high brown boots with the faux fur around the top edge. Then there were the plastic, pink high heels I felt were fitting for any occasion, like attending Barry's championship soccer game. Mom told me I couldn't wear them, but I insisted. She gave in to my hardheadedness, knowing I would learn a lesson in the process. The lesson: listen to Mom. I loved, loved, loved wearing the shoes that night. Honestly, I felt everyone was admiring them as much as I did. However, the sentiment changed the minute Barry made a play, winning the entire game—the championship game!

Before I knew it, the players were huddled together, and Barry was being lifted up over their heads like a prized trophy. He *was* a prized trophy! Because of his superstar moment, the team was going to walk away with a trophy. A big one! It was his moment. And it was our moment, too. Jon took off running out on the field to soak in the victory *our brother* was experiencing. Only there I was, losing a shoe through every other stride of my run. My family was relishing the moment while I was trying to keep my shoes on my feet. Lesson learned. Listen to Mom.

By 1988 I had a variety of my newly found favorite shoe—the jelly shoe. In my six-year-old opinion, the ballet-slipper-style plastic shoes went with practically any outfit. And just as if it were a preprogrammed setting for my female mind, I knew having my favorite shoe in a few different colors just made good sense. I wore them with everything, from shorts to dresses, and for everything, from attending school to adventures at play. They were the shoes adorning my feet when we collided with the truck on the dirt road. And they were the shoes that melted to my feet in the flames.

● ● ● ● ● ● ●

I was intrigued with fashion, performing and theater. Not this kind though. Not this scene I was often being rolled into. The spotlights of the operating theater didn't call. They terrified.

There was a large cast for the surgery to be performed. The leading role was played by whoever was conducting the operation, either Dr. Norberg or Dr. Park and sometimes both. I rarely saw them in the operating room. They usually entered stage after I was already asleep, likely scrubbing in while I was being prepared.

The supporting cast were the ones who made the frightening room feel a little more friendly. The cold environment was warmed through the contact of their compassionate eyes and caring words. From the moment I entered, the surgical techs and my precious operating room nurses extended their love and kindness to comfort me through the experience.

Their hair was tucked up in their surgical hats. Many of them wore a disposable blue surgical cap, but some of them would have a custom one made from a variety of colors and patterns. They also wore their procedure masks covering their mouths. The mask was either tied around their head or strapped over their ears.

If positioned in a lineup, I could never have identified them. I never saw their hair or their faces, but I saw their eyes and held my focus to them for as long as I could. I also held to their voices. As quickly as things move in the OR, I always had someone talking to me. The anesthesiologist would walk me through the process of what I was getting ready to experience. "Heather, I'm putting some medicine in your IV. This may burn just a little." And then, "Okay, Heather, you're going to start feeling sleepy now." All the while the nurse would be by my side, visiting with me, reassuring me I wasn't alone.

Their voices speaking peace and security into this performance were vital in my mental ability to endure it over and over and over. One of the last senses to lose when having an operation is hearing. They provided me with comfort as the last of my senses was sedated.

Waking up was always the worst part. The tremendous pain indicated the brutal performance required as I slept. No amount of pain medication would numb it. It was a symptom I learned to anticipate.

Fever was another cruel experience, causing the most confusing reaction. I felt so very cold, shivering in my bed. Movement alone from the shivers created pain, but the torture became worse as ice packs were applied to my body.

"Please take them off. Please. I'm so cold," I pleaded. I was corrected with, "No, Heather. You're not cold. Your body is very, very hot. We have to get your temperature down."

I couldn't understand the process of what takes place when the body works to fight against infection. The brain is like the thermostat in a room. When bacteria enters the room, the brain changes the thermostat to a higher temperature in an attempt to bake off the infection. Because my brain set a higher temperature for my body to meet, I felt cold. In reality, I was cold in relation to the new set point my brain had determined. The shivering and chills were my body's way of generating heat to warm itself.

Fever, surgeries, bandage changes, repositioning and linen changes. It was all so painful. The linen changes took a team to make it happen. It was a long, involved process.

The nurse taking care of me would get another nurse to assist. They rolled me to one side of the bed, one nurse holding me up on my side and maintaining that position while the other nurse removed the old linen off the edges of the mattress. The old sheets would be rolled up as closely to my backside as possible. While still holding me in position, the new linen would be smoothed onto the mattress, also spreading it as closely to my back as possible. This created a hump of two sheets: the old sheet rolled up one direction, and the new sheet spread out the other direction, meeting in the middle of my backside.

What came next was the *one, two, three, roll!* I would roll over the hump of fresh and soiled linen to the other side of the bed, where my other nurse held my body up on the opposite side, so the old sheet could be removed and the new sheet could be further applied. After it was all done, I was rolled again to my back and made as comfortable as possible through positioning, pillows and pain medication.

All of it was painful. Still yet, I had people surrounding me with the intention to minimize as much of it as possible.

I was given a scale to rate my level of pain. "Heather, if zero means you aren't hurting at all and ten means you're hurting more than you have ever hurt, what number is your pain right now?"

There weren't any charts of faces illustrating the different levels of pain to point at. Just numbers. It was simple for me to understand ten was the worst and zero was the best. Although, I don't think I ever experienced a zero again. Pain eventually took on an entirely different sensation as I grew accustomed to permanent discomforts.

Dad had a way of making me feel like some sort of champion in dealing with pain. The kind of champion like I pictured Barry was with his team: valued and celebrated upon their shoulders as a star player. Dad would motivate me by saying, "You can't hurt steel."

That's right. I was a champion, strong as steel. Nothing could hurt me.

But it could. And it did.

"Heather, pain is gain," Dr. Norberg stated to keep my focus maintained on progressing.

Pain is gain.

It reminded me of Krista telling me pain is beauty when she fixed my hair. My hair was now gone, along with my beauty, but I had an endless supply of pain.

When I couldn't handle any more of it, I reported pain. Whether it was physical pain or pain from the reality of my circumstances, I knew morphine would make me feel better, so I asked for it frequently and it was administered liberally. Yet as I was learning, there wasn't enough medication on the planet to numb the array of pain I was feeling.

While I certainly wanted to hear the praise and affirmation from my nurses, doctors and parents telling me what a good patient I was, my intuition of how unfair my circumstances were occasionally overruled my desire to please. Life was the cruelest reality of unfairness.

Sometimes people would tell me how lucky I was, and it made me fume inside. If I could have screamed my thoughts I would have.

Lucky? I'm lucky to have a dead brother? I'm lucky to have laid in the road on fire? I'm lucky to be lying in this bed? I'm lucky to be alive, but I don't even know if I can wiggle my stupid toes?

I couldn't begin to articulate the grief inside of me. It was too vast and unfamiliar for me to understand for myself. All I knew was there were days I was mad. I couldn't understand why. I was simply mad. There were days I didn't want to endure anything requested of me.

My nurses knew when to push me. They also knew when to comfort me.

Every now and then, Lois would bargain. Her baby, Amber, was not even six months old. She was a beautiful baby with the cutest little glasses. Lois would say, "Heather, if you do this like I ask, then I'll bring Amber in to see you."

When my little mind couldn't wrap around the long-term benefit of the unpleasant things needing to be done, my nurses met me with small immediate rewards to win my compliance. One of the biggest rewards was getting to see Brad.

Children were not allowed in the ICU. Only those sixteen and older were permitted back for the scrubbing-in process and donning of gloves, gown and mask to visit me. I was a kid removed from all kids, placed to spend my days surrounded by a world of adults.

The only exception made had been to allow Krista back a few times. She was fourteen. But on June 6th, Brad got to come back. He was more than our neighbor. He was even more than a friend. He was truly like a brother, part of my life's picture from the time his mom, Katherine, had driven Mom and me home from the hospital after my birth.

Brad wore a burr back in those days, or a buzz cut as some call it. Even though he had recently had his hair cut, he knew mine had been shaved off the month before. In response, he requested a fresh trimming before visiting me. He didn't want me to feel bad about my hair being shorter than his. It was just one of the ways, at nine years old, he could demonstrate his deep sensitivity, consideration and compassion to his best friend's baby sister.

During his visit, I told him about my very first trip to the tank room that morning. Bandage changes were extremely painful, but the tank room offered an improvement to the necessary process.

I was laid on a large cot-like table attached to cables. The lift was operated with a control, hoisting me up then positioning me over the water as the entire table I laid on was immersed into the tub. It looked frightening. The tank looked enormous and caused me to have reservations about going down into it.

The process is called immersion hydrotherapy. It provides improvement to the healing process by removing dead tissue, cleaning the wound and draining pus. Soaking in the tank helped the bandages come off, and eventually physical therapy was incorporated because the tank facilitated in loosening some of the tissue for stretching. Even though the tank room meant the dreaded bandage changes, it was a more tolerable process than having them changed in bed under the heat lamp.

• • • • • •

The hospital bed was both despised and cherished for me. I didn't want to get out of it because I hurt, but I hated being in it. I wanted to get better. I just didn't want to be in so much pain.

A few days earlier on June 2nd, Dr. Park told me I had to get out of bed to sit in a chair. The news was not welcomed. However, by June 8th, he upped the ante and I was told it was time to stand.

My poor physical therapist. I hated her that day. Truly. For being such a loving little girl, physical therapy had a way of tapping into deep waters revealing my most intense emotions.

Biting is a common response for pediatric patients. It's an attempt to protect from harm. While I never bit anyone during my entire journey of recovery, I wanted to that day. Only my eyes would express the deep loathing I had for what she was making me do.

Mom and Dad kept a Polaroid camera in my room for the staff to take photos. Although Mom and Dad were there as much as they could be, they were gone more than they wanted. Life was still happening outside the hospital. The lawn still needed mowing, bills still needed paying, and going to work was required. Even when tragedy hits a home, there is no pause button to press while walking back to normalcy. Extended hospital stays set the stage for juggling two lives—one inside the hospital and one outside. The Polaroid camera helped in that juggling process.

I understood why Mom and Dad couldn't be there all the time. My nurses frequently informed me how I needed the nurses to take care of me now and that Mom and Dad would be taking care of me when I got home. It made sense to me. Nevertheless, I knew they got to escape the hardest parts. When the environment got overwhelming or when they absolutely couldn't handle what had to be done, they got to step out. They had their opportunity to grab some fresh air, a cup of coffee, a night's sleep in their bed.

There was no escape for me. Ever.

This was life. My life.

Daily I was confronted with what was necessary to make it better. June 8th, it was standing.

Normally I didn't wear a hospital gown. Bandages clothed my entire body lying under the sheet in my hospital bed. But for this moment, my arms were inserted into the openings of a small gown as it was tied around my neck.

A tech assisted my physical therapist, Pam, in getting me out of bed. There was a countertop with a sink to the right side of my bed. The area in between is where I stood. Pam was behind me supporting me between my elbows and forearms. I displaced as much of my weight as possible to my arms in efforts to avoid using my legs. They throbbed with the mere change to an upright position.

The Polaroid camera was used to capture the moment for Mom and Dad. Two photos were taken.

One picture was the brief moment first out of bed. I was terrified I would fall, knowing my legs were weak, fearing they may never work. The top of my head was bald with remnants of the remaining bandages from the skin graft. My eyes were looking down. The front of my hospital gown was pulled like a curtain over my left side, gathered around my back to use for support, revealing my torso of betadine-soaked white bandages. The ace bandages were wrapped starting from my feet up my legs; only my toes were left exposed. Blood stains were collected above my right knee and in my groin. The tech helping was positioned on my right, holding my urinary bag and offering support as my hand clinched around her wrist.

The second photo was my picture for Mom and Dad.

A wheelchair had been rolled directly in front of me to use for supporting my weight. The photos were taken back-to-back rather quickly. Pam was still behind holding me up. The tech was still beside me.

I knew they were taking this picture. And I gave it my best smile for Mom and Dad. I hated what was happening to me. I hurt beyond what words could begin describing. However, I knew I had to do this—with or without a smile.

I wanted my parents to be proud. I wanted to make them feel good. So with everything I could muster up within me, I lifted my chin and produced the face of a fighter—a smile in the presence of insurmountable pain. An approach I would employ many times over, becoming my life's greatest performance.

9

Tough Cookie

There wasn't anything I wanted more for the Christmas of 1987 than a Baby Heather doll. She had blond hair, blue eyes, a pink outfit; she talked, responded to voice, and topping it off, her name was Heather. I felt we were meant to be.

My experience with Santa gave me a good feeling I would find her waiting in front of the fireplace when I came downstairs Christmas morning. Only I didn't.

I found a Cabbage Patch doll, a parakeet we named Tweedy Bird and a note from Santa with the following explanation:

Heather, I know you asked for "Baby Heather," but my Chief Elf has informed me that we have had many problems with that doll. Hopefully by March we will have her working properly.

Despite the disappointment I felt, there was still a tinge of hope in my heart that I might unwrap a Baby Heather doll at Grandma Cochrane's house later in the day. Only I didn't.

Could it really be a malfunction in production at the North Pole? It just didn't seem logical to me. What did seem logical was concluding I must not have been a good girl. Everyone knows Santa brings gifts to the good boys and girls. However, my hang-up wasn't in regard to *not* receiving gifts, but rather in not receiving the one gift I had wished for. It derailed my Christmas celebration as I wondered if I had not been good enough.

Freezing rain set in during the day, so we stayed the night at Grandma Cochrane's house. Aunt Margie, Uncle Stoney, Slade and Krista were there too. We always spent Christmas Eve with Mom's family at my Aunt Sarah and Uncle Roy's, had Christmas morning at home and then Christmas Day with Dad's family at his mom's house. The icy road conditions meant we would be having a sleepover—ideal for a kid on Christmas. Only it wasn't.

Mom came and laid down with me in the back bedroom, reassuring me I had been a very good girl, explaining a reality of life I was needing to learn. Sometimes we don't get what we wish for, and it has nothing to do with whether we deserve it or not. Oh, how that foreshadowed what our entire family would encounter just a few months later.

For the time being, I was encouraged to look forward to March, when I would be turning seven, when Santa felt Baby Heather might be working properly. Having a birthday three months after Christmas meant I might receive some of those Christmas wishes as birthday gifts. Only Baby Heather wasn't in with the birthday present pile either. It was appearing this most-wished-for gift was not as meant to be as I had dreamed.

· · · · · · ·

One thing about tragedy is it often brings out the best in people.

Mom and Dad would come home from the hospital and find a note on the front door informing them there was food in the fridge. And although there couldn't be flowers in the burn unit, my room was filled with get-well support, from stuffed animals, balloons and storybooks to personal cards and custom-made posters.

A blue My Little Pony sat to the far right of the shelf in my first ICU room. I found comfort in those initial days after the accident, glancing to focus on the familiar favorite character of mine. It was a gift from Grandma's friend Zettie, who spent every Christmas Eve with our family. Like so many, she couldn't come back to see me but sent a token of her love expressed through a simple stuffed animal.

I was deep in loss, yet rich in love.

Countless people came to the hospital to offer support, encouragement and prayer. Most of those who visited were not allowed into the unit, so Dad had the idea to create a guest book. Mom brought a two-hundred-sheet, college-ruled, yellow spiral notebook to place in the waiting room of the burn unit. Krista wrote "Heather's Guest Book" in bold black marker on the front. Family and friends who came to visit, nurses, doctors, physical therapists, and even strangers I never met wrote messages Mom and Dad would sit at my bedside and read to me.

Entries like the one written on May 3rd by the hospital chaplain:

Heather, your struggle and your expressions of determination have certainly been an inspiration to me. Please continue to get better and to [be] the wonderful being that you've obviously always been. God Bless.

People all over the hospital were learning of our tragedy and offering their most sympathetic support. Including those from the laundry department.

Fisher Price had a line of stuffed animals called Puffalumps. Aunt Donna purchased one that was a gray mouse. The stuffed animal was about sixteen inches in height, had a small tuft of white hair and a pink nose. Her white, sleeveless, apron-style dress had floral eyelets and a pink bodice underlay with a little pink bow on the center waistline. I appropriately named her Mouse.

Mouse was so lightweight she was able to sit on my bed and be close to me without causing discomfort. Furthermore, she was made of parachute material, so any blood or drainage from my wounded body cleaned off fairly easily. She instantly became my lovey of comfort, staying with me even when Mom and Dad couldn't, like going into surgery.

My nurses would put a mask, hat and sometimes even little disposable shoe covers on Mouse to accompany me to surgery. She sat at the very end of my bed between my feet, looking at me as we rolled into the OR, and she would be sitting right in the same place when I woke up afterward. She journeyed with me through the process from bandage changes to linen changes. And it was one of those linen changes when Mouse went on an independent field trip.

It didn't take long to discover she was gone. But the minute we did, the search team went into action. My nurses responded as if a Code Adam were called, alarming for a lost child.

Upon arrival, Mom and Dad were approached with such discernable concern, causing them to anticipate receiving a report like one they had been given before: *Heather's condition has deteriorated.* To their surprise and relief, the nurse informed with palpable seriousness, "We've lost Mouse." They looked for her with seismic intensity by shaking down every area Mouse could be located. She was found in the laundry and came back smelling fresh and clean, dryer-tossed to a fully renewed puffiness. Such intention and efforts illustrated the love surrounding me.

Not too much time passed before I was surprised with the fulfillment of my one birthday and Christmas wish—Baby Heather.

The doll was so popular stores couldn't keep them stocked. Apparently, Santa didn't have any pull either. Mom had enlisted her friends in the accounting department at Saint Francis to help her in finding one that Christmas of 1987 and my seventh birthday in March 1988. There just weren't any available.

Several people were involved to fulfill my one gift wish, and after the accident, a pastor got wind of the story and started off on his own mission to find a Baby Heather doll.

On May 19th, Don Soderquist, the Vice Chairman and Chief Operating Officer of Wal-Mart Stores, Inc., sent a package with the following message:

> On behalf of Wal-Mart and Mattel Corporation, please accept the enclosed doll along with our best wishes for a speedy recovery to Heather. We hope it will help comfort Heather in the weeks to come.
>
> We appreciate being able to help Heather in this small way and thank you for your concern in bringing this matter to our attention. Let Heather know our thoughts and prayers are with her.

Tragedy brings out the best in people. It is a lens to see the kindest attributes of human nature.

Baby Heather sat on the countertop in my room. I couldn't hold her or play with her, but I had the hope of being able to one day.

• • • • • • •

Pain is gain became the maxim of my journey. There was only one way home, and it was a painful one. I was dependent on others to do some of the most emotionally difficult tasks with the most unimaginable strength to get me there.

Bandages dried to my raw flesh were moistened in saline and peeled off. Staples embedded under my tissue were dug out. My body bled red and drained sanguineous fluid. I begged, I pleaded, I even demanded for my nurses to stop. I screamed at the top of my lungs, crying, "Please, stop! Please, stop hurting me!"

Horrendous pain expressed with desperate requests.

They held me down continuing the necessary process, constantly reminding me they were helping me get better, that it would only hurt for a little bit. My health-care team was comprised of the strongest people on the planet. Even when I would fight against them, they fought for me to live a life beyond my injury. And they did it with an observed conviction and passion.

One day I watched and listened as a nurse advocating for a patient played out before me.

Lois and Dr. Park stood at the foot of my bed, disagreeing on some type of cream to be used on my body. He wanted it. She didn't. There was nothing left to interpretation. They were both clear on where each stood in the matter. I don't know how the situation ended, who got their way or not, but I did realize they both cared very much about me. It was my perception people only argued about stuff that mattered, and in that moment, I felt like I mattered very much to them both.

Much love was laced into the loss I now knew. And sweet memories were being made in the midst of so many painful ones. The team caring for me provided it in creative ways. They were flexible to meet me where they could and give in on a few issues—like food.

Nutrition had been delivered intravenously when my digestive tract could not perform. After a few weeks of receiving total parenteral nutrition, a gastric tube was inserted through my nose to administer enteral nutrition directly to my gastrointestinal tract. Caloric intake is a crucial component in wound healing. The metabolic rate for burn patients can be more than twice the normal rate and stay maintained for nearly a year after the burn.[1]

My parents and health-care team were willing to try anything that would deliver calories to my body. I had to demonstrate I could eat and drink enough on my own before the nasogastric tube could be removed, so I could go home, the one place I had asked for ever since being transported in the helicopter on the day of the accident. Perhaps the most unorthodox approach was when Dad asked Dr. Norberg about beer. Surprisingly, Dr. Norberg was eager to provide whatever would accomplish the goal of oral caloric intake. Dad brought small bottles of beer, which were kept in the nurses' refrigerator. What may seem even more surprising, I drank them! Just probably not as many as they hoped for, because everyone continued to hammer me with one challenge—*eat*.

I wasn't unlike any other kid. Hospital food was about as desirable to me as cafeteria food. There's just nothing like Mom's home cooking. So Mom brought my favorite right to the ICU: roast, mashed potatoes, gravy and cooked carrots. Later on, Aunt Donna brought soup, and I received special deliveries of Arby's Jamocha Shakes, along with a plethora of ice cream treats. It wasn't home, but it was as close to home as I could get for the time being.

Little reminders of home migrated into the burn unit. The show *Alf* had been a big hit in our house. Jon and I tuned in to watch as this alien life-form became a part of the Tanner family, who constantly hid him in the kitchen and tried to keep him from eating their cat. Alf was hysterical. He was hysterical to us anyway. Barry brought of bit of that comic relief to the hospital. Burger King released a set of Alf hand puppets. There were four—the baseball Alf, the surfer Alf, the rock band Alf and the cook Alf. Barry went every week to Burger King to collect all four for me.

He also watched *Wheel of Fortune* with me. I looked forward to it in the evening. When Barry's friend Chris would visit, he would get on one side of my bed, Barry would get on the other, and when the show came on, we were ready. Starting on one side, Chris would say, "Wheel." Then I said, "Of." Barry would carry it through with a theatrical tone of "Fortune!"

Smiles appeared. Laughter echoed. Joy was still real.

The staff got in on making some fun too. The day came when no one needed to wear a mask, gown, and gloves anymore. It was a grand day for me. Finally, I would be able to look at Mom's face, Dad's face, Grandma's face, Aunt Donna's face. All the faces of my family whose eyes I could only see for weeks. I would finally look at them completely. No longer would I have to be content with the pressure of their touch, but I would get to feel the sensation of their ungloved skin when they held my hand.

Instead of the staff telling them the good news, they let me do it. Mom and Dad arrived, scrubbed in and put on their gloves, gowns and masks. They entered my ICU room 5417 like every other time before.

The head of my bed was fully elevated where I was sitting up in bed. Mom came to the right side of my bed, opened her arms as she leaned in to place her hands gently on my waist and kiss my head when I stopped her with one sentence. "You don't have to wear that anymore," I said. Off came the gown, the gloves, and the best part, the mask! I got to see their smiles for the first time in over a month!

• • • • • •

Mom, Dad and Aunt Donna spent Friday, June 10th, decorating room 5410. They hung multiple runs of twisted pink, crepe-paper streamers across the ceiling tiles. A few extra-large, pink ice cream cones made of tissue dropped down from in between the streamers. The room packed as much pink and celebration any room could hold.

I had to get up in the wheelchair to be transferred out of the ICU to my new room in what was called the progressive unit section of the burn center.

The door was opened to cheers of "Surprise!"

Aunt Donna gave me a plain ivory T-shirt with one sentence on the front. There wasn't a design or picture on the shirt of any popular characters like Strawberry Shortcake or Herself the Elf. It contained just one sentence. A sentence on a blank canvas that summed up my journey to room 5410 and defined every step thereafter.

Tough Cookies Don't Crumble.

I didn't know what it meant, but Aunt Donna gave it to me, so I loved it regardless. She knew me inside out though. Realizing the words didn't make sense to me, she began to explain that I was the tough cookie, and I didn't crumble when things were hard or scary or painful. I was strong and brave. I was tough.

Pain had become more manageable by the time I moved to the progressive unit. Nevertheless, I still felt pain.

When Mom and Dad left for the evening, I would have the company of my small, extendable, arm-mounted television. They positioned the screen close by my bed before leaving. *Nick at Nite* kept me company, airing classic shows that became some of my favorites, like *Mr. Ed, The Donna Reid Show* and *My Three Sons.*

Eventually I drifted off to sleep. Yet, on many occasions I was awakened from an involuntary jerk in one of my extremities causing extreme discomfort. Other times it was from a nightmare. Whatever the cause, I found myself alone in my dark room, so I hit my call light and said one phrase I knew would help make it better: "I'm hurting."

One particular night, I started screaming in my dream. I woke up petrified, crying. I hit the call light and said, "I'm hurting." My nurse Carolyn came in with two syringes, one of morphine and one of saline to flush behind the med. She pulled up a chair to the left side of my bed and began to administer the medication, asking me more about my pain. I reported the number as I knew I was required to do and then began telling her the events of my dream.

Jon was there. It was dark. The ground was black pavement and it was wet. We were at the end of the street in front of what looked like a white garage, similar to a tire shop or old gas station. There were tall buildings lining the street. All of a sudden, what looked like green vapors came after us. We began running and then Jon was gone and I was alone.

Carolyn sat with me until I fell back to sleep. She didn't leave to complete the duties of her shift. She simply sat and offered the most effective intervention she had—herself.

10

My Way Back Home

Glimpses of life were seen from my new room. Basketball and tennis courts were in view right outside my window. From my bed I could see people play and cars pass on the street. I looked out the window at life but wasn't a part of it. Life happened outside the hospital, not where I was. My time alone gave me plenty of opportunity to wonder if I would ever be a part of it again.

School was now out for the summer. Sarah, the friend I was playing with before getting on the motorcycle for the very last time, accepted my awards at the end-of-the-year assembly. Jon's friend Kenny accepted his. Our family was not there to hear our names called, but our young classmates held us in thought and memory, as they rose from their seats and walked forward on our behalf to receive the paper of accomplishment from our school year. Jon's last school year.

My new hospital room opened opportunities for me to see my school friends for the first time. Sarah came to visit a couple times with her older sister and her mom. Brad came several more times, and my new room meant his little sister, Mary, got to visit too. Aunt Donna was able to bring her daughter, my six-month-old baby cousin, Austin. Little girls love to hold babies. I certainly still did. It took some effort to be transferred over and positioned up in a chair. It was an effort totally worth getting to hold Austin. Aunt Donna would, of course, help by keeping Austin's active hands from grabbing my feeding tube.

The only thing worse than having my feeding tube yanked out was having it reinserted. The unfortunate situation happened on one of my transfers back to bed after returning from the tank room.

I was always so worn out after the tank room. The debriding and bandage-change process was pretty exhausting. One of the perks of coming back to my room was being greeted with fresh linens. It was always a good thing when I didn't have to roll over the hump from an in-bed linen change. Unfortunately, on one of those returns, as I was lifted up and moved over to my bed, my feeding tube caught on the rail and ripped right out. The two nurses moving me felt terrible. I believe they would have each inserted the tube into their own nose in the moment. They apologized profusely. I felt bad because *they* felt so bad, but I felt even worse knowing I would have to gag and swallow that feeding tube right back down again. It's just one of those things that happens. At seven, I was gaining much understanding of those things.

The feeding tube was still in my nose when we had the big party. It was like an open house. Faces I hadn't seen since before the accident were coming to the hospital. Being the social girl I was, the occasion was monumental. I was excited but also nervous about what they would think of me.

Kids I didn't even know had made posters and sent balloons and stuffed animals. In fact, my own elementary school collected two huge boxes of stuffed animals for me. Jon's second-grade teacher, Mrs. Cox, and my first-grade teacher, Mrs. Smith, wrapped the boxes in pink paper and brought them to the hospital. Each day, Mom and Dad would pull one treat out of the box for me. It made me feel special for sure, but even I knew I wasn't the same. I feared it meant my friends wouldn't feel the same toward me, particularly, the little boy who was my first-grade boyfriend.

Some would say I was boy crazy. Indeed I was. But it was a little deeper than just being boy crazy. I had a strong awareness of my sexuality very early. Television and movies were an unfiltered venue of exposure to sexual behavior. Jon popped in the VHS tape of *Sixteen Candles* and watched the bare-breasted scene on numerous occasions, for one, because we weren't supposed to, and two, because it was intriguing. I watched Grandma's favorite television drama *Hotel* with her routinely. She attempted to distract by making conservative comments of disapproval like a little, "oh my," when sex scenes were performed, but I saw them nevertheless. Additionally, I grew up in a sexually geared environment, hearing Dad and his brother casually joke about sex. I pieced together a world where women had beautiful bodies, where men admired and enjoyed the features of such a body. A body I would never have.

Since my perception of love was skin-deep, I questioned if anyone would ever want me in such a way, which were some of the most personal and vulnerable types of thoughts. Furthermore, they aren't appropriate for children to even think, much more express. I knew that, so the way I expressed my concern was by asking questions about my future in regard to marriage and children. "Will I be able to get married when I grow up?" and "Will I be able to have children?" I had a strong sense those components were off the table for my life, before they were even on the table. My first-grade boyfriend coming to visit would be my first opportunity to detect if there was still a glimpse of attractiveness found in me.

By this point in my recovery, I typically wore a nightgown over my bandaged body. Not this day though. This day my mind and intention were not in the place of a seven-year-old little girl. My mind and intention were to answer a question I had been asking myself for weeks: *Will anyone ever want me?*

What kind of life was I getting better to live? What kind of future did I have to look forward to?

I couldn't articulate such grown-up thoughts. Therefore, I would assess the potential for myself. I refused to put on a nightgown, or any shirt. We were having a party, and I refused to wear clothes. I laid in the hospital bed with a white sheet and rose-colored comforter pulled up over my chest, both my arms exposed, extended down my sides, holding down the bed linens as I had seen in sensual scenes. This adult dilemma I faced was on the shoulders of a sweet, little, first-grade boy, who had merely been nothing more than a special friend.

He came for the hospital room party that day. The minute he arrived, I remembered nothing more than what a sweet friend he was to me. Just four months earlier, our class had exchanged Valentine's cards. The one I gave to him was extra special, like a *Be Mine*. Those were the age-appropriate things that made a first-grade girl giddy. After the party started, I forgot about my concerns of growing up scarred. In the moment, I was just a kid again with a room full of friends.

Like any party, there were trays of bite-sized sandwiches, pop and punch, and lots of voices sharing stories, laughter and gratitude over the many answered prayers invested for the hope of this day.

Our family friends from Arkansas, Doyle, Linda and their kids, Sara and Leslie, were part of the party crowd. Dad and Doyle were best friends, and the rest of our family became the same. We celebrated birthdays and holidays and spent summers together. Their long drive to come to the hospital that day connected me with my life before the hospital and the one waiting for me when I got out.

• • • • • • •

I was progressing to a life outside of the hospital. In fact, I actually got to leave the hospital for a short field trip.

My doctors gave approval for an evening excursion. Mom, Dad, Barry and Grandma took me to get brand-new shoes. As they pushed my wheelchair through the shoe department, my eyes were drawn to the display of the black and white 1920s-style button dress shoes but knew my feet were not up for fancy shoes like those. I picked Jon's favorite—high-top Converse. Except mine were hot pink. It made me think about the time he tried to dry his in the microwave. We both learned a lesson: nuking Converse smells like burnt rubber!

I was so excited to be getting new shoes, but it hurt just trying them on. My right foot was much bigger than my left, so Dad had to buy two pairs in different sizes. However, he was more than happy to do it. There wasn't a problem in the world because for the first time, we were doing something normal.

We ate dinner at Taco Bueno and watched *Who Framed Roger Rabbit* in the movie theater.

Going to the movies had always been an exciting treat for me. The last time I had been to the movies was a few months earlier to see *Three Men and a Baby*. As wonderful as it was to be out of the hospital doing something normal for the evening, it just didn't feel normal. Jon wasn't with us.

I loved watching the movie that night, but I thought about the time Dad had taken Jon and me to see *Flight of the Navigator*. Dad was never much for planning—a downfall when it came to seeing popular movies. He typically tried to fit more into the schedule than what time allowed, meaning we ran late when running with Dad. When we arrived, the theater was dark, and the movie was already playing. He scoped out two seats on the very front row and marched Jon and me down to sit in them. Dad went to stand in the very back of the theater. I kept turning around to check on him, seeing the light of the movie reflect on his glasses, as his tall stature peeked just over the partitioned wall behind the back row of seats. I would have rather all of us sit together, but Jon was right next to me. The same place he was when we saw *American Tale*.

Fievel, the story's main character, captured our hearts through his journey to find his family. The movie produced more than an emotional story line. "Somewhere Out There" was a hit song for writer James Horner, scoring him an Academy Award nomination in 1986.[1] The motion picture soundtrack rendition performed by James Ingram and Linda Ronstadt peaked to number two on the Billboard music charts by March 1987 but continued playing on the radio for years following its success.[2]

The song was more than a pretty ballad for me. I was struggling to understand the permanence of death. I couldn't comprehend my life without Jon. In a similar way I remembered Fievel's sister Tanya feeling about her brother. Her family said Fievel was gone, but Tanya still had hope he was alive. In the movie, she and Fievel sang the song at the same time from different places. Fievel was looking for his family, and his sister refused to believe he was dead. Their song to find one another was a prayer and hope I wanted to be for Jon and me.

Accepting the heartbreaking reality of never being together again was a challenge I continued facing internally. Not that I didn't want to share. I simply didn't understand enough to know what to share. My grief was a barricaded dam of powerful emotion. It was an incomprehensible magnitude for me, having no experience with death and no coping skills developed in facing it. The journey was not going to get any easier by making my way back home.

Mom, Dad, Barry and Grandma returned me to the hospital at the end of our evening out. The nurses graciously listened as I shared the details of the night of eating out, watching the new movie and getting new shoes.

My new high-top, hot-pink Converse shoes were a big hit. Their greater purpose was to hold the new leg splints in place, meaning the shoes stayed on my feet even when I was in bed. Ken, one of my nurses who worked the tank room, made jokes about how bright the shoes were when he came to get me. He had a way of making me giggle but brought out the biggest belt of laughter the day he showed up with sunglasses covering his eyes. "Your shoes are so bright I needed my sunglasses to walk in here," he dramatically stated. I always liked Ken doing my bandage change because he let me soak in the tank longer than usual, making my bandages come off easier. Plus, he always brought energy, enthusiasm and happiness to whatever he was doing.

These nurses were my family. When I hurt they'd ask, "Is it on the inside or outside?" Sometimes I didn't know. Sometimes I just hurt. I ached. Whether it was a superficial physical sensation, an underlying unidentified problem or an emotional need I didn't know how to express, they were there. They were there, bringing life to mine by sharing theirs. Through the most ordinary events, they connected me to normal life. Like when Carolyn brought Polaroid photos of her latest litter of dachshund puppies and when Susie would let me count the earrings running from her lobe around the top of her ear. I wondered if I would ever get my ears pierced the same.

The single earring holes I got two years earlier were starting to close off after weeks in the hospital with no earrings to fill the pierced lobes. It had been quite an ordeal getting my ears pierced. "They take a big gun and shoot a hole in your ear," Barry reported. "Are you sure you still want to do it?"

My five-year-old mind pictured myself sitting in a chair, while someone stood back with a large gun pressed against their shoulder, aiming the barrel at my earlobe. Even with that image and anxiety, I really wanted my ears pierced. Imagine my relief when I saw how small the gun actually was. Barry certainly did me a favor by building it up in my mind. By comparison it wasn't a big deal at all. But here I was two years later, after weeks in the hospital, my treasured pierced ears were closing, and I wondered if I'd have pretty earrings like Susie again.

A fellow patient in the progressive unit was engaged to be married when he sustained his burn injury. His fiancée was as sweet as she was beautiful. Her name was Angela. She sat at my bedside, tediously working a pretty pair of red, heart earrings back into my ears, telling me I could have her wedding bouquet when I got better and came to her wedding. In spite of the bald head, Angela helped me feel a piece of pretty with those earrings. Some weeks later, I did attend her wedding and she fulfilled her intention of gifting her bouquet to me. She didn't opt for the tossing tradition at her reception, but rather walked over toward me, knelt down by my wheelchair and handed me her beautiful flowers.

I felt very loved.

Special moments frequently unfolded with feelings of love from the staff, fellow patients, friends and my family. Like Grandma rubbing and rubbing Curel lotion on my skin, Aunt Donna reading *James and the Giant Peach* to me, and Mom polishing a pretty pink on my long fingernails.

An unofficial fan club cheered me on, supported me and encouraged me as I made my way back home. I needed every ounce of strength they offered on the other side of that hospital door.

On the day of discharge, July 11, 1988, Dr. Norberg stated, "People like to throw the 'miracle' word around here, but I can say now, I have *truly* seen a miracle."

11

Not Normal

Every patient in the hospital has one common goal: go home. Home represents security, comfort, safety and normalcy.

In my first television interview after the accident, I expressed my hope for normal. A hospital bed sheet was folded and laid in the seat of the wheelchair, running up over the back of it for me to sit down on and lean back into. Though I never did lean back. I was in a forward-flexed position placing my forearms on the armrests of the chair. My hair had started growing back, looking like a short boy-cut. I wore a white T-shirt that had two bears on the front. Mom and Dad were positioned to my left, sitting behind me on a hospital bed. For some reason, the interview wasn't conducted in my room but set up in an empty one. When asked what I wanted to do, I answered, "Run and play and stuff. And be back how I was before the accident."

I can't recall how many times as a family we expressed we just wanted to "get back to normal." Only our normal was gone. And I would never be back like I was before the accident. None of us would. We would never get back to anything we had known as normal.

I wasn't necessarily ready to discharge by July 11th. My doctors intended on sending me to another facility for rehab. Children's Medical Center was a 108-hospital-bed facility in Tulsa, offering services for developmental pediatrics, pediatric neurology, physical therapy, audiology, speech therapy, biofeedback and such specialty clinics as muscular dystrophy and allergies.[1] The plan was to send me there for rehabilitation, or rehab as everyone referred to it. Rehab, I learned, was a nice way to describe intense, painful physical therapy. It was believed I would never walk again, so whatever activities of daily living I could recover would require a rigorous physical therapy treatment plan.

Nevertheless, what appeared as my biggest physical challenge paled in comparison to the emotional trauma I had not been able to absorb.

I was disconnecting from the life I was supposedly getting better for, forgetting what home was like. I was losing memory of our old beagle dog, Schultz; the pool; and what our house looked like, the only home I had ever known. Dad used the Polaroid camera to snap pictures of those fading pieces of my life, pinning the photos to a corkboard on the wall in my hospital room. Mom and Dad felt it was imperative to get me home. They were willing to do whatever it took to provide some portion of normalcy.

It was agreed I would be discharged home with a demanding outpatient rehabilitation program at Saint Francis, the hospital where Mom worked.

July 11, 1988, was on a Monday. It was also Barry's 18th birthday.

One might imagine a big to-do leaving the hospital seventy-five days after the accident, people who prayed for my survival there to celebrate as I exited the entrance of the hospital. However, there was no applause, confetti, bubbles, balloons, nor were there any people. It was just Dad. Dad was there to take me home. Only him, as he requested it be.

Before leaving I was commissioned to drink a small Styrofoam cup of warm prune juice. Since narcotics can slow the bowel and lead to constipation, it was determined I needed prune juice to promote gastric motility. I couldn't. I wouldn't. I refused. *Are you kidding me?* I thought. *This is the day I'm supposed to go home, and after all I've had to do, it comes down to this?* There was no way in the world I would drink that yucky stuff. So I thought, anyway. I drank the disgusting warm prune juice and finally was placed in my wheelchair to roll out of the burn unit.

Leaving wasn't a big deal at all. Not even a close staff member walked us out. Not Lois, Kelly, Vicki, Susie, Ken, Carolyn, Bobbie or Mary. It was without fanfare, a relatively somber and stoic atmosphere.

We made our way out of the burn unit's front doors, into the waiting room where so many prayers were prayed over my life. We passed the restrooms on our left, the very place Mom had told Dad Jon didn't survive. Making a turn to the right we entered the elevator corridor where Dad pressed the down button. It dinged, opened and we loaded on. We descended from the fifth floor, getting closer and closer to life outside the hospital. Upon exiting, the wheelchair rolled so fast it created a strong breeze against my face. We entered the main lobby of the hospital, passing by the information desk. The first set of automatic glass doors on the right separated. There was a slight slope down in the floor toward the second set of automatic glass doors opening up to life outside the hospital.

I looked around at the outside, the clear canopy covering the walkway over me, the red-colored brick pavers jostling my wheelchair as the wheels rolled across them.

The four-door brown Oldsmobile was parked in the circle drive at the end of the walkway. Dad loaded a few things in the car before opening the front seat passenger door. He walked over to me, slid his right arm behind my knees, and his left arm around my back with the fingers of his left hand flexed around my left shoulder. I couldn't lift my right arm enough to wrap it around his neck, but his six-foot-four stature held me securely, lifting me out of the wheelchair and transferring me into the car. We pulled away from the hospital, heading for our first stop.

The cemetery.

Dad made several turns after entering the cemetery. We drove to a dead end. Dad turned around and positioned the car so the passenger side would be nearest the sidewalk. The car inched up slowly to a stop. I looked out the window on my right and saw three steps with a single wrought-iron handrail on the left leading up somewhere.

Dad put the car in park. He got out and opened the trunk to retrieve my wheelchair. He walked up the steps, carrying the wheelchair with his right hand. He disappeared out of my view for only a moment. Dad walked back down the steps, opened the passenger side door and lifted me out the same way he had placed me in just moments before. Dad carried me up the steps and as gently as he could, he placed me in the chair and knelt down beside me, grasping the left armrest of the wheelchair with his right hand.

I looked at the bronzed grave marker.

The marker was flat on the ground, rectangular in shape. There were raised gold grains of wheat adorning each side of the top.

Jon Michael Cochrane
1979–1988
With Jesus In Heaven

I looked at his name. I looked at the numbers. I tried to understand his body was buried under the ground beneath us. I attempted to comprehend the reality of the moment, that the dash meant time was already gone and so was Jon. I don't even know if I cried. I simply could not grasp my life without him.

Dad began to cry. His crying turned into sobbing. He broke as he knelt beside me, hanging on to my wheelchair. I believe he spoke words, but the weight of the moment was too heavy to recall what those were. I didn't know Dad very well. None of his kids really did. In that moment at Jon's graveside, I believe he was grieving that very harsh reality and making the determination to do life differently.

Our life as we had known it ended at the grave of a nine-year-old child. Nothing would ever be the same.

Our next stop was home. Whatever home was going to mean now.

• • • • • • •

The drive home was unremarkable. Until I realized we weren't taking Highway 51B. I didn't know the names of the roads, but I knew the way. We weren't taking the route I was familiar with. Instead, we continued heading east on the main highway, Highway 51. I realized where we were when I saw Lawg Caybun, Mike and Katherine's store. It was a gas station and a bait and tackle shop sitting on the south side of Highway 51.

Dad turned right onto the road beside the store, driving south toward the location Jon and I had our accident.

The road was no longer dirt. It had been paved, so it already looked different. And although only seventy-five days had passed since I had last been there, it felt vaguely strange, like a bad dream. Dad stopped at what was our point of impact. The place where Jon died and I burned. He encouraged me to look around. This was something I had to face. This was part of my life, a road we traveled before the accident and one we would travel after. Like everything else, there was no option to avoid it; no option to run away, never seeing it again; no option to put it as far behind us as remotely possible. This road was now a part of my story, the last road Jon and I traveled together.

On July 11th, Dad took me home, completing the journey Jon and I started seventy-five days earlier. It was a journey I have been on every day since.

The car came to the end of the road. Dad turned, right off the new pavement onto dirt road, driving toward the bridge over the turnpike. Past the bridge, we made a curve to the left and then angled back to the right. Those bends in the road had made me nervous when Jon and I were on our way to see our friends. Dad proceeded up to the next intersection by Mike and Katherine's house. I saw their house and the McColloughs' next door to them. It had been so long since I had seen everything, it was almost as if I were seeing it for the first time.

Dad turned heading west on our dirt road. Our house came into view on my right. There in the front yard was an eight-foot-wide roadside sign with a yellow arrow at the top pointing toward our house. The board face was white with black letters spelling out *Welcome Home Heather! We Love You!*

I was finally home.

My pleas from months before during the helicopter ride to the hospital, "I want to go home," were met.

I was home.

However, unbeknownst to me, I was no longer the same little girl. My family was not the same family. And our home didn't feel like the home I had known, the one I had longed to get back to.

Mom and Dad set me up on our brown-striped couch in the living room. I spent the daytime on the couch, and at night, Dad carried me upstairs to my bed. But even my room didn't feel right. It was too quiet. Like the house, my room felt so empty.

Jon's bedroom and my bedroom were right next to each other. When Barry lived with us, Jon and I shared a room, but anytime Barry would leave for his mom's, Jon would promptly move me out to my own room, whether Mom had given the go-ahead or not. Being the very reason why those moves commonly took place in the middle of the night.

Jon woke me up for one such move. He enthusiastically convinced my sleepy head of his grandiose plan, and we were transferring hangers of clothes from one closet to another before I knew it. There must have been much more to do than I had the energy for, because I found myself lying on the bed in my new room, the light shining bright over my face, dozing off with David Letterman on the television. Jon commissioned me, "Heather, get up! Get up!" I got up, complying with his command, only to take a short break from the task a few moments later. Jon and I went downstairs for a snack. Trying to be quiet and not get caught, we returned upstairs to eat in the closet. Our hearts stopped when the closet door opened. Sitting on the floor, we looked up to see Dad standing there groggy and grumpy. We were braced for the worst. To our surprise, we didn't get in trouble. Dad simply grumbled, "Get back to bed." That was that. We got to bed. And to Jon's satisfaction, we had made enough progress that our going-to-bed was in different rooms.

It was the last time we would shake up the sleeping arrangements. That was the room where I stayed, the room straight across from Mom and Dad's. Upon reaching the top of the stairs, Mom and Dad's room was on the right. There was a bathroom on the opposite wall facing the top of the stairs. My room was to the left of the stairs. Jon's room was the next door past mine. We shared the wall separating the spaces.

Those rooms had been an area of assertive independence and creative exploration. Jon and I spent hours building tents and forts, playing with cars, Legos, board games, and even dressing up. Jon's persistent intention to make others laugh generally involved dressing up as a girl or flushing his head in the toilet, creating a customized hairstyle he called *swirlies*. He always succeeded in getting laughs.

Those rooms of ours were filled full, from pillow fights to eighties pop music. The radio was on and ready at all times with a cassette tape for us to record an array of our favorite songs, like "Dancing on the Ceiling" by Lionel Richie, Prince's "You've Got the Look," "Walk Like an Egyptian" by The Bangles, "Bad" by Michael Jackson, "Faith" by George Michael, and Bon Jovi's "You Give Love a Bad Name." Jon must have been just as confused as I was because he never corrected me, but I wholeheartedly thought if someone got "shot to the heart"[2] like Bon Jovi sang, then it only made sense for the words to be "you give love a Band-Aid." Wouldn't you need a Band-Aid after getting shot to the heart? I thought so. And that's just what I sang—at the top of my lungs.

I was home in the rooms where Jon and I read our Golden Books, played our board games and drew our pictures. I was home where we spent summers riding our bicycles and motorcycles, making mud pies, swimming, fetching frogs out of the pool to dissect, and running with our arms straight out through the tall stalks of corn in Mom and Grandma's garden.

I was home—but far from comfort.

At first, Mom and Dad thought I must be in pain. Physical pain. Lying on the couch, emotion overcame me. I began crying hysterically. Inconsolable crying.

"Heather, what's wrong?"

"I don't know," I answered.

"Are you hurting?"

"No," I responded.

Dad carried me up to my room, attempting to bring comfort with a change in my position or just a change in scenery. Despite intervention, the torture of emotion came every day around 5:00. A few evenings passed before Mom and Dad began seeing the pattern. They were caught off guard, considering the fact I had no knowledge of what time our accident happened and that this attack of grief never occurred in the hospital. But I was home now. I was home where Jon had been all my life. I was home, but he wasn't.

His place at the table was empty. The same table we ate at every night. It was still there. The same chair. Still there. The same plates. Still there. Everything the same but nothing the same.

Mom and Dad wanted me to come home to the way things had been, not as they were now and would be. Thinking it would be more difficult to return home with nothing of Jon left, they waited for me to go through his things. It was a necessary process that had to be done at some point. He wasn't there anymore. Keeping his stuff wouldn't change our brutal reality.

It was just Dad and me. Mom wasn't there. It was too much for her.

Dad placed me at the foot of Jon's bed facing the closet. I watched Dad retrieve the clothes from the hangers, fold them and place them in a bag to give away. Jon would not be coming home. He would not ever be back to wear them again. Nor would he be back to move me out of his room in the middle of the night. He would not be back to chase me around the pool or dare me to drink Pepto-Bismol. He would not be back to carry out all the big brother duties he so perfectly performed.

Jon would not be back to finish the book left in his room. The bookmark would stay between the pages where he left off. The place he intended to return indicated by a pencil mark at the start of the second sentence on the top of page thirty-seven. The last words he read from *Charlotte's Web* were:

> At last, Wilbur saw the creature that had spoken to him
> in such a kindly way. Stretched across the upper part of the
> doorway was a big spiderweb, and hanging from the top of
> the web, head down, was a large grey spider.[3]

I did not know what I felt. I did not even know to call it pain. I could not understand the sheer emptiness of my being, the complete loss of my existence, the shattering of my identity. My soul felt what my mind could not understand.

Normal was no longer.

12

Returning to Life

Memory can be the greatest gift and the cruelest curse.

Over the years, I've been asked if I remember. I've been asked if I remember the accident, the hospital, or the pain. People wonder how much a seven-year-old could possibly recall. Furthermore, some assume there is a natural protective mechanism in the brain, which blocks out the darkest moments of life.

In an article for *Psychology Today,* Dr. Batcho explains otherwise: "The earliest childhood memories recalled by adults are often of emotional events. . . . The extent to which an experience is understood in a meaningful way affects the likelihood that it will be incorporated into the permanent repertoire of the events of our life."[1]

Studies have reported only 3 percent of life events are memorable, meaning we forget more of our life than we remember. However, those we do remember are significant emotional experiences or events.[2]

Much of me wanted to forget, but more of me worked to remember. If I forgot the worst day of my life, then I might potentially forget Jon. As hard as it was, I wanted to remember every detail I could possibly hold on to.

Mom says Jon loved being a big brother. Around four years old, he began saying, "I'm Heather's big brother, like Barry's my big brother." Despite her explaining Barry was a big brother to both of us, Jon remained fixated on his big-brother status to me, demonstrating pride and ownership in our relationship.

During his early preschool years, he had difficulty connecting with other kids. He expressed feelings of loneliness and sadness. Jon had challenges in learning to play with others but never with me. I was his built-in buddy, and he was mine.

If it weren't for our rural roots, I'm not sure Jon and I would have developed the special bond we did. We seized every moment we could to play with someone else, whether it was our friends and neighbors, Brad and Mary, or our cousins, Krista and Slade. We welcomed the company of other kids. And Jon commonly pushed the mark on trying to impress them. Whether throwing money out the car window or riding his bike in the pool, there was no consequence too great for the satisfaction he got in the moment.

I wanted to remember everything. How he spoke so loud Mom would say, "Jon, we're right here." How he hardly ever used a napkin at the table; rather, he'd utilize the arm of his sleeve to wipe off his face. I didn't want to forget a thing.

Preserving my happiest memories meant preserving my most painful ones. Remembering Jon meant realizing my loss. Every day.

Memories were one of many challenges I faced simultaneously. Physical therapy, further surgeries and returning to school made for a buffet of misery I had no emotional experience in tackling. There was no choice. This was the process of returning to life.

As every effort had been given to save my life, every effort was then invested into rehabilitating my body. There wasn't much optimism I could regain my ability to walk. The function simply was not present. Muscle mass was lost. Extensive nerve damage was sustained. Dr. Raptou, the head of the physical therapy department, didn't sugarcoat the situation during a conference with Mom and Dad.

"She will never walk again," he proclaimed.

It wasn't the first time they had been given a grim report. They had experience in believing against bleak circumstance, to the point of once being described as living in a fairy tale. Considering how far we had come, they were defiant against his conclusion.

"It would be a waste of my therapists' time," he continued, "but we will give her three weeks."

"No," Mom corrected. "Heather connects quickly with people. I don't want her forming a bond with her therapists and then having to move her somewhere else. We will give her two weeks."

Dr. Raptou's note to Dr. Park outlined the plan: "We will begin this patient on an intensive program of physical and occupational therapy in an attempt to aid in her rehabilitation. We will treat her each day for the next two weeks. I will recheck her on July 25, 1988, for disposition and further care."

With that my physical therapy program began.

After two sessions, Dr. Raptou sent an update to Dr. Norberg, informing, "Heather promised me today that she would try her best to cooperate with the treatment regimen that is outlined for her." In another note dated August 9, 1988, Dr. Raptou wrote, "The patient refused stretching activities during her last few days of treatment, probably because of the anxiety associated with her forthcoming hospitalization. Overall, this child has done quite well and has put a great deal of effort into her treatment sessions, as you will note in perusing the therapy notes."

I went in for surgery the next day, August 10th—back in the hospital within thirty days of finally leaving. This surgery, though, was performed at Saint Francis, the hospital where I was receiving my physical therapy. Having surgery at Saint Francis was intended to provide the benefit for recommencing physical therapy while still inpatient. Plus, Mom worked there, so she could be with me in my room over her break and lunch during my hospital stay.

The approach was meant to make what had to be done work the best way it could, aiming for Mom to be with me as much as possible without having to take off work. She had already been off more time than was available to her. Coworkers had generously donated from their own accrued hours of paid time off to help with the burden of missing work. Her job in accounts receivable at Saint Francis provided the health insurance for our family, which in light of the hospital bills was actually more valuable than her paycheck. It was a job she had acquired only seventeen months before our accident and was one our family couldn't afford for her to quit.

Dr. Norberg performed the surgery with Dr. Park assisting. Dr. Park carried out an anoscopy, a medical procedure to identify abnormalities in the gastrointestinal tract, notably in the anus or rectum. In the time I had left the burn center, it was suspected my lack of bowel movement was due either to the effects of pain medication or an insufficient amount of nutritional intake or both. This resulted with me on the floor in the small upstairs bathroom, completely distressed while Mom and Dad attempted to administer an enema. After shrills of screaming, tears of pain and pleas of resistance, it was discovered that scar tissue had formed over my rectum. The moment was traumatizing for all three of us. Trying to rehabilitate at home presented challenges that were overwhelming at times.

Burn scar contractures behind both knees, right armpit, right elbow, perineum and rectum were released during the August 10th surgery. Split-thickness skin grafts were taken from my back and placed in the wounds, anchored with skin staples.

The four days in the hospital proved to be overwhelming for the staff taking care of me. Nurses who work in burn care have received specialized training and education. Presenting a nurse who has never had such experiences to care for such a patient is not only an unfavorable situation for the patient, but an unjust expectation for the nurse. However, it was a situation we found ourselves in.

I perceived the uneasiness of the nurses caring for me. They didn't have the confidence and assurance I had known before. This was confirmed when I expressed to one of them, "I'm scared," and she responded with "I'm scared, too." With that conversation, Mom and Dad had me transported back to Hillcrest where I continued with treatment. It was apparent that while it would have been ideal to be at Saint Francis with Mom and with my physical therapists, the importance of a specialty service could not be overlooked.

Surgeries were performed routinely. Physical therapy was a normal part of life. I would ping-pong back and forth between the two. The progress being made couldn't afford breaks; otherwise, scar tissue constricted and regression was a threat.

At home, Dad carried out dressing changes and therapy. He structured his life and career around my care. He'd carry me up the stairs, place me in the tub and let me soak as long as possible, slowly pulling off the dressings adhered to my body. As physical therapy progressed, he implemented stretches and activities to promote movement. Much of what he did came with pleas to stop, like putting me against the wall and working to straighten my torso.

Scar tissue constricted as I slept through the night. I had an array of splints for my torso, my legs, and even my face. But it was hard to sleep while braced flat. I wanted to curl up in a position of comfort. Which came at a cost. My body was drawn up each morning. The trunk of my body contracted, hunching me over like an old woman. The tissue behind my knees constricted, pulling my heel up off the floor. The skin in the crease of my arm tightened, drawing my wrist up against my stomach. Mornings meant ripping, tearing the tissue to stretch the extremities. In order to get my heel to the floor, tissue behind my knee tore open. In order to extend my arm to my side, tissue in the antecubital area tore open. In order to straighten my trunk, tissue ripped on my torso.

Dad tried to make the necessary process as natural as possible by incorporating activities of daily living. Like making breakfast.

There was a wooden step stool kept under the built-in desk in our kitchen. The underside of the stool was stained with drops of Jon's blood from an accidental head wound. Memories of him were never lost in our home. Dad put me up on the stool in front of the stove and had me scramble eggs in our black cast-iron skillet. The daily life challenges continued to the dinner table. Mom and Dad placed things outside my reach, making me stretch my arms to get them. Grandma couldn't stand it. She left the dinner table many evenings and retreated across the driveway to her house. Rehabilitation was not for the faint of heart. It required the strongest determination from all of us.

My schedule for physical therapy started with twice a day for an hour every day of the workweek. Over time it tapered off, until I had surgery, and then the intensity recommenced.

It was an excruciatingly painful program. I'd have given anything to avoid it or just delay it. I'd try any excuse I could find. Going to the bathroom was a common one. Bowel movements had come to be an important happening in my world. Whether I could make it happen or not, I'd waste as much time as permitted pretending to produce one. Therapy was going to happen one way or the other, but I gave my best to postpone it.

When CNN came to our house for an interview to share our story, Dad described it like this: "If I told you every day that I'm going to hit all your little toes with a ball-peen hammer, I think after the first day you'd say, 'I don't want to come back.' But you know you have to come back. You have to come back day after day after day after day."

The strongest people were the therapists who worked to rehabilitate my body despite the loss of muscle mass and the absence of nerve conduction. Jeff, my physical therapist, and Cathy, my occupational therapist, worked together during the sessions. They fought for me, even when that involved fighting against me. In order to stretch my trunk, they laid me prone on the mat on my tummy. Jeff would straddle me and sit on my bottom. Cathy would straddle me and sit on my back. Impressively, my seven-year-old, 49.8-pound body could hold them up in painful resistance to pulling the tight tissue on my chest and abdomen. One particular time, after they had succeeded in flattening me out on my stomach, Cathy began to slowly abduct my arms until we all heard the tissue rip like the sound of a T-shirt tearing. I belted out a bloodcurdling cry. They immediately released all pressure and provided complete comfort.

Upon leaving that day, the secretary summoned my attention. "Heather," she began, "a lady heard you crying today and left this for you." I was astonished as she handed me a twenty-dollar bill!

I was used to people having to hurt me. I wasn't afraid of them. I knew they wanted to help me, even though that meant pain. Getting twenty dollars from a compassionate patient made me feel a little bit guilty, but it was a major score nevertheless!

Jeff and Cathy incorporated praise and rewards into treatment to promote my cooperative behavior and compliance. We always started with time in a stainless-steel whirlpool tank. From appearance it looked too small for me to fit in, so I initially opposed the idea. As with most things, I eventually had to comply. The whirlpool became an enjoyable part of therapy. Especially because I would bring my radio and Jeff would sing. At the time Janet Jackson's "Escapade"[3] song was very popular; however, when Jeff sang it, he changed the words:

> Come on baby, let's get away
> Let's save our troubles for another day
> Come go with me, we've got it made
> Let me take you on an Ice Capade (on an Ice Capade baby)!

It made complete sense to me. I had been to the Ice Capades before. On the other hand, I had no clue what an escapade was. Embarrassingly, I was an adult before I figured out what the lyrics really were!

The journey was hard fought, but Jeff and Cathy got me where no one thought possible—walking!

Ambulating was truly attained one step at a time. First with a few feet, and as time progressed, so did the distance. I despised ending therapy with the challenge to walk down the hall from the physical therapy door to the accounts receivable's door. I had to get to Mom for my ride home. It was good motivation. Within four months I was not only walking but also climbing up and down the physical therapy department's training stairs.

A camera crew came for one of my therapy appointments. I quickly came to know I was living a story others wanted to hear about, or at the least, were curious about. Furthermore, I had met enough reporters between newspaper and television to discern whether or not they just wanted a story or if the reporter really cared about me. Jerry Webber, from our local NBC station, was a journalist who genuinely cared about people. He came to capture my accomplishment and reported, "Heather Cochrane of Porter, cute as a kitten with the heart of a lioness, making a comeback at the age of seven."[4]

There were many setbacks; nevertheless, Jerry Webber was right. I was making a comeback. Yet I was gaining a lot more than my basic ability to walk. A key component for carrying the physical reminder of our tragedy was developing within me. Placing the painful memories in a box at the back of my mind was not an option. My body carried the evidence of the accident. Scars keeping the memory tied to my present. Never would it be a mere piece of my past but part of every single day of my life. Forever carrying the memory was cultivating the character and quality necessary in transforming this tragedy.

An overcomer was in the making.

13

Healing Hurts

Healing can feel absolutely miserable. It sounds like a good thing, but it's only good once it has been completed. *Healed* is the place to be. *Healing*, not so much. The process is not a positive experience. It hurts to heal.

Even though I despised hearing it, *pain is gain* continued to be my mantra. It was a phrase I had come to live by.

Surgeries were a part of normal life. I'd go in for three to four each month, and then it eventually tapered off to three to four each year. Releasing contractures of scar tissue and skin grafts was routine procedure. There was a lot of growing my seven-year-old body had in store. Since scars don't stretch, each bit of growth meant surgery to cut something.

It was a dreadful process. I had immense anxiety the night before an operation because I knew what awaited me. I'd get in the bathroom and stare at the location being released, sometimes getting a mirror to see. Whether it was my arm, my armpit, stomach, side, back, groin, thighs, legs, backs of knees or feet, whatever the area, I tried to see it, preparing myself for what it would look like the next day. And worse, what it would feel like. But I always knew it was something that had to be done, so I tried my best to approach it with the right attitude. Surgery was going to happen whether I wanted it to or not.

My attitude determined either the level of misery or the level of peace I experienced. Not that I was always cooperative. I certainly had my moments. Overall though, my nature to please others and make them proud made me a pretty compliant patient.

I tried to make the most of it, finding good things about surgery. Like all the attention I would get. I loved adults wanting to visit with me and ask me questions. The fact I had a captivated audience while awake was certainly something to enjoy. Plus, I knew I'd get warm blankets, a total perk! And I knew I'd get good medicine. Anything to make me sleep was welcomed in my world.

Above the blankets and meds were the treasures of precious people like Fred. He was Dr. Norberg's personal surgical assistant, so he was there for many of my surgeries. Fred had a gift. A talent of sorts, perfect for the apprehensive pediatric patient.

Like clockwork, before strolling out of the pre-op area, Fred would come see me. He'd be ready in surgical scrubs with his disposable surgical cap covering his red hair. His caring blue eyes and bubbly personality made him just the person to make it all seem okay.

Fred was full of fun. When I'd visit Dr. Norberg's office for appointments, he'd offer occasional entertainment, balancing the leg of a chair on his chin. Wherever he went, joy and laughter showed up. From the pre-op holding area to the surgical suite, he brought happiness. And he did it with help from his sidekick cricket. No, it wasn't really a cricket, but I wouldn't have known it. The chirping was completely convincing as Fred pulled his cupped hand out of his pocket, making the noise like a professional ventriloquist. Once in the OR, I'd hear it chirp again and fall asleep feeling like a kid should feel—impressed with the sounds of an imaginary cricket.

The falling asleep part of surgery was always a little scary. I felt anxious before ever getting into the operating room. Most of the time I was rolled in on a gurney, but some of the time I entered in a wheelchair. Occasionally I walked in. Whichever the route of arrival, the environment was the same. White walls. Cold room. Echoes. Electro adhesives stuck on my chest and back. A blood pressure cuff wrapped around my arm. A pulse oximeter placed on my index finger. A mask positioned over my nose and mouth providing oxygen.

Out of all the times I underwent general anesthesia, I only had complication with one induction. It was one time too many. The experience heightened my anxiety for future surgeries, changing my mental process of going to sleep.

It was a surgery like any other. The nurse came down close to me while the mask was positioned over my face. She instructed me to count down from ten to one with her while I fell asleep. The plastic smell of the mask was an overpowering aroma. I could hear the sound of my pulse beeping on the monitor. As I transitioned to sleep, I felt like I was falling down a black hole outlined with neon green lines. Each time I heard the *beep* from the monitor, the hole expanded, feeling as if my body expanded with it. To make the experience even worse, the nurse stopped counting and everyone in the room started talking to each other. I'm sure the moment was incredibly brief, but I was terrified they were starting the surgery without realizing I could still hear them. Scarier than experiencing the sensation of falling down a black hole was the fear of not being fully asleep for the operation.

Regardless of how long it lasted, I was petrified when I woke up and shared what had happened. Unfortunately, many more operations were ahead of me. It was a way of life. I had no choice but to move forward from the experience and hope it never happened again. For every surgery thereafter, I have requested no masks be placed over my face until I've been given some sedation. In addition, I distract myself from focusing on the environment by engaging the staff in normal conversation. Since that one bad induction event, I have never once obliged to counting. Thankfully, I have felt surrounded by compassionate people who have always met me where I am, giving their best to care for me in a caring way. Even if that simply involves some casual operating room chitchat.

After surgery comes recovery. The recovery period is when the healing process immediately begins. One of the worst parts of a surgery is having to wake up, because the healing process can be so very painful. The healing process can also itch!

As if pain isn't bad enough, itching is awful, driving a person absolutely mad. If I invested a dime for every time someone said, "Heather, that means you're healing," I'd be sitting on one cushy mutual fund.

Along with the agitation of dry skin was the irritation of the Jobst suit. It is a compression garment suit used to treat the hypertrophic burn scars. Hypertrophic scarring is considered an inflammatory illness creating raised red scars due to excess collagen production. While collagen is necessary for healing, too much of it leads to hypertrophy, a common outcome in children. It is considered an adverse wound healing factor because these types of scars can limit a patient's level of function. The pressure garments are used to make the scars smoother as they heal. Not quite registering on my fashion radar. Not in the least.

With growth spurts came measurements and fittings for a new suit. I had the pants and full long-sleeved shirt, not the kind of "custom-made" people are standing in line for. Let me just say, it was hot and itchy and absolutely miserable, especially during the heat of an Oklahoma summer. To top it off, I had a piece of silicone gel that applied to the scar on my face at nighttime. Trying to sleep with a sheet of slimy gel ace-bandaged to my face and in a complete pressure garment suit did not make for an effective night's rest. The day Dr. Norberg said I no longer had to wear them, I placed every single piece of Jobst garment on my bed, took scissors in my hand and randomly started cutting. I knew I had gotten a little carried away when I ran a cut into my bedspread. Normally Mom and Dad would have been upset with such a decision, but they never said a word. I think they felt just as liberated as I did to close that chapter.

Scarred skin is different. The tissue is not elastic and is more fragile, about 20 percent weaker than normal skin.[1] The wrinkly inelastic skin on the back side of my elbow and on the top of my right knee are common places for skin tears. They become wrinkled when extended and tight when reducing the extremity. Shoes are my biggest source of skin tears, rubbing wounds on the back of my right heel and on the medial malleolus, the bony prominence on the inner side of the ankle. Even after healing, mine protrudes against certain styles of shoes, rubbing open sores. Band-Aids have become my best friend in providing cushion and protection to my thin-scarred skin.

Scarred skin is also drier, so lotion is another friend of mine. Sebaceous glands produce oil to lubricate and moisten the skin, but burns destroy those glands. Whoever in my family was willing spent countless time rubbing innumerable bottles of lotion on my arms, legs and back. Sadly, it was never long enough for me. Being gently massaged with lotion was such welcomed relief despite the areas of decreased sensation, numbness and tingling. We learned there were places to avoid—like my left scapula, or what's referred to as the shoulder blade. I never regained full sensation from the incision made for my open-heart surgery. Another area we avoided was behind my right knee where there is a round bump containing a bundle of nerves. Touching it shoots painful pins-and-needle signals down my leg and on into my toes. It's like an electrical shock. Nevertheless, the lotion was welcomed relief for every other area of my body. It became an essential product, not an optional one—part of my world forever.

Scarred skin doesn't sweat and is more sensitive to the sun. For the summer after the accident, I wore a big wide-brimmed hat to block the sun. But I wasn't outside very much. Dad did get me in the pool a few times, and although being in the water was a good sensation, the joy just wasn't there. I couldn't swim like before. I could hardly move. So sun exposure wasn't too much of an issue that first year after the accident. Years following, I implemented habits of lathering on sunscreen, never having any major issues with sensitivity to a particular brand of sunscreen. Any of them seemed to work fine. Sweating, on the other hand, was an issue.

Burns destroy sweat glands. Sweating allows the body to regulate temperature. With over 80 percent of my body burned, there aren't many places capable of producing sweat. My left armpit and my back are the two. This means overheating can happen from the most ordinary events, such as outdoor activities and aerobic exercise. My face gets really red, like a harsh sunburn, and I feel my heart beating in my head. But it doesn't mean it kept me from those types of activities.

Mom and Dad had me working in the yard and helping with home construction projects just like any other kid. And once my love for the ocean was realized, I couldn't imagine avoiding those tropical climates. Like everything in life, it came with consideration of the challenge and minor modifications when necessary, such as increased hydration, making sure there was the option for shade, and breaks to cool down.

However, some things were beyond modification. Some things were just ugly and hurtful. Going back to school was one of them.

• • • • • • •

My family explored every possible way to help me face the world. It's not an easy navigation for any kid to make, especially for those who look a little different. Namely, little girls with burn scars and no hair challenged with returning to school.

Mom, Grandma and Aunt Donna felt getting a wig would help. I was against the idea, but they persisted, convinced I would like one once I saw the options. It wasn't apparent how deeply I despised the idea until we got to the parking lot. I refused to get out of the car. Moreover, I refused to allow anyone to get me out of the car. I did not want a wig. It made me mad because it made me feel like even more of an old woman. Hunched over. Can't walk. In a wheelchair. Now a wig? No way! How I was going to face the world was going to be with what I had or didn't have. Fake hair couldn't change that fact.

My life was completely sheltered up to the point of returning to school. The burn center and physical therapy department staff and every medical staff individual I had been surrounded by were not shocked, aghast or taken aback by my appearance. The rest of the world was a different story.

Certainly, the process of accepting my new body was difficult, but I had enough denial to cushion the cruel reality. No doubt, Mom and Dad were in denial too. We focused on each day as it came with hopeful optimism for future advancements in medical technology to provide astonishing reconstruction. Specifically, I contended the challenge of living with scars with hopes of one day having new skin.

Burns are described as a grossly disfiguring injury.

Those words. *Gross. Disfigured.*

It's a heavy description to carry. It's hard to have a positive body image and a healthy self-esteem in light of those words.

Kids think concretely. Who they see is who they think they are. Much is the same for how kids view others too.

My family was so proud of me. They didn't have an inkling of embarrassment for the looks we received in public. No. They were completely confident in sharing me. Mom and Dad actually wanted people to see me because I was alive. I had made it! But more importantly, they wanted me to feel their same pride for myself. They wanted me to face the world as the brave, strong fighter I had been, proud of my miraculous story.

Social interaction provided some experiences that were just normal parts of life. However, I did not look normal. The responses of people reinforced the grossly disfiguring description of my injury. Shortly after my initial discharge from the hospital, the farmer who leased our family land stopped by our house with his wife. Mom and Katherine were so excited for the visit and the opportunity to let them see how I was doing. The couple came in eager to find me recovered. Only I didn't look recovered to them at all. The farmer's wife quickly dismissed herself as politely as possible with tears welling up in her eyes.

A few months later, Mom and Dad took me to the state fair. Outings were uncomfortable—physically, socially, and emotionally. I experienced discomfort with pretty much any activity requiring me to get out of bed. But here we were wandering around the fair. I was in a wheelchair being jostled and jolted as Dad tried to navigate the wheels over large electrical cords powering food trucks and fun wheels. Nothing about being there was fun. And people stared at me. Imagine that! Even at the fair with some of the most puzzling people to see, folks were staring at me. Almost as if they had paid a quarter to see something crazy like the world's largest pig.

Returning to school wasn't that bad. Attending *regularly,* on the other hand, was a completely different situation.

I started back in the second grade. Jon's second-grade teacher, Mrs. Cox, was my teacher. I didn't make it for the beginning of the school year, so I had a homebound teacher who came to the house with worksheets and readers. To start, I attended half-days on Fridays, eventually transitioning to full days on Fridays. With therapy and surgeries, I wasn't there very much over the course of the year. Although during the time I was there, I experienced a mixture of diverse emotions.

It was strange going to school without Jon. Being in another place he had been but wasn't anymore. Especially being in the exact classroom where he had occupied a seat just months before. Much of everything was the same, but it felt like a completely different life. School was another reminder of that reality.

Yearbook pictures were a few weeks after school started. Grandma tried to make it special by fixing what hair I had into a spike. I wore a white bib dress. Two blue buttons adorned the top of the V-neck bib, one on each shoulder, with one red button centered at the bottom of the angle. The short-sleeved dress had a pattern of primary-colored circles in the black and white gingham checkers. A matching belt with a red square buckle wrapped my waist. It was the perfect dress for picture day. The Jobst suit was under my dress, covering my arms and legs. Since I wore it every day, only the scars on my left hand, right side of my face and right ear were visible, as well as the quarter-sized wound on the right temple of my head. It took a while to completely close, and hair never grew back in that spot.

Most of my classmates were very sweet for my time there. I didn't know it then, but the students had been prepped for my presence. Dad coordinated with the school to present information about what had happened and what to expect. It helped for reassimilating over that initial year, but like most things, the kindness wore off. If we want to see authenticity, then wait a while. It eventually surfaces.

In terms of physical appearance, I had made strides toward significant healing over the year. For a little girl who wasn't even supposed to live, it was pretty incredible I was back at school for anything. Nevertheless, Mom and Dad made it clear I was not to be given special accommodations.

When the tornado drills were practiced the next spring, I lined up with the rest of the class filing into the hallway. As a second grader, I knew the drill. I knew fire drills were easier. All I had to do was get outside. But for tornado drills, students had to get down on their knees in the hallway facing the cinder-block wall. Hands were clasped together around the back of the head. Next, the students sat their bottom on the back of their heels, leaning forward up against the wall for protection.

I could not raise my arms enough to get my hands behind the back of my head. In fact, Dr. Norberg frequently teased me, "Heather, if a robber came in to the 7-Eleven with a gun and told you to put your hands in the air, then you need to put your hands in the air." It was something I was working toward, but the scar tissue was so constricting I couldn't stretch that far. Nor could I bend my legs to sit my bottom on my heels.

So there I was for the drill in second grade and then again the next year in third grade, on my knees in the hall a head above the rest while my classmates practiced protecting themselves from potential flying debris in the event of a tornado. It's not the way a student would prefer to stand out.

It was the same for school assemblies. When I was growing up, teachers told students to sit *Indian style*. That's been replaced with telling kids to sit *crisscross applesauce*, meaning to get on the floor, sit on their bottom, and cross their legs, tucking their feet under the opposite legs. If students didn't want to sit on their bottom, they could get on their knees and sit their bottom back on their heels. Neither position was possible for me. So there I was for school assemblies on my knees again, my head poking above the crowd of kids. Although my modified position was uncomfortable, increasingly so as time passed, Mom and Dad didn't want me to be given special consideration, which would have made it more embarrassing than it already was.

Mom and Dad were confronted with one of these special considerations during my second-grade year. My tissue was tight from the time sitting at my desk over one particular morning. It came time to line up for lunch. I was at the back of the line. On the walk over to the lunchroom, my class got farther and farther ahead of me. I couldn't straighten my leg, so I was walking with more of a hobble, hunched over, my knee bent, heel up off the ground in a forward-flexed position.

The other second-grade teacher, Mrs. Lewis, came upon me with a friend who stayed behind. Mrs. Lewis was a small lady herself, no taller than five-foot-five, surely. Nevertheless, she carried me over to the lunchroom and made contact with Mom, offering to bring a wagon to school for me. Mom was deeply grateful and expressed such sentiment to Mrs. Lewis but informed her as to why I had to be pushed. We had come so far. The journey hadn't been easy. It wasn't easy and it wouldn't *ever* be. But it would be worth it.

Healing was hard. Healing hurt. However, what was made in the process wasn't worth any shortcuts. Transforming from the state of *healing* to the goal of *healed* was miserable in many different ways, on many different occasions, but the long-term outcome was oh so valuable.

14

Hit Head-On

There are a few things I've gathered regarding head-on collisions. For one, they come unexpectedly, out of nowhere, completely unanticipated and unsuspected. Second, the smaller vehicle is more vulnerable. The larger vehicle in a head-on collision has greater ability to absorb the impact. Third, collisions resulting in a fatality are more likely to occur in a rural area over an urban one.

At least these are true aspects in regard to my experience.

I didn't have any fear of harm the day Jon and I collided with Adrian Ruby. We were absolutely unsuspecting of the danger, so much that I was confused after it occurred. I had no idea what happened.

Adrian too was caught completely off guard. Never would anyone imagine passing a vehicle going the opposite direction and then crashing into two kids on a motorcycle. It was unbelievably unimaginable.

I never saw Adrian after that day.

His family sent a beautiful arrangement for Jon's memorial service: blue carnations and white poms made into a wreath on an easel display. His dad was amongst friends and relatives who signed the guest book at the funeral. They were compassionate people with two heroic sons who didn't hesitate to face fire and fear to save my life.

I was so curious to know them—the driver we collided with and his brother who rushed from their home to help.

Lots of people *wanted* to see me. Several were out of pure curiosity, merely wanting to know what someone looked like after their body burned. Some didn't connect with me or have a care at all about the person under the wounds. Like the man who came to my bedroom after I got home and asked me to show him. He was a friend of our family's friends, and the two families came by to visit one evening. Dad had already carried me up to bed, a place I often preferred to be, but that didn't deter the man from making his way up the stairs to see what he came to see. Yes. The sick-minded man wanted to see my raw flesh. As if I could have shown him anyway. The process involved unwrapping layers of bandages.

The creepy moment didn't last too long. He migrated back downstairs when he realized there was no possibility. After I told Mom about it, I knew Dad would never allow that man to step foot in our house again. It didn't take much intuition to know I was just a free freak show to some people.

However, to others like Adrian, I was a reminder of one of the worst days of his life.

So I never got to see him. I never got to hug his neck and thank him for being the hero I needed in having the chance to live beyond that dirt road.

Mom and I took a platter of home-baked treats over to his family the first Christmas after the accident. I felt so uncomfortable thinking I wasn't wanted there. My seven-year-old mind reasoned that Adrian must blame me for the bad things that had happened. In all reality, if I had left with Jon when he first came to get me, we would have made it home just fine, because Jon had already made it home once. The danger came in him having to come back for me. It was a guilt I worked to bury. One of many things I faced in living beyond the tragedy.

Christmas of 1988 was anything but *merry and bright*. It was routine. It was painfully routine.

My letter to Santa indicated how much Jon was still a part of my world.

> Dear Santa,
>
> I would like a Nintind and litte miss makeup.
> OH I want a bird and a stuffed bear and a
> playpen for a baby cabbage patch. And I want
> a baby cabbage patch too.
> I hope you have a good Christmas.
> Well you please fill Jon's stocking for Jon?
> How is your wife and reindeer? You are getting
> eggnog and chocolate chip cochies this year.
> Barry is here this year.
> This is Austin's first Christmas.
> Have a good Christmas.
> Heather Cochrane

I had a few things correct in my letter. Barry was indeed with us for Christmas that year, although it was not my cousin Austin's first Christmas. I must have been looking forward to celebrating the holiday with her in 1988, lending to my inaccurate report. Additionally, filling Jon's stocking would not make him feel more present. His absence was absolutely overwhelming. Coming downstairs on Christmas morning without him was the most dismal experience.

We were all being happy for each other. Mom, Dad, Barry and Grandma were putting on faces for me and I for them, a face I maintained through reading the annual letter Santa left.

I hobbled over to the end table closest to the fireplace. Hunched over. Short hair. One brace still secured around my right leg. The pictures are pitiful.

The photos captured the moment. *The moment.* The moment I relinquished one of the remaining pieces of my childhood. Santa's penmanship looked awfully familiar to me. Mom and Dad had written many notes over the months I was in the hospital. I watched them sign consent after consent, learning to identify their handwriting.

This letter I so greatly wanted to be from Santa was instead from Dad. I didn't have the heart to tell Mom and Dad I knew. I didn't want them to be sad, or rather sadder, than what all of us already were but didn't talk about.

Instead, I played along while the eager desire to believe in the magic of Christmas was laid down in a letter on the end table closest to the fireplace. There was no room for fantasy, no allowance for fairy tales, as they collided with the unfair realities of a dead brother and a make-believe Santa.

There was much more I would unexpectedly hit head-on.

• • • • • • •

Within a few months after I was born, a bright red area began developing on the uppermost part of my left arm. Our family physician told Mom it was a type of vascular birthmark called a superficial hemangioma, also known as a strawberry mark. He said it would regress and eventually disappear when I got older. He was right. The area I referred to as my *strawberry patch* was completely gone before our accident happened.

I liked my strawberry patch. Mostly because it made me feel a little more connected to Strawberry Shortcake, but it also gave me a sense of uniqueness. The same was true of my first scar from my first fall that required my first set of stitches.

It was very ordinary for us to walk down to the bridge after a big dinner. This one particular evening, Mom, Grandma, Jon, Katherine and her kids, and

I were doing just that—taking a walk down to the bridge. On the way out of our wrap-around driveway, everyone stopped to grab a pear off the pear tree nearest the road. I was always lagging behind. Always. My pear selecting took longer than everyone wanted to wait, so they went ahead and began walking. They were barely ahead, although to me, it seemed far, so I started running to catch up. The gradual decline of the driveway meeting the road, combined with the gravel and my inappropriately matched shoes for the activity, resulted in a fall slicing open the front of my right knee.

I had not known pain. And I wasn't too good at controlling my response to it.

Mom and Katherine took me to the emergency room, and Mary went along too. My hysteria heightened when the hospital staff came at me with shots of lidocaine to numb my skin, so it could be sutured back together. Mom tried to motivate some self-control in me through flattery.

"Mary is watching you, Heather," Mom said.

At the moment I didn't care who was watching me. People were coming at me with needles! It was do or die as far as I was concerned. Being the "big girl" for the three-years-younger-than-me Mary was not effective incentive. Apparently, someone offered something that calmed me down. It wasn't the obligation to set a good example, but whatever it was did the trick. And when I got home, I was so proud of my stitches. A battle wound so to speak. Jon had already had stitches from the incident with the wooden step stool. Now I was in his league.

I looked for that scar after the accident. It was replaced with new scars. Burn scars. And burn scars were not nearly as impressive to people as the clean-cut scar from stitches. It was a uniqueness that was completely opposite of special.

"I don't like people staring at me," I would say.

"How do you know they are staring at you?" Mom would ask. She aimed to give reassurance. "They're not staring at you, Heather."

Oh, but they were. They still do.

How do I know?

I just do.

There is a feeling that comes when you catch the sight of someone's eyes. It's almost like they freeze you with their focus. No matter what you're doing, you are aware of their stare. And it holds you until you remove yourself from it, or the looker gets distracted. The only thing that makes it worse is when they have someone to share their bewilderment with. When they lean over, cup their hand and whisper to their friend, enlisting even more attention, as if you don't already feel like a complete spectacle from theirs alone.

It's not the kind of *uniqueness* anyone wants to know.

It's not the kind of *stand out* anyone wants to experience.

I could handle it with strangers. As a little girl I was able to withstand the stares, knowing they would only be momentary. The name-calling, on the other hand, would stay with me forever. I said what we all said, the lie we learn as children to fight the battle of bullies: *Sticks and stones may break my bones, but words will never hurt me.*

Nothing could be further from the truth. I know.

I know because I've literally had my flesh ripped off my body with the process of innumerable bandage changes. I've dug staples out of my skin too many times to tell. I've pressed through the pain of physical therapy trying to improve the function of my insufficient body. But nothing, nothing in all my experience, has surpassed that type of temporary hurt like the permanent pain from words.

An apology doesn't compensate for being called *French fries*. Hearing *I'm sorry* doesn't cushion getting labeled as *Freddy Krueger.*

After my first official boyfriend broke up with me in the sixth grade, a fellow classmate informed me the boy had just felt sorry for me, that he never really wanted me to be his girlfriend. And when it came down to it, he just didn't like *fried chicken.*

Choosing not to cower to those comments didn't make much of a difference. By junior high a guy interrupted me talking to some friends, telling me, "Shut up, handicap. No one wants to listen to you." Whatever that was supposed to mean. The fact that it didn't make sense didn't matter. While I would have never wanted him to know, the arrow of his statement punctured right through me. I rolled my eyes and responded as any nineties teen would with a "Whatever!" Internally, I felt like my heart was bleeding out. A piece of me truly wished I could have died.

The same scenarios played out even in my own backyard when swimsuit season came.

Summertime is one of my favorite times of the year. I have loved and will most likely always love the water. Thoughts have crossed my mind why a water girl like me grew up in a landlocked state. Nevertheless, I felt lucky, 'cause this water girl got to grow up with the most treasured amenity right in her backyard. A pool.

Our backyard pool revealed a sad truth to me. People who come swim in your pool don't necessarily like you. It doesn't even mean they are your friends. It seems an obvious reality that fun in the pool is the goal, not the relationship. What is not so obvious is realizing this truth applies to family too.

I don't look good in a swimsuit. That's just the way it is. My body isn't my strongest feature. And that's okay. It motivated me to focus on strengthening attributes scars can't ruin, like character. However, when I put on a swimsuit, I put the evidence of this injury on display. The unwanted attention it created was something I mentally prepared for in public. It was not something on my radar at home and with family.

That opinion changed when a distant cousin took note of my groin. My legs were burned from my feet all the way up to my buttocks and my perineum. My chest was burned extending down and covering my entire abdomen. The very small patch unclaimed from the fire held hope for me to have a future family of my own. It was a gift, but the small remaining skin on my pubis protruded in comparison to the lack of skin and fatty tissue around it. This distant cousin of mine was not hesitant to point it out in front of other kids, yelling, "You look like you have a penis!" As if I didn't know that already; he provided confirmation for what I hoped others weren't thinking.

Words wound.

They come unexpectedly like a head-on collision catching you off guard to the trauma they leave. There is no fixing or undoing their damage. Words create an energy, an atmosphere, an environment. It's a hurt that walks in and never leaves.

Furthermore, the mere absence of mean words doesn't void or cancel out the heaviness of hurt from ugly words that have been spoken. There are many more people I've encountered who never said anything harmful. They just never said anything one way or the other. How commonly children and adults alike consider the goal "be kind or be quiet," not realizing how crucial their words could be in combatting the cruelty or healing the hurt.

It's a collision requiring first responders to make the rescue to diminish a bully's satisfaction and outmatch a bully's effectiveness. The kind of rescue that further overshadows the memory of being attacked with the outlasting one of being defended.

I had professional help to navigate through these rough waters.

From the time I had been admitted to the burn center, I had a therapist involved in my care. His name was Howard. I don't remember much about him. He was tall and slender. His hair was a reddish color and he had a full beard, neatly kempt. Howard was gentle and soft spoken.

Mom and Dad were cognizant to the physical, social and emotional challenges; therefore, once I was outpatient, they set me up with a psychiatrist who carried the reputation for being the best in Tulsa. I didn't think so. He scared me. He was very tall and thin. I was used to tall, because Dad was tall. But this man seemed even taller because of his lean stature.

We never did counseling as a family, so I went in alone while Mom or Dad stayed in the waiting area. His office was dimly lit. He had me sit on a couch across the room from him. I always sat closest to the arm of the couch for whatever sense of security I could find. The doctor sat in a chair next to a floor lamp. His legs seemed even longer when he sat down in the low chair, his knees nearly coming up to his ear lobes! Maybe childhood memories are a bit exaggerated. Still yet, his knees seemed to come a lot closer to his face.

From his chair he'd ask me questions. He looked down mostly, writing on the pad of paper in his lap. He seemed to write a lot. A whole lot.

We did not have a connection in the least bit. There was no way in the world I was going to open up and tell him my thoughts, my disappointments, grief, sadness, anger, fear or feelings on fairness. No possible way.

I'd beg not to go. My pleading did not avail me in the least. Mom and Dad continued taking me. I became strategic, thinking if I stayed with Aunt Donna I wouldn't have to go. I was wrong. Despite my pleas, she took me too. After half a dozen appointments or so, Mom and Dad conceded. It was pointless to pay for therapy that wasn't going anywhere. Counseling was something I'd have to come back to later in the journey.

In the meantime, I continued the quest for answers on my own. My pursuit led me to another head-on collision.

It was unexpected. I was unsuspecting. And it made me realize how very incredibly small I was. It was a collision that changed the trajectory of my life and started transforming this tragedy into something else.

15

Anger and Blame

Have you ever been asked a leading question? It's when someone asks a question with the answer embedded into it. This style of communication is commonly played out in a courtroom setting. At least it does on *48 Hours* and from what I used to watch of *Perry Mason* and *Matlock*. Courtroom drama has always been interesting to me. I realize it's not a completely accurate portrayal of real life, but it's fun to watch and it helps in illustrating a leading question I've been frequently asked.

"Now, third-degree burns don't hurt as much because of the damaged nerves, right?"

It's constructed as if the questioner expects me to answer, Right. It doesn't really hurt that bad.

Only someone who has never been around this kind of injury would think to ask such a question. I *want* to answer with, Well, maybe if you had a third-degree burn, you would know how untrue that assumption is.

I don't say it though. Not out loud anyway. Those sassy responses are contained because honestly, I really do see how someone could think that's the way it'd work.

The body is truly phenomenal and so is pain. Signals are sent when something goes awry. The brain gets notified. These experiences of pain after a burn injury involve what is known as nociceptive pain, neuropathic pain and hyperalgesia. Nociceptive pain and neuropathic pain are the two main categories.

Nociceptive pain is due to chemical, inflammatory or mechanical mediators responding after injury. It results from direct activation of pain nerve fibers. Neuropathic pain is pain generated or sustained by the nervous system.[1] Hyperalgesia is a form of neuropathic pain, because it results from changes to nerve pathways, causing a person to have an overreactive pain response due to initial tissue trauma and inflammation.[2]

A cascade of reaction occurs from third-degree burns. The brain knows it and the body feels it.

Now, keeping that physiological response in mind, imagine the body sending the brain a positive message while the body is experiencing agonizing ones. What the what?

Yes. And although I mistakenly thought Mike and Susan Cochrane were the ones to develop this hypothesis, they were no doubt ones to test it.

The facial feedback hypothesis was actually established in 1872 by Charles Darwin who believed expressing a particular emotion intensified it, and on the other hand, suppressing an emotional expression repressed it.[3] Basically, it means frowning at a party will minimize the level of fun to be had, and likewise, smiling through a challenge will decrease the depth of misery experienced.

Ross Buck published his article in 1980 acknowledging a bit of truth to this notion. He informed that "skeletal muscle feedback from facial expressions plays a causal role in regulating emotional experience and behavior."[4]

Mom and Dad demonstrated such behaviors in our home. So much that one could have thought they were participants in Buck's research. For the record, they never even knew about this hypothesis. It was just part of their fabric to put on a smile and good attitude in the face of challenges. It was their approach to life, believing that while a smile wouldn't change the circumstance, the facial expression would certainly influence their attitude in it.

We focused on having a good attitude, smiling and laughing.

Their personalities were geared this direction. It suited them. Grieving was not in their nature. They simply weren't comfortable with sharing their brokenness. So we minimized the pain by joking. Lessened the load with a witty remark.

They preferred to laugh rather than cry. The only time I saw them shedding tears was during personally delicate, soul-touching moments at church. They never openly wept, grieved or sobbed from the emptiness we all felt.

My family didn't like sorrow, an emotion they so automatically suppressed. Yet it was still there. The grief lurked under the surface of our lives, masked in arguments of heated exchanges. Anger feels more powerful than sadness. At least it looks that way.

Mom and Dad never went to counseling. The hurts and hang-ups that had their marriage hinging on divorce when the accident happened were not revisited with the help of a professional. The complexity and commitment for my care provided consistent distraction to their issues. But every now and then it would blow. They would have a fight full of slamming doors, curse words, screaming, yelling and threats to leave. Ever so often anger erupted, the pain seeped through the cracks of imperfections and loss, and everyone crumbled. What it looked like was anger. But blame was there too.

Blame lived with us. And Blame had a best friend named Anger. When Anger showed up, it was because Blame had brought him along. However, no one talked about Blame. No one. Ever.

I think everyone assigned their self-blame for the accident.

Grandma felt blame for letting us go to begin with.

Mom felt blame for not going after Jon when he went back to get me.

Dad felt blame for not being there. He carried the weight of being an absent father that day, along with the many days before.

Even Barry felt blame. He wasn't even living here at the time, yet he expressed feelings of responsibility, thinking Jon and I would have never gone had he been home.

And there was my own blame. I was the bratty, spoiled little sister who refused to leave my friend's house the first time. If I had simply obeyed my big brother, we would have got on that motorcycle and made it back home safely. Jon would never have come back to get me. He would still be alive. Adrian never would have had the horror of colliding with two kids on a dirt road. My family would not have known the loss, grief and pain. They would not have had to construct their lives around surgeries, doctors' offices and physical therapy appointments. We would have all been a family without tragedy.

There was enough blame within each of us. And although no one ever, ever said it, many suppressed their anger from the blame they laid on others. Quelling the thought, *There are just certain things you don't let kids do.*

The responsibility had been considered. On April 28th, the day after the accident, Social Work Services wrote the following evaluation note: "Social Work referral received this date. At-risk orders also written. Discussed with staff and social worker regarding concerns about the accident, etc. At-risk order cancelled by Dr. Norberg and the writer will assume the case."

In all tragedies there could be one decision to make things different. Just one. It could have been mine, Grandma's, Mom's, Dad's—I suppose by extreme consideration, it could have even possibly been Barry's. Changing one factor could have produced a completely different result. But that's what makes it an accident.

Yet some questions can't be averted. Such as considering, Why would something like that happen? Some emotions can't be suppressed, emotions like blame. Blame steps in and is concealed by its friend Anger. And when Anger is around, the hurting keep hurting, because Anger keeps Comfort from coming in.

• • • • • • •

I was quite the thinker for my young age. Lying in a bed provides a lot of time for thoughts.

When Mom busied herself with laundry, meals or mowing, I lay still with my thoughts. When Dad kept focused on meeting sales quotas with calls and at-home appointments, I lay still thinking. Insight, acumen and reason were developing in those quiet moments alone. Lots of questions crossed my mind. One of them was not well received in our house.

Why me? I thought.

It was more frequently a thought than an audible question because pity parties were not celebrated in our home. Mom and Dad reminded me of others who had it much worse than I did. They corrected me to concentrate on how grateful I should feel for the things I had, like my fingers and toes, and for what I was able to do, like regaining my ability to walk again, ride a bike and run.

The question wasn't just from me feeling sorry for myself. I no doubt had many of those moments. The question was more often me aiming to understand why I was alive. Why did I live? Why me?

Death eluded me. I couldn't make sense of it and continued to be puzzled by it. In time, it didn't get any clearer to me. It actually got more complicated.

I had been in the principal's office before. Not to see the principal but to see Dad. It hadn't been a good experience.

Dad came right to the school to confront me about some numbers that came up on our phone bill. Apparently, they were expensive calls. My friend and I thought they'd be funny. Dad was not laughing. He was madder than a wet hen, holding the phone bill in one hand, waving it around, laying in to me with his words.

It was back in the day when kids would pull out the phone book and randomly call people to ask if their refrigerator was running. Oh my. Well, my friend and I upped the ante and decided to prank call the nine-hundred number advertised on television. I learned the caller didn't only pay per minute, but per call. So the fact that we called a sex hotline multiple times and then hung up made for a hefty bill he was not keen on paying.

Bad situation.

So the day I got called out of class in fourth grade and saw Dad in the principal's office, I could only think, *What did I do?*

Dad had been crying. I could tell by his eyes. Although we didn't share our sad feelings of grief and loss, Dad was nonetheless an emotional guy. Mostly he cried when we were at church. Something there brought so many tears he'd end up having to blow his nose. Mom cried at church too. I had no idea why we'd make the forty-five-minute one-way trip to go, if it was just gonna make everyone sad.

Still yet, going to church meant I was going to see my great aunts and uncles: Aunt Florence and Uncle Frank, Aunt Frances and Uncle Ernie. Uncle Ernie sang in the choir, which I found to be extremely fascinating. The choir wore long white robes and were contagiously charismatic in their worship. I watched and wondered if I'd ever get to sing in a choir like Uncle Ernie. Or more like Madeline Manning-Mims, a tall gorgeous black lady who was a former Olympic runner with a voice as beautiful as her face. She added angelic echoes to worship as the choir led the congregation in "Turn Your Eyes upon Jesus." My love for music was a constant in my life, before and after the accident. Actually, even more so after. Songs helped me articulate and convey the complicated emotions I had no idea how to express.

The other perk of making that forty-five-minute one-way drive to church was going to Aunt Florence and Uncle Frank's house afterward for lunch. Aunt Florence and Uncle Frank were more like grandparents to me, and their home was warmly nostalgic. They raised pigs and chickens on their small farm located amidst lush neighborhoods of doctors' homes in south Tulsa. Schools in the area often took students to their house for field trips to see the new baby pigs. Their home felt calm, simple and peaceful, including an abundance of comfort from Aunt Florence's cooking.

Other than the delicious lunches we savored after service, and the treat of getting to see my great aunts and uncles, I didn't really get *why* we went to church. Many times, Mom and Dad would even argue on the way. It seemed to me that if it made everyone mad, maybe we should just not go. I thought, *Who wants to go to church mad?* And while I loved Pastor Beller who supported us in prayer the first night of our accident, and many thereafter, Mom and Dad cried during the singing and while listening to his message. Seemed like a lot of work to drive all that way just to be sad. However, we didn't attend every week, so I didn't normally see Mom and Dad cry.

I knew something was not right this day of fourth grade in the principal's office with Dad. Nothing could have prepared my ten-year-old mind for what I was about to hear.

Samantha had died.

I didn't understand. Samantha was my baby cousin. We had celebrated her first birthday not quite three months earlier. She could not be gone. It couldn't be possible. She was a baby!

We went straight to Aunt Donna's house. She was sitting at the bar in her kitchen by the sliding glass door. I went directly to her arms and squeezed as tightly as I could hug her, tears of emptiness and confusion flowing from my face. I listened as my three-and-a-half-year-old little cousin Austin learned her baby sister wasn't home but was in Heaven.

Samantha's birth was so special for us. She arrived the day after what would have been Jon's eleventh birthday. We were marking the third year of having his birthday without him when Samantha came. She brought happiness and joy in the midst of that difficult time of year. She was our gift and the surprise Aunt Donna never anticipated.

Aunt Donna had one ectopic pregnancy, which often occurs as a tubal pregnancy, where the fertilized egg gets stuck in the fallopian tube, presenting a risk of that fallopian tube rupturing as the fertilized eggs begin to grow. The diagnosis requires medication or surgery to remove the tissue in order to prevent further complication. In addition to the ectopic pregnancy, she miscarried three times before Austin was born. So when Aunt Donna found out she was expecting Samantha, we relished the joy of her upcoming arrival. She wasn't Aunt Donna's baby alone. She was all of ours—our worlds touched with hope and healing through the miracle of her life.

Samantha was extra special. She was extra everything: extra loving, extra happy, extra smiles, extra hugs, extra baby laughs. Her makeup had one extra gene copy on her twenty-first chromosome. For our family, her diagnosis of Down syndrome meant she was extra cherished. She was a fighter too. Congenital heart defects are not uncommon for trisomy 21 babies. Samantha had one that required open-heart surgery when she was six months old. She recovered beautifully. Apart from the scar down the center of her chest, no one would've known her heart wasn't properly routed. Her heart had been fixed, and she was our precious strong girl full of smiles.

A common cold was the uneventful reason her dad took her to the pediatrician's office that Friday morning. No one could have anticipated the devastation that followed after getting her to the exam room. Samantha started seizing. There were no oxygen masks to fit her baby face. She was flown to the nearest hospital. Aunt Donna left her first-grade classroom and rushed to the hospital. Samantha was gone. Aunt Donna rocked her for hours.

She died fifteen days before we marked the third anniversary of Jon's death.

Her funeral was the first I had ever gone to. *This is what they did for Jon,* I thought. I went from trying to wrap my mind around a child's death to a baby's. Some experiences people live a lifetime and never know. I was working to comprehend and digest this experience at ten years old.

Her casket was so tiny. It was beautiful and she looked beautiful. But it was so small. She was so small. She looked like she was sleeping. I had watched her sleep many times before. Aunt Donna was very willing to involve me in her life. I felt like a big sister to her and Austin rather than their cousin.

I stood next to Aunt Donna as they lowered Samantha's casket into the ground. I watched Aunt Donna pick up a handful of dirt and release it over her casket. *This is what they did for Jon.* And as we drove off in the family limo, I sat next to Aunt Donna, feeling nauseous inside that we were leaving Samantha there. I saw her dead. I touched her cold face. But I couldn't grasp leaving her body in a hole. The baby we rocked, fed, sang to and loved, we were leaving behind alone in a cemetery.

Death was a robber. Death was a thief. Death stole every good, pure happiness life held.

The day played over and over in my mind for weeks, months and years to come. So did the song that was sung: "Give Them All to Jesus." The lyrics were about giving Jesus "the shattered dreams, wounded hearts, and broken toys."[5] For me, the *toys* part of the song meant even children have broken pieces of their lives to give to Jesus. I most certainly felt I did. However, I didn't know what it meant or looked like.

The next year Uncle Roy passed away.

Mom, Dad and I went over to say our final goodbyes the night Uncle Roy was passing away. Aunt Sarah said he wanted his family to stay with him while he left. Even though Uncle Roy and I weren't deeply bonded, I wanted to stay. I longed to understand more about what happened to Jon. I needed to know what death was. Even with cancer, Uncle Roy's death was much more peaceful than Jon's. Uncle Roy passed surrounded with a room full of his family and their love.

We lost Uncle Frank too, followed by Aunt Florence's passing four weeks later. I knew it was more appropriate for older people to die. Jon, and then Samantha, were deaths not taking the normal pattern of life. Their passing was out of order. Children are not supposed to go before their parents. While I realized both Uncle Frank and Aunt Florence had lived good lives, I was deeply sad to say goodbye to them, my unofficial grandparents. I loved them both so much.

The next year, Mom's first cousin took his own life. Jon and I played with his daughters at family gatherings before our accident, and he served as one of the pallbearers for Jon's funeral. He was such a nice man, a good-looking man with two beautiful girls and a wife. But his life had been its own trauma.

His mom, Grandma's sister, was an attractive mother of four when she collapsed on her kitchen floor and died from a brain aneurism at thirty-seven years old. His father, a Tulsa fire chief, who was so deeply in love with his mother, didn't know how to live without her. He connected a gas hose from his truck and fell asleep, passing away from the poison of a grieving heart. Losing both parents so tragically at a young age does not dissipate in adulthood. Grief, pain, loss, depression and darkness expand in the soul if nothing enters to heal it.

Mom's cousin dying was the first time I knew death could be a choice. I had wanted to die many times but never felt I had a choice. I hadn't been too happy I had lived. I missed Jon every single day. I didn't like my body. I didn't like my life. I didn't like death and funerals. There wasn't much I had experienced after the accident that made me grateful to be alive. Although I knew I was supposed to be.

• • • • • • •

Small deposits were made into the empty places of my life through Dad's love language of buying gifts. He experienced much joy giving things to others. Despite their fragility, I had been given a couple Precious Moments figurines at my young age. I really loved them—their teardrop-shaped eyes and delicate features, innocent and happy as children. Even the ones who were depicted as adults rendered a youthful gentle joy. Dad started a collection of Precious Moments for me, including some figurines, the children's Bible and storybooks.

I read the books and took the Bible when we went to church. Seeds were being planted. The soil in my own individual spiritual garden was being tilled and prepared. Each simple story planted a seed in my soul.

In the sixth grade someone asked me, "Have you been saved?"

Saved? I had no idea about this new term.

"It's when you ask Jesus into your heart as your personal Lord and Savior, so you can go to Heaven when you die." The student continued, "If you aren't saved when you die, then you go to Hell with the devil."

What?

Okay. I knew you needed to be a Christian to live with Jesus in Heaven. We had been to church enough through the years for me to understand that much. Plus, I came from a family of Christians. Little Grandma Ward was a Christian, so were all my great aunts and their families. Grandma was a Christian, and although I heard colorful words flow out of Mom's, Dad's, and even Aunt Donna's mouths, I knew they were Christians too. It's just what we were.

I had this impression that if you were born into a Christian family with a Christian heritage, then you must be a Christian. My fellow student told me that was not the way it went. I was informed I had to make my own choice whether or not I wanted to invite Jesus into my heart and have a personal relationship with Him.

Well, yes! I thought. *Of course, I do!*

I attended the very next youth event at the little church next to the school. I couldn't wait on getting this squared away. Seemed like something that needed tending to immediately.

All the students sat in the sanctuary and at the end of the message were asked to bow our heads. My heart started beating just a smidge faster when I bowed my head. The group was then asked who wanted to accept Jesus into their heart as their personal Lord and Savior. My heart started beating a skosh more quickly as I thought, *That's me.* Then the rubber met the road when the Preacher Man asked those who wanted to make that decision to raise their hands. *Raise my hand? Oh, my word!* My heart was seriously racing by this point. With my head still bowed, I slowly raised my right arm. *All right. It's done. I did it. He's in there.*

But the stakes got even higher. Preacher Man then asked those of us who raised our hands to stand. And not only that. Walk to the front. Oh, my dear Lord of mercy! I was not quite even twelve years old yet. I couldn't take this intensity.

But I could. And I did.

I stood and felt the weight of people staring at me. A weight I was so familiar with experiencing. I began to shimmy down the pew to the center aisle. My heart continued pounding like it was coming plum out of my chest.

On the journey out of the pew and into the choir loft, something was awakening inside me. My spiritual self was coming alive.

I took a seat next to Rhonda. I hadn't seen her in a while but was so glad she was the one to pray with me out of all the people there I didn't know. She had babysat Jon and me when we were little.

This church, where I hadn't even realized was the very place our friends, family and community gathered together nearly five years earlier for Jon's memorial service, was the very church where I was laying down my life and being born into a new one. I didn't know what to do with this tragedy but felt like something good could come from it if I put it in the right hands.

On this Friday, February 12, 1993, I accepted Jesus as my personal Lord and Savior. I put myself all in His hands, *the shattered dreams, wounded hearts and broken toys.*[6] I believed if anyone could make the weak strong, the ugly beautiful, the scared brave, the grieving joyful, if anyone could fill the empty and bring peace to the anxious, it would be Him.

16

Scary Changes

A shower revitalizes the body. When I'd been sick from illness or hurting from surgery, I knew if I could motivate myself to get through the bathing process, I would feel better.

There's just something about getting cleaned up that changes how we feel. There have actually been studies on it. Neil Morris, a University of Wolverhampton psychologist, created a poster summarizing the information titled *A Clean Bill of Health: The Physiological and Psychological Effects of Bathing.* He reported that bathing in a bathtub radically improved general psychological wellness. The benefits don't stop at bathtubs alone. While baths are best, he also included positive outcomes from both hot and cold showers. He even shared that studies have found that a person feeling more isolated will take a hotter bath or shower and stay in longer.[1] Overall, it can be concluded getting cleaned up isn't just necessary for our personal needs of hygiene, it's good for our mental disposition too.

Accepting Jesus into my life and heart, making my own choice to have an individual personal relationship with Him, felt like getting a revitalizing shower!

I was on cloud nine by the time I got home. I had barely made it in the door to share my news, thinking how ecstatic Mom and Dad would be for my decision. However, I didn't get the response I had anticipated. Dad seemed mad. That's how he came across anyway. Disappointment was the root of his emotion, but Dad didn't say he was disappointed. He didn't say he was proud of me and how deeply disappointed he felt for missing such a monumental moment. Instead, he gruffed, "You couldn't have done that in *our* church?"

The reaction broke my heart. I was angry he couldn't just be happy for me and tell me that. It felt like nothing I did was the right way or the way he would want. Here I thought "getting saved" was a good thing, something my parents would be rejoicing over. I mean, at church they told me angels were celebrating in Heaven over my decision. Angels! So why not my parents?

I headed upstairs and got on the phone to call someone I knew would be happy for me. Aunt Donna.

Aunt Donna had moved nearly seven hundred miles away. I missed her terribly. So much so I asked Mom for the two perfumes Aunt Donna wore: Beautiful and Oscar. I didn't just rotate wearing them. I also sprayed them on my stuffed animals so I could smell her scent. No doubt it was difficult having her so far away, but we talked on the phone pretty consistently. Because we only had the phone to share life together, I imagine I talked to her much more than I would have if she had been close. Sometimes we're satisfied with presence alone, but when we don't have that commodity, we utilize our words more, building a much deeper connection.

For some reason or another, I wasn't in my room, but instead lay on the center of Mom and Dad's bed, talking and talking to Aunt Donna. The response at home didn't subdue my joy. I was full of zeal when I phoned her, sharing every single detail of what transpired. From the kid who practically told me I was on my way to an eternity of pain and suffering without Jesus, to the youth event, and to my moment of walking the aisle in that Baptist church.

I'm sure the entire time I talked to Aunt Donna, Mom was talking to Dad. Dad never said he was sorry. Not about that or about anything ever. He had his own way of apologizing. For him it typically included buying a gift or doing something special like going out to a nice dinner. A relationship with him meant overlooking the hurtful things to see his heart. He had a really good one. He just got it caught up in the barbed wires of an inability to express vulnerability, disappointment or sadness. Realizing this helped interpret the real meaning of a blowup.

Despite the hang-up, Dad and I had a strong relationship. I spent more time with him than any other person. He took me to school every morning. Before I got out of the car, he leaned over to kiss me right in front of everyone, smack dab on the lips! By the time I was in sixth grade, I wanted him to still kiss me goodbye; I just didn't want anyone to see it. I would have been mortified if they had. There was always a large group of kids outside the school waiting on the first bell to ring. So I started getting ready to get out of the car before we pulled into the school parking lot. I practically hugged the passenger side door. As he'd come to a stop, I'd all but jump out of the car, avoiding his affection.

He wasn't reserved with love. Because of the tragedy we lived with, we always, always said, "love you, bye." We never ended a phone call or parted ways without saying it. Sometimes it was lathered in teenage daughter attitude, rolling my eyes behind Mom and Dad's backs, but no one needed to explain to me the fragility of life, how we're never guaranteed tomorrow. That was a reality we woke up with every morning and were tucked in bed with every night. We understood each day had the potential for being the last day to say, "I love you."

Dad and I spent a lot of days together. On numerous occasions during the short drive to school, he'd ask, "Do you want to go with me today?"

I'd think, *Really? Skip school?* No need to ask me twice. "Of course, I do!"

We never talked about it with each other, but I'm pretty sure Dad knew the misery I felt at school. Riding around with him picking up paperwork from clients, going to lunch meetings with fellow professionals or visiting with adults was more natural to me than being with my peers at school. I had become used to being in a world of grown-ups. Trying to assimilate back to one with kids, moreover, trying to return to *being* a kid felt unnatural.

I spent Friday nights with my parents. Typically starting off with *TGIF* television shows on ABC. *Full House, Boy Meets World, Family Matters* and *Hangin' with Mr. Cooper,* followed by the ever-so-grown-up *20/20.* Oftentimes I watched either the beginning or the last half of the Friday night line-up. Mom, Dad and I would load up and head into town for dinner. When we got back home, Dad would say, "Ya want a malt?" or he'd make blueberry muffins while we drank hot tea. The Friday evenings concluded as I'd crawl up in between Mom and Dad watching *OETA Movie Club* on our local PBS station. They ran old movies into the late night like *The Thin Man* movies, *Penny Serenade* and *It's a Wonderful Life.* On Sundays Dad and I watched a British comedy on PBS called *Fawlty Towers* about a man who didn't like people but ran a hotel with his wife. The poor chap had all sorts of trouble, and we had all sorts of laughs watching and making memories.

The weekend routine wasn't what most kids my age were doing. My life didn't look like most kids though. Even though our family had baggage of pain, loss and hang-ups, we navigated through it the best we knew how and had found much happiness in moments along the way.

• • • • • • •

In the spring of 1994, Dad had a client extend a simple invitation.

"Mike," he began, "we have this new preacher at our church, and I really think you'd enjoy his messages. Would you like to come Sunday for service?"

By this time, Dad had an office just seven miles from our house in a nearby community. He had started selling insurance as an independent agent while maintaining his bookkeeping business. He had outgrown the ability to office out of our house, as he had done for the years following the accident. He purchased a piece of property on the main street in the little town over, demoed the old dilapidated home, and built a building with six office spaces.

As with all projects, Dad had Mom and me, and even Grandma in there too. We were the cleanup crew sweeping floors and the painting crew staining trim for the baseboards and doorframes. We were all in it together just as we had been with building his business all along. It's what happens from homegrown businesses. The home grows it.

Dad had me sorting receipts in the second grade. And I knew very early how to speak to a client on the phone. When someone called, I was trained to inquire, "May I ask who's calling?" Once the person answered, I'd hand the phone to Dad, reporting who it was. If Dad wasn't there, I apologized with, "I'm sorry, he's not available. Can I take a message?" I was very good at phone etiquette. I was not, however, very good at getting off the phone.

One evening Dad realized he had probably been missing calls when he heard me click over to answer the call waiting. Without saying a word, he anticipated being handed the phone. Completely oblivious, I handled the situation, implementing my well-mannered phone skills, saying, "I'm sorry, can I take a message and have him call you right back?" The client gave me the information. I informed Dad of the call as I clicked back over to my friend. Surprisingly, he wasn't mad. Instead he determined he needed another phone line. It was a win for me, for sure, getting my own line out of the situation.

There had been some kinks in running the business out of the house. The new office helped as most business calls were directed there. However, self-employed people always have clients call their home. It is just part of being self-employed. Work isn't a separate part of life. It's in *every* part of life. Nevertheless, Mom was thrilled to have our dining room table utilized for one purpose and one purpose only. Family dinners. Which is what we started having on Sundays.

Mom and Dad liked the idea of attending church closer to home. They felt we could be more involved if we didn't spend so much time traveling to get there. If we were closer, maybe we'd go more. They had tried finding a church closer to home a few times before. For a period of time when Jon and I were little, we attended a new Lutheran church getting started. Mom taught Sunday school. But for some reason or another, we ended up making the drive back to Evangelistic Temple. So when this client invited Dad to his church to hear the new pastor, Dad was intrigued.

We went the following Sunday, and Mom and Dad enjoyed it. Grandma did too. So we went back. I wasn't too keen on it. For one, we only ever went to church on Sunday morning—if that. This church had service on Sunday morning, Sunday evening and Wednesday night. And my family thought it'd be great going to all of them.

Two, I'm not big on change.

Those two things coupled with my misery of insecurity and teenage hormones made for quite the protest. I did not at all want to attend this new church. I liked our old one. I liked slipping in and slipping out.

This church was tiny. Tiny as in maybe a hundred people were there. And matters only got worse when we showed up on a Wednesday night a couple weeks later. It was bad enough going to the Sunday morning services. Now Mom and Dad wanted to go for a Wednesday night one! But that wasn't the half of it.

The pastor's wife, Paula, came up to us and invited me to join the youth upstairs. I'm pretty sure I politely smiled while declining the offer. But she wouldn't take no for an answer. She persisted with her sweet smile. Before I knew it, she was taking me by the arm, enthusiastically sharing about the youth group. I was giving Mom all kinds of facial expressions to signal her to save me, but she didn't. She totally knew how much I did *not* want to go with this Paula lady, but she didn't say a word as I was led away. If looks could kill, Mom would have died on the spot.

Paula led me up the stairs opening to an area with a few classrooms. She walked into the room on the left summoning some girls my age. I was a little lamb, a helpless sheep being led into a pack of wolves. At least I thought that anyway. I quickly learned how wrong I was. I met a group of girls who would become some of the greatest treasures of my life. Something of great value was in that room. True friendship.

It was a big summer, that one of 1994.

The last Sunday night of July, the church had cake and punch for those with a birthday in that month. Mom and Dad wanted to stay, especially with Dad being a July 6th baby. It was hysterical, the days following, overhearing him tell his clients about the new little church we were attending and how they threw him a birthday party! He knew it wasn't just for him, but there was a sense of excitement to this process we didn't even know we were in—the process of becoming part of a church family. The excitement was laced with some anxiety, because it's hard to do new things, to be in unfamiliar places with unfamiliar people. But the possibilities that can come from those very places of getting outside the comfort zone are what lend to the excitement of it. We had gone to church but had never known what it was to be in a church family. The two were completely different. We were learning that.

The same month I went bowling with the youth after the service for what they called an *After Glow.* Soon following, we were informed the church was looking for a new youth pastor. Some of the students seemed upset. I hadn't had enough time to get to know the guy, so it didn't affect me one way or the other.

August brought even more change.

Despite encouragement from my new friends to change schools, I decided to stay at the school where I had been since kindergarten. I had known students from my school to change to Coweta (pronounced Ko-wee-tah). In the seventh grade, one of the popular pretty girls at my school transferred to Coweta. For one day. She was back the next. I kept thinking, *If she couldn't fit in there, there is absolutely no way on earth I would.* So I started the eighth grade at the school where I had been since kindergarten.

Over the course of a week, I walked the familiar halls of a school I knew I didn't belong in. But I was scared. I was incredibly terrified to transfer to a new school. I wrestled my thoughts. *If I don't feel acceptance with these people who have known me since before my accident, how in the world would new students who have never known me accept me?*

It's puzzling how we will stick to what we know even if we are miserable, solely for the sake of it being familiar. There is a sacrifice at stake if we can't face the fear of the unknown. It's the sacrifice of what could be. Albert Einstein said it best: "I must be willing to give up what I am in order to become what I will be."[2]

After one week of school, I mustered up all the courage I had within me and transferred to Coweta Junior High, starting with my new student body for their very first day of school. It was a pivotal decision. One I could have never known to be so crucial.

Every future event of my life would point back to that one choice.

17

The Broken Side of Brave

Right after the school year started, a young man and his wife visited the church for consideration of filling the youth pastor position. They joined us for Sunday morning service, and then the youth pastor candidate preached that evening. This twenty-three-year-old guy incorporated his farm experience of harvesting cantaloupe to illustrate the message.

I wouldn't have thought anything farm-related would connect so deeply in me. I grew up on a farm, but I didn't know a single thing about what was involved in farming. Whether it involved crops or cattle, I didn't have a clue. Nevertheless, the message given by this potential youth pastor resonated in me.

He spoke about the qualifications for becoming a worker for Jesus, saying, "There are none." He said we didn't have to worry about wearing the right clothes, whether we were male or female, rich or poor, what part of town we lived in, how good looking or ugly we were, or what color skin we had. He said there was no interview process or waiting period to see if we get hired. Just ask Jesus to be your personal Lord and Savior and you've got the job.

He shared about his job of bringing in the cantaloupe. The rows were half-a-mile long, and on a foggy morning, he couldn't even see the end of one. But he knew it was there, so he just kept picking one cantaloupe at a time down the line.

It wasn't easy work. There were obstacles of weeds to get through. Hot temperatures and heavy loads made for a grueling task. Still yet, his job accomplished something of value, bringing in fruit for the nourishment and enjoyment of others.

This analogy came together when he connected it to the cross. Jesus faced the most agonizing row of work. There were challenges, pain, turmoil, suffering and agony, but He stayed committed for us! He provided a way to bring us in to an eternity in Heaven.

It all meant something to me. According to this message, it didn't matter that I didn't look the way I was supposed to. Jesus could use me anyway. There was value in what was difficult. I knew pain. I knew suffering. I knew agony. Jesus knew it more. That reality brought much comfort to me. Furthermore, Jesus not only *knew* my pain, He could *use* my pain.

The message was more than about being committed to picking a row of cantaloupes to the very end, even when it got difficult. It was much more to me. It gave meaning to the past, brought comfort in the present and encouragement for the future.

At the end of the message, Pastor Gary declared, "Church, I think we just got ourselves a youth pastor!" Steve and Michele Lee's investment and influence of ministry started in my life that night. And it propelled me forward through a variety of seasons to come.

When my decision was made, it was more than grabbing a ticket for Heaven. For me, choosing to accept Jesus was more than a fire escape from an eternity of pain, even though that's the way the kid at school presented the need. After experiencing all the deaths in my family, I felt I had finally received a power that defeated the grief and despair of a grave.

It was *not*, however, a fix. My life did not necessarily get better. In some aspects, it got worse.

Just as my body, years before, had undergone escharotomies to relieve pressure from the tough, rigid, inelastic eschar restricting flow in my blood vessels, I felt my soul was now undergoing the same process. Cutting away the dead tissue of my spirit and restoring perfusion for me to live—fully and abundantly.

The emotional trauma was just beginning to surface. I didn't even know I was broken. God knew I was to quickly find out, strategically putting help in place before the storm began brewing. My new youth pastors were equipped with faith, the Word of God and prayer to minister to me, speaking healing, vision and inspiration into my heart, into my life, into my bones.

• • • • • • •

When I was around twelve years old, Mom and Dad took me for a makeup class in the burn unit with special makeup for burn patients. They bought it for me, but I didn't use it much. It was complicated mixing a little of one color with another to accomplish the right skin tone. The scar on my face was slightly red, making it difficult to blend the color to my unscarred skin. Plus, it didn't make me feel very pretty. My issues with beauty were much more involved than the scar running under my cheek line on the right side of my face.

While my discontent with beauty was growing, Mom and Dad had additional concerns. There wasn't much education provided regarding HIV when my seven-year-old body was receiving reoccurring blood transfusions. My parents had been informed there was a potential risk I could have contracted the disease and possibly not know until after a ten-year period of dormancy. Hepatitis B and Hepatitis C were two other blood-borne infections they hoped against. Today there is an extensive screening process for donated blood. The risks of contracting a blood-borne infection are very low. Overall, the immediate benefit of blood outweighs the potential risk, as those who need transfusions would die without them.

The potential unseen risk of an underlying disease was overshadowed by the obvious deficiencies in my physical development. Body image was my most apparent problem, capturing my focus and my parents' attention. My peers were discussing their changing bodies. Although I was one of the first to start the anxious onset of menstruation, I didn't realize the event should have occurred alongside breast development and the growth of armpit, leg and pubic hair. When the subjects arose, I just listened, hoping no one noticed my lack of contribution.

I felt totally insufficient. I felt like I wasn't a complete girl. The same way I felt when I returned to school in the second grade, putting on the girliest outfits I had and yet still being called a boy because of my short hair. I wanted to be a beautiful woman with a beautiful body. I felt a piece of femininity was robbed from me when I lay in the burn unit, and the loss stayed with me for every single day thereafter. Some days it seemed like the loss was slapping me in the face.

Mom and Dad frequently told me I was pretty. But they had to say that. They were my parents.

I wanted the world to see me as pretty. Beautiful. Delicate. Treasured.

Not scarred. Not peculiar. Not weird.

Over my eighth-grade year, it seemed I had found someone who saw me exactly that way.

He was a grade older than I and attended Coweta Junior High. I had actually met him a year earlier through a mutual friend. The meeting took place on three-way phone calls. Before long he called me to visit on his own. I had no idea what he looked like, but I knew I liked him. He had an enthusiasm about him. He had deep thoughts, was funny and had a contagious laugh. We eventually met face-to-face when a group of us went to see a movie. A friend and I were already in the theater waiting on the movie to start and for the rest of the group to arrive. While munching on our popcorn, they walked in and Michael jumped over the back of the theater seats to grab one beside me. No boy had ever seemed so eager to get a seat next to me.

We continued our phone chats after our meeting at the movie. Our friendship continued growing when I transferred the next year to the same school he attended.

Even though Michael attended the Baptist church in town, he came a few times with me to our church. Mom and Dad would pick him up, and all of us went for ice cream. It was the first time I experienced a boy interacting with my parents. Dad was witty and so was Michael. Observing their exchanges of jokes was enjoyable. Mom and Dad treated all of us to dinner a few times, but the most special for me was my fourteenth birthday.

Number fourteen was one to go in the books. If every year of misery before was building credit, then my fourteenth was my cash-out!

It started with several people, from a couple of Mom's coworkers to my newly made friends, calling two different radio stations to give me a birthday shout-out. When I arrived at school, I received birthday cards from countless people, as well as balloons and flowers. One boy in my history class walked up to me with a folded note. Apart from history, I didn't really know him. The note felt awfully thick, causing me concern something was folded into it—like a bug. When I opened it, there was a twenty-dollar bill! His note said he just wanted to give me something for my birthday. I couldn't believe I had been so hesitant in moving to this new school. It's like God had these people packaged up for me and was just waiting for me to open His gift.

The special birthday ended with a celebration dinner at Outback Steakhouse with Mom, Dad, Pastor Steve and Michele, and Michael. Nothing could have made me feel more valued and loved.

More moments came. One day I opened up my locker to find a light bulb and a note from Michael saying, "You light up my life." As time passed he shared an expression that captured my heart as I had never known. "I love you, Heather," he said to me.

My friendship with Michael was unique to say the least. It was confusing too. Aren't all relationships in junior high?

To my absolute astonishment, I found out he asked another girl to be his girlfriend. She was of course popular and athletic, and in my mind, perfect. A real girl. One who had to shave her legs and had boobs. I was devastated. I believed someone had seen me for me. He said he loved me. Loved. Me. He said he loved the person I was on the inside. All those long conversations on the phone, trips for ice cream and dinner, a light bulb, and for Heaven's sake, an *I love you* and then he goes and chooses someone else? The biggest hurt was the fact that I had truly come to love him.

Nothing had ever made me feel more inadequate than this painful experience of rejection. I was just starting to believe I was enough. I was starting to believe the person I was on the inside could be loved. The rejection caused me to question if I would ever be desirable, cherished and loved.

It was just the crack leading me to complete brokenness. Brokenness isn't always a bad thing. Facing it requires a completely new level of courage. Bob Goff wrote in his best-selling book *Love Does* about the benefit of brokenness. He shared, "It has always seemed to me that broken things, just like broken people, get used more; it's probably because God has more pieces to work with."[1]

It didn't feel like it, but I was becoming so much more in my brokenness.

• • • • • • •

At seven years old, lying in a hospital bed in the ICU, I determined no one would ever want me. Michael wasn't the cause of my brokenness, but God used the experience to confront the lie I had effortlessly received many years earlier. The enemy feeds lies. We see that in Genesis chapter 3 when the serpent spoke to Eve about the fruit from the tree of the knowledge of good and evil. In Genesis 3:1, he asked Eve, "Did God actually say, 'You shall not eat of any tree in the garden'?"[2] Truth is twisted with one word. *Actually.* Verses 4 and 5 inform us of the lie Eve bit into. "But the serpent said to the woman, 'You will not surely die. For God knows that when you eat of it your eyes will be opened, and you will be like God, knowing good and evil.'"[3] Bite taken.

It's crazy to me that Eve thought she was missing out. She only knew good in the Garden of Eden. The things she was missing out on were the very things I was longing to escape as a little girl—pain, hurt and tragedy. But one lie placed her and all humanity into a sinful, imperfect world we were never created for. I guess it's more fathomable for big people to buy into the lie. However, the enemy lies to everyone. Even to children.

I had no ownership of my body. I felt like a lifelong science experiment. Repeatedly standing naked in front of countless people. Being prodded and poked. Pictures were taken of my bare body, mapping out the surgery plan on how to make it better.

Reconstructive surgeries commenced. My first breast reconstructive surgery was the first semester of ninth grade. I was fourteen. I didn't know one person my age who would understand breast reconstruction. There were no breast cancer survivors in my peer group to navigate through the physical hurt and emotionally humiliating process.

The first surgery was brutal.

It would have been beneficial to begin with placing tissue expanders in my chest. A tissue expander is basically a balloon with a small amount of fluid in it. There is a port just under the skin for the surgeon to access and instill more fluid in the balloon over time. This gradually stretches the tissue. Unfortunately, this is not what we did.

Instead, I went from a flat chest to a B cup in one surgery. The crease created in between the two implants didn't look at all like cleavage, but rather resembled a rubber band from the tight inelastic scar tissue. It was one of the most painful procedures I've had. Seriously. The pain ranked up with that of a skin graft.

More breast reconstructive surgeries followed. I had endured five by the time I was eighteen.

The left implant fell after the first surgery. It wouldn't hold in place. Scar tissue is not only tight; it's incredibly weak. Dr. Norberg referred me to Dr. Mathers who specialized in that field of plastic surgery. I underwent another operation with the addition of nipple construction made from my own donor skin. After it healed, I went for a few appointments to tattoo them. I was grateful to have the feminine appearance of a woman, but under my clothes, my boobs didn't look real. They weren't real. They weren't natural. I cringed on the inside when jokes about fake boobs were made. Nothing about my body felt authentic or special. It felt purchased and plastic.

The challenge was seeing myself apart from my body. I hated my body, but I couldn't tell anyone. I knew I wasn't supposed to feel that way.

I was supposed to feel grateful for the life I had been spared to live. I was supposed to be happy. I could walk when doctors once thought it wouldn't be possible. I was supposed to be strong and resilient, not bothered by the superficial deformities of my flesh. I was supposed to be encouraged by how many more people had it worse than I did.

I couldn't disappoint or hurt the people I loved. I wanted everyone to be proud of me, to be proud of their investment into saving my life. So I kept my pain quiet. I embodied the *pain is gain* mantra, beginning a process of hurting from the inside out.

The onset of eating issues was subtle. In the sixth grade, I chose the salad bar each day for my cafeteria lunch, having only cucumbers. It was the first time I started experiencing how long I could go without food.

Fasting wasn't a new feeling for me. I was familiar with hunger pains from all the many surgeries and procedures I had to be NPO for, meaning nothing by mouth. It was the well-known *nothing to eat or drink after midnight* speech. One thing I realized: it hurts to be hungry. I was hurting. But I had no clue how to face it or express it. Remember, my family wasn't comfortable with crying, nor were pity parties acceptable. And being sad sounded an awful lot like feeling sorry for oneself. Therefore, my emotional pain slowly manifested from the inside out into an eating disorder.

I hadn't stepped into a full-blown eating disorder yet. The decline was gradual. From time to time when my emotions felt overwhelming, I would go without food. This approach was utilized here and there starting in the sixth grade. But when I encountered Michael's choice of another, and then his unexpected move out of state to live with his dad, I coped as quietly as I knew— with no food.

Would anyone ever see *me?* Would anyone ever truly see *me* apart from my body? What kind of future did I have? Would my scars always define me? Did I fight to live a life I had already lost? If so, then why didn't I die with Jon? Why did I have to go through all the pain for a life of rejection? Would this always be the outcome for potential relationships? Would someone connect with and care for me only to decide I wasn't cute enough to carry on one's arm?

I couldn't change my scars. Oh, how I wanted to, and oh, how I silently held on to hope for medical advancements to one day give me new skin. However, I had to face the present day I was living, not the future I hoped would fix me. So I decided to live thin. Maybe I wouldn't look good in a pair of shorts or a swimsuit, but I could be uber thin in my jeans and sweaters.

It was an intense commitment to live nutritionally deprived. I avoided anything I thought would be good for my body, even multivitamins. I didn't want to consume any calories, so when I got really hungry, I'd allow myself three to four saltine crackers. Eventually, this transitioned into a routine of bingeing and purging. I would get so hungry I'd eat. And then I'd throw up. Thinking that maybe I couldn't empty my stomach completely by puking, I decided to implement laxatives too—in my mind, the more the better. One night I took eleven. Eleven laxatives. I lay on my bedroom floor and surely thought Mom or Dad was going to find me dead the next morning.

By the time I was in the tenth grade, I wanted someone to know something was wrong. I wanted my internal pain to be obvious. I wanted to be rescued from the turmoil. However, I wasn't happy when it happened.

My friend had found my laxatives in my bathroom. She didn't confront me. Instead she punched the remaining ones out of the foil package and into the toilet. She flushed them away and never said anything. I knew something was up when I found the package completely empty.

This friend of mine told Mom. Mom told Dad. But no one was mad.

Mom took me to see a pediatrician who came recommended in dealing with young girls and eating disorders: Dr. Anne Harrington.

Dr. Harrington didn't make me go into a treatment facility. I committed to her that I wanted help. I didn't want to feel the way I did. She started me on protein shakes for nourishment. No instructions to stop at our local ice cream shop and binge on banana splits, no suggestion of steak dinners. She didn't want me to eat much, just drink the shakes. Furthermore, she prescribed medication—an antidepressant and an anxiolytic to reduce anxiety. She also referred me to a counselor.

Mom made an appointment for me with a therapist named Susie. That name sounded nice to me. Mom's name was Susan, and her side of the family often called her Susie. The therapist's name offered a small detail of comfort to face the first session.

I was completely broken. I had been for years, ever since the moments on the dirt road with a dead brother and a body burning. This brokenness was long neglected, convoluting over time.

Now came the moments for piecing myself back together. And I was brave enough to try.

18

Holding On

From the outside I looked like I had it all.

I had a closet full of name brand clothes and shoes. I wore department store makeup. I went to the salon for regular appointments to highlight my hair. And when it came time for me to drive, I got my dream car right off the showroom floor! I had so very much, and I wanted to be happy. Genuinely happy. I was very grateful. But when it came down to it, it was all just stuff. I knew no material possession in all the world could fulfill the emptiness in me.

I felt totally disqualified. Written off. Voided. Unworthy. Unwanted.

My friends and family were determined to influence my outlook. Mom sat on my bed countless evenings listening to my pain, speaking optimism into my heart. My youth pastor gave innumerable hours toward counseling and discipling me in grasping the plans and purposes God had for my life. My friends consistently wrote and spoke words of value and encouragement into my life. They never hesitated to share how they saw me.

Like friends do, one of them assumed meeting another guy would resolve the problem. Oh, how I wish those problems had been teenage-guy-rejection deep. Unfortunately, the experience of losing a first love did not create my pain. It merely unveiled it.

Nevertheless, this friend wanted to help. She invited me along for a group date to a Drillers baseball game in Tulsa. I was supposed to meet this guy named Brandon. As if he were going to be some knight in shining armor or something. I wasn't interested in the least bit. My heart was scattered in fragments. Meeting another boy to grind down the remaining? No thanks!

Mom was about as bad as my friend, insisting I go. I felt like the fifth wheel, or third leg, or whatever it is they call it when you feel absolutely awkward tagging along on someone else's date.

It was August of my sophomore year. My friend was turning sixteen the next month, and her date was a grade older than us, so he was already driving. He came to my house to pick the two of us up. She and I crawled into the cab of his truck heading for the baseball game. I met the guy they were all so eager to introduce me to.

There wasn't much to report from the night when I got back home. Mom persisted for details. I mean, the guy hardly spoke, so there truly wasn't much to share. Heading up the stairs, I casually commented, "He was cute. And he had a nice butt." Had I not ascended the stairs so quickly, I would have seen Mom picking her jaw up off the floor. I never spoke like that. She was stunned at my response but realized there truly wasn't any more I had to tell from the evening. I didn't have the slightest interest. Apparently, he didn't either. In all fairness, he didn't even know I would be coming to the game. He drove there with another friend, not realizing this was supposed to be some double date, with a big blind date component to it.

Although we attended the same school, we didn't know each other.

Brandon had moved back from Texas a couple school years earlier for the start of his ninth-grade year. We were both the new kids but in different grades—he was one grade ahead of me. He moved to the high school for tenth grade, so although we both attended the same school system, we were in different buildings. We met just before the start of my tenth-grade year and his eleventh-grade year.

I never saw this guy around school, and then it seemed I saw him all the time. We politely said "hi" in the halls at school and during extracurricular events like football and basketball games. I even saw him pass by my French class one day. My teacher, Mrs. Brown, routinely left her door open at the start of class. My seat was in the very front. I noticed someone out of the corner of my eye walk by. The person captured my attention when he took steps walking backwards. It was Brandon. He waved and communicated a silent "hi." I wasn't sure he was waving at me. Thinking he must be trying to get the girl's attention behind me, I just smiled. As soon as he walked off, I turned around to the girl sitting in the desk behind me.

"Did you see him?" I asked.

"Who?"

"Oh, no one," I casually dismissed.

I really thought he *had* to have been waving at her. She was super gorgeous. Tall. Long, straight hair. Smart. She was super sweet too. And she was a junior. In his same grade. I realized he had been waving at me. But I certainly didn't want her to know whom I was talking about, because I wasn't completely sure I really even cared. I mean, I kinda did. Just not totally certain.

The very last day of tenth grade, my friend Mandy was pushing me to do something.

"He likes you, Heather!"

I wanted to believe that. It seemed he might like me a little. He *did* ask me to dance at the Valentine's dance and at prom. We had each gone with different dates but found ourselves dancing with each other. And he *had* asked me about going to a hockey game with him sometime. For some reason, I heard myself saying I loved hockey, which was the furthest thing from the truth. I was starting to think I might just like him. Just a little. He was so quiet, though, and somewhat mysterious.

Mandy gave me the best motivational speech to make a move. I had business cards in my purse Dad had made for me to take to a music conference. So I pulled one out and wrote on the back, "Call me sometime." Mandy drove up to the baseball field parking lot where Brandon was practicing. I jumped out and quickly stuck the card on his driver side window. My heart was pounding as if I were robbing a bank and she were driving the getaway car! I couldn't believe I was giving this guy my number. He hadn't even asked for it.

I gave myself a list of reasons why I shouldn't have done that. It was so impulsive. And what girl gives a guy her number when he didn't even ask for it? My only consolation was the possibility it may have been long forgotten by the time school started back after the three-month long summer.

He called.

We started spending some time together over the summer. Before long there was much more I liked about Brandon Meadows than I'd have imagined that night at the Drillers game. He was more than another cute guy. He was becoming a good friend.

● ● ● ● ● ● ●

In spite of my incessant declaration about how I was not a pageant girl, I participated in our town's Miss Fall Festival pageant my tenth-grade year. The winner received gifts from area merchants along with scholarship money and served as a representative at ribbon-cutting ceremonies when local businesses joined the town's Chamber of Commerce. I sang "I'm a Believer" by Amy Morriss. It had a gospel feel starting off with an organ and then coming in with a catchy beat and trumpets. Moreover, the song communicated a message I wanted to share. I won Miss Talent and Second Runner-Up.

I competed again the next year, and this time Brandon was serving as one of the escorts. He accompanied the contestants to the Main Street stage for the business wear introduction, the talent performances, the evening gown final question and crowning moment. However, Brandon never escorted me. No matter how he tried to make it happen, it just didn't work out for him to walk me from the building of our holding area to the stage. Which probably benefited me by helping me keep my focus.

Contestants were individually asked one question for the final category. They were ushered to and from the holding area one at a time, so no one would hear the others' answers. Then the contestants returned to the waiting area. Before walking to the stage, each girl received a flower to carry. We were all lined up waiting on the final ones to be questioned, when it was discovered that the very last girl to go out didn't have a flower. Someone yelled she didn't have one, so I instinctively handed her mine.

Instead of her marching back to the building, all the contestants joined her on stage after she answered the question. I realized then that someone must have missed the count when ordering the flowers because there wasn't another one to grab before going out on stage. It seemed my contestant number thirteen was not looking so lucky. I felt awkward, the only girl in line with nothing in my hands. I just stood with my arms extended down and fingers clasped together.

The results were announced.

My heart sank when I wasn't called for Miss Talent. I felt solid in my deliverance of "I Now Live" by Crystal Lewis. It was a strong song. It was upbeat—ideal for an outdoor audience. And again, the message was powerful. But the girl who won it was definitely deserving. We were in choir together, and she was just about as sweet as they come. I really was happy for her.

They proceeded to announce Second Runner-Up. Not me. Then First

Runner-Up. Not me. While the girl's sash was being wrapped around her, I consoled myself, *This is their year. I had mine last year. Be happy for them in their moment.*

A camera captured my face as I heard, "And Miss Fall Festival 1997 is . . . Heather Cochrane!"

My mouth dropped. *No way!*

It was the most incredibly humbling moment. The girls all gathered around me and hugged me. I kept looking into the faces of the ones I had personally envisioned winning. *This should be yours,* I kept thinking.

In the grand scheme of life, it may not seem like a huge accomplishment winning a small-town pageant, but it was the greatest correction to the determinations I had made of myself. Scarred-skin girls *can* wear crowns.

• • • • • • •

By appearance I looked well assembled, like a small-town pageant girl. But my battle was as intense as the one I had faced nine years earlier. Unfortunately, no crown could compensate for the agony inside. My life was being consumed with the fire of internal suffering.

I had been placed on an anxiolytic for anxiety and an antidepressant for depression. The first antidepressant made me so happy. Euphoric. I wasn't even in this realm. I went from being in a depression-drained energy state to a nothing-could-get-me-down state. My therapist and pediatrician worked together and decided to change the antidepressant I was taking. A short time later, I was deeply depressed. More so than ever before. But I had just won a pageant. I was on the praise and worship team for my youth group. I was an honor roll student. I shouldn't be depressed. Everyone thought so highly of me. I couldn't let them down.

It all hit me coming home from a youth service. I started crying the minute I got in the car. I was like a dam holding strong around others, bursting the moment I was alone.

I got in, buckled up and started the car. Programmed robotic routines.

The tears were accompanied by prayers. I talked to God all the time. All. The. Time. He was the only One I shared with about my deep desire to go to Heaven. As I stood in the shower, He was the One I asked why I had to live in *this* body. As I lay in bed at night, He was the One I begged and pleaded to allow me to come live with Jon.

In counseling I was asked repeatedly if I wanted to kill myself. "No," I'd answer.

I didn't at all. Truly. But I failed to relay how much I didn't want to live. I didn't connect that my desire to go to Heaven may transpire into me actually pursuing that possibility.

That night on the way home from the youth service, I continued accelerating until I lost control of my car and landed it in a ditch. I wanted to die that night. I hoped I'd die that night.

But just as a Divine hand was upon me the day I burned in the road, so was that same hand upon me the day I lost complete control of my life in the car. My car hardly looked damaged. My moment was so impulsive I hadn't even thought to unbuckle my seat belt. There were other plans for me. Overcoming the brokenness was part of it.

I lied to my parents about the accident. Said I avoided hitting a dog. I know they didn't believe me but went with it. It all came out in counseling.

Susie took me to a back room with a bat and a punching bag. She said, "I want you to hit this bag for everything you're mad about in life." I wouldn't take the bat. "I'm not mad about anything," I said. She persisted, saying, "Yes, you are." She demonstrated as she hit the bag with the bat. *Whack!*

"You are mad that you are burned." *Whack!*

"You are mad that you are scarred." *Whack!*

"You are mad that you have felt so much pain." *Whack!*

"You are mad that Jon is dead." *Whack!*

With every *whack* I cried until I broke on the last one. Tears flowing down my face, I interrupted, "But I'm not mad! I'm sad! I'm just *so* sad. I'm sad." Susie sat the bat down, wrapped her arms around me and I collapsed into her.

This pain demanded my attention. My existence was in a critical condition. It could not be avoided. However, I was not in it alone. God was coming ever nearer to me. C. S. Lewis wrote, "We can ignore even pleasure. But pain insists upon being attended to. God whispers to us in our pleasures, speaks in our conscience, but shouts in our pains: it is His megaphone to rouse a deaf world."[1]

I turned to Him in my suffering and was becoming closer and closer to Him, thus stronger and stronger in my pain.

At a back-to-school youth rally, I received a supernatural touch of His power. After praise and worship, I sat down on the pew for the message. When it concluded, the praise and worship team got up as usual, migrating up front to play for the prayer time. However, I stayed where I was. Typically, I sang, but this night I knew I needed to sit. I just kept my head bowed as student after student raised their hands and moved toward the front, responding to the message of praying for our school year. But I sat. In the back of my mind, I considered how bad it looked that I wasn't going to sing, nor was I going to pray. Nevertheless, the thought wasn't strong enough to move me. I stayed. Head bowed.

Eventually, I stood up and walked to the front right of the sanctuary where the youth rally was being held. This one wasn't at our church. We had them about once a quarter, and different Assembly of God churches within the area took turns hosting them.

When I got to the front, most of the students and adult leaders were already involved with praying for one another. I wasn't there to pray for my school. I was too empty. I had nothing left within me. I didn't even have words to pray. I stood on the right side of the church, cupped my hands over my face and said, "I can't do this." I repeated it. "I can't do this. I can't do this. I can't do this."

With every confession came emotion. A flood of emptiness. Oceans of grief. Rivers of tears. I echoed, "I can't do this" until I started speaking words I did not know. Everything was gone within and only my spirit was left to pray. Even though I knew about the baptism of the Holy Spirit by evidence of speaking in other tongues, I hadn't really felt that was something for me. I just wanted to stop feeling the agony inside.

That night, while the depths of my being were praying, I felt the Lord reply, "I know you can't, Heather. But I can."

19

Power Tools

I grew up on a whole lot of Grandma's cooking. Her rolls and pies were legendary. There are lists of dishes I loved, like her goulash, her home-made applesauce and the way she'd make rice for breakfast. Who knew rice for breakfast could be so good? Well, apparently Grandma did. She made everything so tasty.

Before Jon and I had our accident, the farm Grandma and Grandpa Creekmore left our family looked somewhat more like a real farm. Mr. Jones leased the land for his cattle, but in addition to the cows, we had a large garden, goats, rabbits, geese and fresh eggs from the chickens. Moreover, we had the constant convenience of preparing another one of my favorite meals—chicken and dumplings. All I pretty much had to do was ask Grandma to make it and she would. Well, I also had to catch the chicken.

It was somewhat disturbing watching Grandma chop off the head of the chicken I caught. But even more intriguing was observing it run around full force with no sense of any direction whatsoever, being that it didn't have a head. Then seeing it *kerplop*, falling over dead.

Tragedy does something like that to a person on the inside. We continue moving through life without being fully alive but not fully dead either.

The loss consumed me.

More so than sustaining the burn injury, or people staring at the scars, or being what the medical field labeled as a deformity, was the loss of my brother. Jon's death was the hardest part to live with, a challenge that never passed in time. It was a pain that would never go away. The void could not be minimized nor compartmentalized. The reality of emptiness weaved through every piece of my existence.

Something was happening in this process of persevering through my painful places. Something was forming through this persistence to overcome my darkest moments. Something terrible was being used to make something even better and longer lasting happen.

The goal shifted from waiting for the pain to end to learning how to live with it. Discovering the reason for living in light of the loss and tragedy. There was a joy buried under the emotional turmoil, and I had some power tools to excavate it.

I never uncovered a how-to manual or a step-by-step guide to healing. It was a journey commissioning my greatest resources: people, music, writing, reading, and prayer.

On May 5, 1988, Grandma's sister wrote in the hospital waiting room guest book, "You are loved by so many people. You must remember this because it will help you to be strong. Much love, Aunt Venita."

Aunt Venita was right. There is strength in people's love. I needed that strength. Not just in recovering from a burn injury, but in regard to the person I needed to become on the other side of it. When it came time to deal with the emotional trauma of it all, I realized I was weak, my gauge had hit empty and

I had nothing left to keep going. I needed the strength of others to get through the darkness I was facing. It required some looking around. It required some reaching out. And in doing so, I benefited from a gold mine of people lending their strength through love.

I had a troop of people. I had a great group of friends. Solid friends. They were truly treasures to me.

It's hard to be thankful for some of the things we've never gone without. Like running water. How often do we feel grateful for taking a shower, running the dishwasher or flushing the toilet? Most likely we never even think about it. Friendship for me was something like that. My core group didn't shift from being friends one day to being foes the next. Surely our connections weren't perfect. Nothing involving people ever is. But our friendships were dependable.

One opportunity to realize this occurred over the first Christmas break at my new school. Dad was driving me as he usually did. I never said a word, but my mind was swirling with anxious thoughts. *What if they've changed their minds over the break and decided they don't like me anymore?* I was considering the possibilities and preparing for the worst. However, these were firm friendships. I had the gift of people who genuinely loved me. And because of that, I was finally facing the obstacle course in becoming a true overcomer.

I had my parents, my peers and some incredible mentors. My youth pastors, Steve and Michele, counseled me, discipled me, and mentored me. They stepped into my battles of suffering, grief, acceptance and value, not giving up on the victory I had in store. Or on the person I was becoming through it. Furthermore, they allowed me to discover my place in ministry, plugging in my passion for singing into the outlet of the praise and worship team. Revealing to me that nothing is more liberating than shifting a hurting heart to the glory of God and the needs of another.

● ● ● ● ● ● ●

I had always loved to sing since those moments when Jon and I would do our little performances in front of the fireplace and those moments of my cow serenading in our backyard. Music was always somewhat of a light switch connecting me to a sense of energy inside.

There were a variety of genres I liked. I loved the tape Barry made for me of Fine Young Cannibals and REO Speedwagon songs. I also loved Aretha Franklin, The Temptations and Lesley Gore from Mom's era. So much so, Mom made comments several times over that I must have been born in the wrong generation. Fifties and sixties music was some of my favorite. But again, the admiration was quite diverse. I enjoyed musicals through movies like *The Sound of Music, Fiddler on the Roof, My Fair Lady* and *Grease.* Songs from practically all genres were in my repertoire.

The passion grew when I went to my first concert at nine years old. We saw Richard Marx. Hearing the hit songs live and seeing the artist sing them in person was phenomenal to me. Richard Marx was on a dark stage as the piano rose up out of the floor for him to perform "Right Here Waiting for You." That was an impressive stage effect for a nine-year-old in 1990!

Grandma was the only one in our family who listened to country music. By way of her radio station, I was exposed to an artist who became one of my all-time favorites: Reba McEntire. Her voice was strong and dynamic. Whether she was singing in her head or her chest voice, whether she was begging her love to come back or kicking him out, she had persuasion and passion. Reba was the second artist I saw live. I seized more opportunities to return for future concerts, and I learned every word to every song.

Music was always enjoyable. Much of it merely captured my attention by the vocals and the beat. But sometimes the lyrics connected inside me, giving words to my emotion. Like Bette Midler singing "Wind Beneath My Wings" from the movie *Beaches.* My life was moving on without Jon as if I were leaving him behind, but the song painted an image of him being with me in the future. As the unseen wind contributes to an eagle's flight, so Jon would continue to be a part of who I was to be.

It took some time for Mom and Dad to realize what a power tool music was for me.

I was supposed to go to softball practice the night of the accident. Mom wanted me to try a season. I didn't really want to. Barry and Jon didn't play baseball; therefore, I wasn't necessarily wanting to play softball. Barry was a soccer player, so Jon and I followed suit and had just finished our second season of soccer.

Three years after the accident, while I was in the fourth grade, Mom had me signed up again for softball. Apparently, she was determined I decide if the sport was for me or not. The heat was horrendous. Due to my inability to sweat, my body didn't tolerate it. I'd stand out in the sun and feel my heart beating in my head. My face turned beet red, but no one said a word. Everyone knew how hard I was trying, so even what was obvious was not acknowledged. And I surely didn't want to request special treatment. I wanted to be like everyone else, but I just wasn't. There really were some things I could *not* do like the other kids. However, we did not ever use the word *can't*. Instead, I pushed through and expressed my preference to not play again.

I also tried basketball. Wasn't any good. At all. Moreover, I didn't care to be.

By the sixth grade, I concluded athletics was a place I just didn't belong. I don't know if it necessarily had everything to do with the burn injury. Mom always said I was a good soccer player with a strong right kick before the accident. But then again, what parent doesn't think their child is a rock star?

Instead of a basketball court, softball diamond or soccer field, I felt drawn to the stage. It terrified me, but overall, a microphone felt more natural than anything else I tried. None of my peers were involved in vocal performance at the time Mom and Dad considered the possibility of that being my niche. While it's always easier to blend in with the norm, I was already *not* blending in. Not in the least bit. Even though it took courage to step into vocal lessons and competitions without a friend to face it with, the experience was liberating. I was finally letting go and pursuing something unique to me.

A whole new world opened. And a whole new set of friends.

After one of my first solo competitions in an organization called Oklahoma Kids, I got connected with George and Rose Earley. They invited me to join a show they were putting together with a group of kids my age called Rock On. The show was a compilation of fifties and sixties music. It was right up my alley. We practiced three nights a week with shows on the weekend. The consistent experience performing at different festivals and business parties around Oklahoma cultivated my comfort of being on stage.

The experience also developed some confidence in me. Singing gave me something to identify with. When adults made casual conversation and asked, "Do you play any sports?," I could respond by saying, "No, I sing."

Those details laying the groundwork for my individuality contributed to my mustering up the courage to change schools. If I hadn't already branched out from the familiar to join this vocal group, I don't know that I could have faced the risk of changing schools. When I did make that change, I came with a confident assurance of my talent. I didn't feel good about the way I looked, but I felt good about the way I sang. So I joined the choir and met an influential mentor in my life. Traci McDaniel.

Traci was the choir teacher. She then became my vocal coach. It was a convenient change for my parents. They had been driving me into Tulsa, ninety-minute round-trips for lessons, plus trips in for the Rock On group rehearsals. Having a vocal coach close to home was a valuable gift of time for them. For me, it was the most unexpected gift of friendship.

I never had problems connecting with adults. At some stages of my childhood, it felt easier connecting with adults than other kids. I had transitioned out of that world so early. My vocal lessons were an opportunity for deep conversation, mentorship and counseling. Traci deposited nuggets of discipleship, affirmation and motivation into me. Teaching me far more than what it was to be a strong vocalist.

She recorded the lessons, playing back the areas I needed to improve. It provided a way for me to hear what I did wrong. So much of singing is learning how it feels to produce a certain sound. It was embarrassing listening to myself, but it helped me know what to avoid and what to continue.

By the time she started coaching me, I was regularly attending church, getting plugged in to being part of a church family. I was also getting plugged in to singing as a ministry rather than just as a performance. It was a whole new world to me, which was apparent in the area of vocal music. I had been trained to always say "thank you" at the end of a song. It was simply the polite thing to do. However, after singing in church, I was informed the expression was "self-glorifying," taking the credit and focus for myself. The interpretation broke my heart. That wasn't my intent at all. Traci kept me grounded. I wasn't well versed in the way things went in church. She reiterated that God knew my heart and He was the ultimate One I sang for. All other opinions could fall to the wayside.

Music was taking on a more meaningful place in my life. As lyrics provided a natural way for me to identify my emotions, I was discovering the Christian music genre connected to a deeper place within me. I didn't grow up memorizing Bible verses, having family devotional nights or playing Bible trivia in children's church. Listening to this music and learning the lyrics of the songs was a seamless way of embedding God's Word in my heart. The messages gave definition to who I was, where I had been and what kind of future was in store for me.

This transforming process was made evident during a surgery in my eighth-grade year. I woke up in recovery singing "I Have No Doubt," a song by the group Point of Grace about having confidence in God's presense no matter where we are. I was realizing God was with me through it all. Through many of those moments when I felt alone, He was there. During those times in the burn unit having bandage changes and nightmares, rolling in and out of surgery, feeling isolated when Mom and Dad had to go, God never left me alone.

Sometimes singing the words of those songs for congregations or audiences overwhelmed me. The messages connected deeply within me. Nerves and emotions frequently caused my body to tremble and shake while I sang. As much as I didn't like my physical reaction, the opportunity to sing was a greater fulfillment.

More fulfilling was receiving affirmation from others. But Traci mentored me through the positive and the negative. "God doesn't owe us compliments from others," she taught. "We're called to be obedient regardless." She explained it as an icing-on-the-cake kind of thought. If someone provides positive feedback, it's a gift the Lord is allowing us to receive, but it's not required or necessary for us to give to Him what is already His.

It's a natural tendency to question our contributions when we make ourselves vulnerable to an audience. But it's a crack for self-doubt and insecurity to seep in. When that happens, it takes our focus off our calling to serve. It's liberating to lay our offering on the altar and trust Him to honor it, bless it and use it. We're simply called to give it. The rest is in His hands.

●　●　●　●　●　●　●

Although music was a good way to feed my mind and heart encouraging words of truth and hope, I also began daily devotionals of reading God's Word. Steve emphasized the importance of reading and memorizing Scripture. I began with a daily devotional book the church provided quarterly. Eventually, I sought out my own guides, reading devotionals like Oswald Chambers's *My Utmost for His Highest.*

Seeking out Scripture was medicine for my soul. Just as my body needed treatment to heal, so did my soul. I began piecing a bigger picture together from my quiet moments of reading God's Word. Peace was found not in ignoring the painful realities but in confronting them through His Word.

Was God watching that day? Did He watch as we crashed? As Jon's neck crushed? As my body burned? He didn't keep me from harm that day. He didn't keep Jon from harm, so how, how would I trust in Him?

I trust Him because I see more of the good He gave than the pain He allowed. I trust Him because I know His love is not proven by lack of suffering but *in* suffering, trial, persecution and hardship. I trust Him because I know He didn't spare His own Son but gave Him up as the perfect sacrifice so I might be saved and have the greatest hope beyond what was robbed on that dirt road— the hope of eternity. Moreover, through Jesus' work on the cross, God the Father provided for everything I would need after that day. Emotional healing. Physical healing. Psychological healing. Spiritual healing.

Do I measure His greatness, His love and His faithfulness by the comfort I have in this life? Or do I measure it by the awareness that He is in control regardless of what the circumstances are?

God allowed Joseph to be thrown into a well. God allowed Daniel to be captured and later thrown into a lions' den. God allowed Job to suffer the loss of his home, his family, his finances and his health.

In his book *Thriving in Babylon,* Larry Osborne shared, "Despite the fierceness of the battle, we still have reason for hope. Though we are sometimes pushed *to* the limit, we will never be pushed *over* the limit." He continued using the life of Job, saying, "The purpose of Job's trial was not to see how much it would take to break him. It was to confirm and display the depth of righteousness that God knew Job already had."[1]

We have much difficulty in trying to understand why God doesn't stop bad things. We know He could have. God could have prevented us from hitting that truck or Jon dying. He allowed my body to burn in the road. He saw it all. He didn't prevent any of this turmoil and pain, yet I will hope in Him. He never left me. He never forgot me.

Stories like the blind man in John 9 gave me a different interpretation of the tragedy that unfolded. So many in our family quietly assumed their own individual blame. Whose fault *was* it? Who was to blame? The same questions were being asked of Jesus regarding a blind man. The disciples asked Jesus if the man was blind because he had sinned or his parents had sinned. Someone must have been the reason or cause for this man's blindness, right? Actually not. Jesus said, "It was not that this man sinned, or his parents, but that the works of God might be displayed in him."[2] The work of God displayed in humanity. That is a power-tool game changer. If anyone was going to see something when they saw my scars, I wanted it to be a display of God's work. He entrusted me to carry the story.

This is an imperfect world where imperfect things happen. But I look toward eternity where the troubles of this temporary life will be outweighed. The pain today is gaining something of far greater value for all eternity. "For our light and momentary troubles are achieving for us an eternal glory that far outweighs them all. So we fix our eyes not on what is seen, but on what is unseen, since what is seen is temporary, but what is unseen is eternal."[3]

I was gaining much hope. Evidence of God's goodness was all around. And I wrote about it.

• • • • • • • •

I loved the idea of writing before I was even old enough to spell. When I was about four, Dad gave me a large hardback notebook he received as a promotional item through his sales career. I sat at the upstairs desk, penciling waves on the pages, pretending I was writing a letter in cursive.

After our accident I wrote more. Sometimes I wrote about the accident. More often, I just made up stories. I had received some small hardback notebooks that I used to make children's books, along with the illustrations too. It was apparent I didn't have an artist's knack in drawing, but my stories hinted at possibly having one for writing.

This became more apparent to me through school. When writing assignments were given, I always felt debilitated to work within a certain word count. My peers were groaning and grumbling at just trying to meet the requirement.

I found strength in writing words. It was a power tool toward healing. It takes courage to explore the darkest areas of our emotions, and sometimes we have them so buried it takes some digging to find them.

My process of journaling daily started as a food log. Susie wanted me to write what I ate and at what point I threw up to help me identify what triggered my desire to do that. This food log turned into a journal expressing those painful places too hurtful for spoken words.

At times, my meticulous regimental personality has been an asset. It certainly was for my start to journaling. Every night I crawled into bed and wrote one front-and-back page in my journal. I was committed to the process even when I didn't think I had anything to say. Frequently, I wrote the nitty-gritty details of the day.

"I woke up late this morning and had to rush to get ready."

"My hair looks crazy."

Those meaningless details often led to thoughts I never considered writing.

"[So-and-so] had on the cutest new Guess shorts, wearing some little shoes with no socks. I wish I could wear shoes without socks. And I really wish I could wear shorts, but I'll never have legs I would want people to see."

My circumstance wasn't changed through writing. Still today, I don't wear shorts in public, but just being able to write the reality of it, without having someone try to make me feel better or pretend it wasn't true, was a tool that strengthened me.

Before long, my journaling turned into prayers.

"Lord, I don't want a serious relationship. I just want someone to go out with, someone to like me. When my friends are all going out with their boyfriends, I don't want to be the fifth wheel on the group date."

People often say they don't know how to pray. Sometimes we make it more difficult than it needs to be. Prayer is simply presenting our requests to God. It is simply speaking our heart. Prayer isn't about getting God to change His plans and purposes. It's about getting us *in line* with His plans and purposes. But we can't get in line with Him until we start genuinely and authentically sharing our heart with Him.

I wrote prayers about everything. Prayers about my pain. Prayers about my hurts. Prayers about my desires, disappointments, questions and fears. I let it all out.

Journaling provided numerous benefits. For one, it slowed down my mind. Instead of my thoughts running multiple directions, the function of writing those thoughts took more time, making me slow down and process those topics more thoroughly. In addition to it being a safe place for expressing the things I could never say aloud, journaling was self-revealing. Some of the things I ended up writing I never knew were tucked inside my heart. It was a beneficial path of self-discovery. Finally, it gave an account of my life's moments providing evidence of growth and change. When I read back through some of my journals, I am reminded of memories nearly forgotten, and I see how I've evolved since writing it.

I must have had an idea about the long-term value of writing. At seventeen, I wrote,

"In English today, we read Shakespeare's 18th Sonnet. He said that the only way he could forever and eternally love someone is to write about it. The per-

sons would die and the seasons change, but the words would live on after everything has passed.

It made me think of my journal. I usually write every day, and by writing I, and the ones I love, will live on through history. Maybe not history to the world, but history to my children and grandchildren and maybe even great grandchildren."

Nothing made for an instant fix or miraculous cure. But my power tools of people, music, reading, writing and prayer put me on a positive path forward: making progress in the process.

Unearthing the painful places was building me into a stronger person. Facing the darkness to excavate the hurt, loss and disappointment was developing a true spirit of an overcomer within me. It wasn't pretty, pleasant or desirable. But if allowed, God can make good of *all* things.

I had no idea He was just getting started with bringing good from the tragedy I had known. He was working it together in ways I would have never thought or imagined!

20

Noticed

Over the holiday season of 1987, Walt Disney Pictures re-released their enchanting classical love story of *Cinderella* to theaters. Mom and Aunt Margie took Krista, Slade, Jon and me to see it. The movie was released for the first time on home video the next year.

Cinderella sang "A Dream Is a Wish Your Heart Makes." It was just a fairy tale, but I believed the lyrics. I believed no matter how my heart was grieving, if I continued believing, the dream I wished for would come true.

I wanted a real-life love story. But I didn't want to bank my happiness on whether or not that happened for me. My determination came in junior high when staying the night with my friend Amanda. She had a book of quotes I was thumbing through when I read something along the lines of *Happiness should not be dependent on others, but rather enhanced by others*. The concept struck me and always stuck with me. Never again would I put that responsibility on someone else. Happiness, first and foremost, needed to come from within me.

My other determination was love should, above all, come from my relationship with God.

In the summer of 1997, Traci took me to a Christian music conference in Estes Park, Colorado. It gave me the opportunity to gain some insight into the industry, receive feedback on my vocals and meet current recording artists. One of my favorites, Crystal Lewis, was there, along with Point of Grace and Phil Keaggy. I had the chance to hear Sandi Patty speak about the personal cost of success in music—the time traveling and missing moments at home, both common and monumental. The perspective was certainly eye-opening.

Of all the highlights from the conference, my most meaningful one was being able to visit with the vocal group Avalon. In my moment with them, I had the chance to tell them what their song "Let It Be Forever" meant to me. The lyrics greatly influenced my understanding of love: how it is our testimony as Christians, how we shouldn't take it lightly and how it should come with a sacrifice because love cost Christ everything. Furthermore, love shouldn't change. Love should be forever.

I was very guarded with my heart, mostly out of fear. I couldn't imagine someone loving me beyond my appearance. The thought was an ever-present reality in my mind but not one I shared with others. Until accidentally one day, I did.

Our church was growing—in family and facility. It was an exciting season as our church built a larger building on a new campus. In some way or another, the entire church body was able to get involved in the process. I went for a designated workday to clean the new baptismal. I paired up with a lady about my parents' age. As we scraped and scrubbed patches of dried sheetrock mud off the fiberglass tub, she expressed visions of all the people who would be baptized right there, including my future family in her vision. But I informed, "I doubt I'll ever get married."

The comment was quite casual. So casual, most people, especially adults, would not have really even heard it. Not this lady. She jumped on it like bees on honey.

"Do you *want* to get married?" she asked.

"Well, yes, of course, one day I do. I just don't think I will."

"Why not?"

For the first time in my life, I was thinking it would be great if Jesus came back and raptured His church right about then. Since that twinkling-of-an-eye moment wasn't happening, I found myself sharing one of my deepest, most vulnerable, insecure feelings with this lady.

"Well, I just feel no one would ever want me, and if they did, it will probably be when I'm old and just for companionship."

Oh. My. Goodness.

How in the world did I share that with her? *Why* in the world did I share that with her?

The Book of Proverbs says, "Trust in the Lord with all your heart, and lean not on your own understanding; in all your ways acknowledge Him, and He shall direct your paths."[1] I didn't know why at the time, but God directed me to that lady in the baptismal. She didn't offer a counseling session or pursue pouring her opinions into me; instead, she poured a prayer of faith over me, claiming the hope in my heart to one day have a family of my own.

In the meantime, I had much to sift through. My objective was *don't let the past define the future.* Life had been very tragic so early. For a young person, there aren't many other life experiences to clarify the lens of loss. Many more of my days included this pain than those existing before the accident. Instead of tragedy being something that happened in life, it *was* my life.

The internal turmoil began manifesting during my eighth-grade year. I started having headaches. At first this wasn't much of a concern. It wasn't alarming, considering my age and all the hormonal and social changes taking place. However, they were more than headaches. I felt nauseous, I couldn't tolerate the light, and the pain was localized as a stabbing sensation in my right eye.

Through treatment for the eating disorder, two determinations were made. One, the headaches were migraines related to post-traumatic stress disorder. Two, the eating disorder was a result of my depression, not vice versa. It was explained to me that depression often results from nutritional deprivation, but my eating disorder appeared to be an expression of my emotional trauma. In other words, the depression came first, causing a cascade of symptoms.

For example, my incessant struggle for perfection. I had highly obsessive tendencies—constantly striving, feeling I had to compensate for the imperfection of my outside appearance by making myself valuable and productive.

I wasn't enough.

Not that I wasn't enough to others. I wasn't enough to *me*. So much so that it blurred my focus to see myself in another's eyes.

Most of my relationships with boys were as friends. When a few of us girls would talk about it, I'd ponder aloud, "Why?"

One friend informed me it was because I was intimidating. I think it was meant as a compliment. But really? Intimidating? Of all the things I thought, I certainly didn't consider myself intimidating. I concluded it was her way of avoiding the real reasons why romance wasn't part of my picture. No balloons, teddy bears or roses were happening in my world.

However, it wasn't because there weren't any prospects. And it most certainly didn't have anything to do with me being intimidating. But rather, it had everything to do with my opinion of myself. It clouded my ability to see what others saw. Until this one quiet guy was persistent enough to change my view.

● ● ● ● ● ● ●

Brandon Meadows was similar to most guys in my life—he was a good friend. I liked him, but our relationship had not grown beyond a friendship. There was never this *oh, I want to date him* kind of purpose.

206

We had many phone chats and had gone out numerous times with groups of friends since the day I had placed my number on his truck's window. We went to concerts, bowling, the movies, games at school and dinner. By the fall of 1997, my junior year (his senior year), I was repeatedly asked the same routine question: "Heather, are you and Brandon dating?"

"No," I answered, in a tone as if the question was completely preposterous. "We're just spending our extra time together." Eventually someone countered my passive explanation by commenting, "Well, you both sure seem to have a lot of *extra* time then."

Brandon gave me a little white teddy bear when I had oral surgery to remove my wisdom teeth. It was kneeling and had closed eyes and the paws were sewn together as if it were praying. A few weeks later, he came over to hang out at my house. He asked if I had ever seen a shooting star. Honestly, I had never found it productive to sit and stare at the night sky. He urged me outside to lie on the trampoline and wait for a shooting star. During our watch, I asked, "Do you have a piece of gum?" I thought maybe he had a packet in his pocket. He replied, "Yes." I turned my head toward him to get it. Instead of a packet of gum, he held the piece he was chewing between his teeth.

I was shocked in both an excited and disgusted kind of way. I declined, "No thanks, it's okay. I'm good."

That was probably the first moment I thought, *I think he may like me.* Shortly after, he joined my parents and me for Mom's birthday dinner. But I knew he liked me for sure when he asked to take me to see *The Nutcracker.*

I liked him too. And had he spoken French, he would have known much earlier.

Mrs. Brown taught us a term of endearment in class, and I used it as a secret way to express my feelings to Brandon. "Mon petit chou," I would call him. It translated "my little cabbage head," which doesn't sound very romantic, but nevertheless, it was an endearing term for the French and he was becoming endearing to me. So it fit.

I enjoyed my time with him, despite my friends' and family's bewilderment. Mom would say, "Heather, he's just so quiet. He doesn't talk." No one in our family was quiet. No one. The decibels escalated at family functions. We were passionately emotional people, whether laughing or lecturing. It was just a loud group. Since Mom and Dad were both like that, bringing home a quiet guy was rather unexpected.

"Well, he talks to me," I simply stated. It was actually a quality that made me like him more. The fact that he was so quiet around others and yet was such a conversationalist with me made me feel special. Like he was giving something to me he didn't give to just anyone.

There was never this uncomfortable effort-to-impress feeling. We joked so naturally. One of the times he dropped me off at home, there was an obvious skunk stench. (It's a downside to country living.) As I was getting out of the truck, I said, "Oh my. Excuse me!" As if to say I had caused the offensive smell. We burst out laughing.

Laughter felt comfortable. I just couldn't stand the thought of trying to measure up to the pretty girls. It wasn't me. All I had to offer was the *me* on the inside. And I was feeling unsure even about that.

One evening I flat out said to him, "You don't want to date me."

"Why would you say that?" he asked.

"Because. I'm a freak. I go to counseling. I take medication. I'm a mess. Not dating material." I was so scared of getting close to him. I didn't know what he saw in me, and I was afraid he'd lose sight of it quickly anyway. I didn't want to be hurt by some casual high school romance. While there were no guarantees, something felt special about him. Something was familiar, relaxed, at ease, peaceful. Something nudged me to just be me with him.

At my New Year's Eve party, he asked, "Heather, would you be my girlfriend?" We were official, and we kissed the night away.

• • • • • • •

Brandon didn't fix my struggle with beauty and body image. In some ways, my relationship with him magnified it.

Once we were officially dating, I started preparing myself for our breakup to happen when summer came. I obsessed over the thought of him seeing me in a swimsuit—to the extent of wanting to break it off with him before he had the chance to dump me.

Coming into my teen years, I avoided any activity that would show my legs. If above-the-knee dress attire was required, I was out. I didn't want people to stare at my legs, so I kept them covered as much as possible. People notice "different." That's just the reality of it.

After winning Miss Fall Festival, people genuinely asked if I would compete for Miss Coweta. I thought, *What? As if!* As if I had a body I could show. The winner of Miss Coweta went on to compete in Miss Oklahoma, who could go on to compete in Miss America. And all that adds up to . . . wait for it . . . swimsuit competition! I didn't have a body in shape to show up for that kind of opportunity. I didn't even want my boyfriend to see me in a swimsuit.

In her memoir *Getting Real*, former Miss America and journalist Gretchen Carlson wrote, "There's ultimately only one way to combat the struggle with body image: to know in your heart that your body does not define you."[2] Getting to that realization was a painful process, a long road, a difficult journey. But I was making progress accepting what I couldn't change, improving what I could and discovering the beauty remaining despite the burns.

Mom embedded the concept of beauty long before the accident. She laid the foundation by way of a full-length antique mirror in my room. As a little girl, I stood in front of it admiring myself. I sought out confirmation by asking, "Mom, am I pretty?" I never got the answer I wanted, which was a simple yes. Instead, as consistently as I asked, Mom consistently responded with, "Heather, pretty is as pretty does. You're pretty because you're pretty on the inside." There was no way to fathom how crucial of a deposit her instruction would be for my life. All I had to offer was beauty from the inside. Over time I came to see it was of far greater value, the most authentic beauty to have.

Brandon didn't run when summer came. A scarred-skinned girl in a swimsuit didn't influence his opinion of what defined beauty. Wherever our relationship was going, experiencing that possibility alone was already a dream come true!

And maybe, just maybe, there was potential for a real-life love story somewhere in my future.

21

Starting Forever

"Heather, will you marry me?"

Brandon and I had been dating seven months when he asked the big question in July of 1998. We were all of seventeen and convinced *forever* was for us.

Convincing our families, however, would be a completely different ball game. We decided to keep the news between the two of us. It's not like we were going to be getting married anytime soon anyway. We both wanted to go to college. Brandon had been dreaming of becoming an engineer since he was twelve. He had a specific goal in mind: complete direction toward a degree. I, on the other hand, simply knew college was something my family expected and therefore was part of my plan. I figured I'd follow in Aunt Donna's footsteps and go into education. Who knew at seventeen? What I did know was this guy wanted to spend forever with me. Whatever the future looked like, he wanted us to be together to face it.

It seemed too good to be true.

Brandon wasn't someone I had imagined for my future. He was beyond what I thought possible. This good-looking, six-foot-two athletic guy pulled me into his heart through the window of his smile. He had a gentle, patient nature. He was genuinely comfortable in who he was, never trying to impress others or capture attention. He was just so pleasantly himself, and I had an incredibly peaceful feeling with him.

He said all the things a girl longs to hear. "I'm just so happy when I'm with you," and "I feel joy when we're together." But I felt concern when he said things like, "You are different. You're not like anyone else I know."

Oh, I *was* different.

Would he be okay with *how* different I was? What guy imagines marrying a no-nipple-fake-boobs-scarred girl? A teenage boy at that! I couldn't wrap my head around it.

Everyone wants a unique love, a special story like no other. But it's mind blowing when something is so far off the path of normal. I scrutinized the treasure of the gift, trying to make it reasonable. I was concerned he just didn't quite understand what he would be getting himself into. As hard as a breakup would be, it'd be better than a rejected wedding night or a lifetime of crushed expectations.

Our relationship gradually became more physical. The process was downright conflicting. We both desired to have a pure relationship. Honor God. Marry first. However, I had so much doubt. I wanted to believe love transcended physical appearance, but when it came down to it, I just didn't know for sure. I knew Brandon would never be able to brag about having a hot trophy wife. I questioned if the excitement and exploration of our relationship would wear off, taking with it his attraction and desire for me. Was the person inside enough for a lifetime?

Delicately pursuing me one evening, he gently began removing my shirt. My convictions wanted to stop. My insecurities wanted to escape. My curiosity wanted to discover his thoughts and feelings about what he'd see underneath. Of all the eyes I had undressed for, all the ones that had assessed my body, poking and prodding and cutting, never had I felt so vulnerable as I did to have Brandon's eyes viewing me. He looked upon my bare, burned breasts. I raised my arms to hide myself. Tenderly he grasped my hands, held me with his eyes and said, "You look beautiful." I began crying in his arms. His words were ones I felt were lost long ago in a burn unit at seven years old. I knew he sincerely felt I was beautiful.

"God gave you goggles, Brandon. If you think I'm beautiful, then I know He gave you special goggles to see me that way." Nothing about my life had been normal. And as I found out, this teenage boy wasn't either.

From then on, he became a strong influence on what I put my body through in regard to additional reconstructive surgeries. I wanted to gain whatever improvement was possible. Had it not been for his opinion, I would have endured procedures irrelevant to progress. After one of the breast reconstructive surgeries, my plastic surgeon referred me to a hair transplant specialist, because puberty resulted in only patches of hair growth on my body.

When a burn is deep enough, it destroys the hair follicles so that none will grow. Some hair was growing in expected places, like my armpits. Unfortunately, even sprouting up through seams between scar tissue in my right armpit. Getting the razor close enough to shave the hair also cut the protruding scar. The smooth skin on the lower front portion of my left leg grew hair along with one tiny round patch in my groin and then some outlining the pubis. Apparently, my surgeon felt this abnormality would be an issue for any future intimate relationships, although I would have never confessed to the surgeon, or my parents, that I was already in an intimate relationship.

I decided to get Brandon's opinion before putting myself through a process of gaining hair in places women spend their money on removing it. His input was incredibly liberating and gave me the assurance to pass on a procedure without wondering if it would be a potential problem in the future. My future was feeling much more settled.

• • • • • • •

Brandon turned eighteen on August 2, 1998. He left for college a week later.

Whoever came up with the phrase, *distance makes the heart grow fonder*, knew a thing or two about the hardship of separation for those desiring to be together. Our hearts were fond. Very, *very* fond. By November we abandoned our long-term goals of finishing college before getting married. There was no way we'd hold out four or five years. We couldn't wait to start spending our lifetime together. So Brandon took me to Helzberg Diamonds to pick out a ring.

It was an exciting evening perusing the cases of engagement rings. I love pretty things like jewelry, which made it fun. But the whole reason for being there, the fact this incredible guy wanted to marry me, made for a deeply meaningful moment. A moment I never imagined for me and certainly one I never imagined happening at seventeen.

Our apparent age didn't deter the jeweler who greeted and welcomed us right in. We began looking at rings, pointing to which ones were intriguing and attractive. She retrieved each one from the case. I'd put it on, examining how it looked on my hand. After every ring I slid off and gave back to her, she unfolded the small price tag reporting the figure. Brandon would say, "I'm so sorry. I can't afford that." He had a certain amount to spend, using his stash of cash from his summertime job cutting steel.

After I tried on a few out-of-budget rings, the jeweler finally asked, "What is your budget?" He shared and we moved down to the cases at the back of the store. It was obviously amusing where we were in life, which was nowhere. Wherever we would go, whatever we would do, we would be together. Nevertheless, Brandon felt bad, apologizing for not being able to afford one of the rings we had already looked at.

"Babe, I don't care," I said. "I want to marry you. It's just a ring."

The conversation felt as if only the two of us were standing there. But we were reminded there were actually three of us when the jeweler naturally reacted with, "Awe!" We looked at her and she injected, "I'm sorry. It's just I see so many couples come in here and get in fights over what ring to buy. It's super sweet seeing a couple like you two." Her observation and opinion were encouraging, since getting married as teenagers wasn't such a popular thing to do.

We found a beautiful gold ring with a modest marquise-cut diamond. Brandon planned to purchase the optional top and bottom bands after working over his spring break. We both liked the ring and decided on that one. Although it wasn't necessary in the least for him to say anything, he sweetly promised, "I can only get this one for you now, but in five years I will upgrade to one of those you really liked up front." We set our wedding date for June 19, 1999, and began sharing our news.

Not everyone was thrilled with our announcement. Rumors started circulating at school that there must be a pregnancy. Why else would we be getting married so young? Of course, it hurt me, but I thought it was so stupid. As if those people couldn't count. If we were getting married to supposedly "make a wrong a right," then why wait seven months to do it? For the first time, I was experiencing the feeling of not caring what others thought. But that resulted from a little bit of loaned encouragement.

I stopped by the church to tell Pastor Gary our big plans. Part of me wanted to see which side of the fence he stood on.

"Heather, you're an SWW, so it doesn't matter too much what anyone thinks about it. What date are you two planning to get married?"

An SWW! He couldn't have paid a greater compliment to me. It was his acronym for strong-willed woman. Sometimes we just need a little reminding of who we are in light of what we face. I gave Pastor Gary the date for our wedding, and we penciled in some premarital counseling sessions along with it.

Those counseling sessions before we got married were fundamental for our relationship. We met with Pastor Gary about six times before the wedding to discuss the marriage. We could have never realized the countless times we would return over and over again to the topics we discussed. Like always saying, "I need you." Of course, we communicated this emotion over the time of our engagement. It's natural to need and love someone when you're happy with them. However, it's harder to express such emotion after a fight. But those are the times it's even more important. This was a valuable game changer. We weren't complete in and of ourselves. We each needed what the other had to give. Lisa Bevere said it like this: "*Healthy* lions and lionesses know they need one another. In their world one strength is no less important than the other. The lion protects; the lioness provides."[1]

We were also educated about the triangle in marriage. God is at the top, and we are on each side of the base. The closer each of us moves toward God, the closer we move toward each other. Our relationship hadn't been without blemish; we weren't the picture-perfect couple of purity. But we rested in the fact that God knew our hearts. We desired our marriage to be founded *in* Him and blessed *by* Him.

Pastor Gary also had us individually write a ten-year plan. Through the assignment, he instructed us to write about where we saw ourselves in ten years. Where we wanted to live. What we wanted our house to look like. Where we wanted to be working. How many children we wanted to have. It was quite interesting when we brought them together. The only apparent subject needing discussing was that of children. I wanted six. Brandon wanted two.

Before our next counseling session, we were to combine our plans into one. I told Brandon I just couldn't marry him if he was set on only two children. I didn't even know if I could physically have children, but whether by adoption or birth, my heart desired a big family. Although I was not an only child, I was raised like one. I knew the feeling of a sibling. I knew what it was, and then it was over. I had felt so very lonely. My greatest dream was to have the family I could have had if the accident had not happened.

Through my experience with my vocal performance group Rock On, I was exposed to a family who captured what I desired and longed for. Two of the group members were brother and sister. They were two of six kids. Their lives were chaotic in a very appealing way. One of the siblings would drop them off for practice and someone—the mom, the dad, or another sibling—would pick them up. They talked about large loads of laundry, big meals and crazy schedules. They were their own group. No matter if they didn't have a person in the world, they all had each other. I wanted that type of family in my future.

Those were the benefits of counseling, bringing up important subjects and sharing the why behind our goals and dreams. Six seemed like a lot to Brandon, but four felt right. Who knew how it would pan out, but four children were part of our plan.

• • • • • • • •

Promises like the one found in Romans 8:31 strengthened our hearts to overcome the obstacles of objection. "What then shall we say to these things? If God is for us, who can be against us?"[2]

That's right! Who could be against us? Well, important people.

Mom for one. She thought Brandon was fabulous. While she didn't express it at the time, he was the picture of everything in a husband she and Dad began praying for me right after the accident. Mom and Dad were confident the Lord had someone for my life. They knew the man I would marry would be set apart, not typical or of the norm. However, never in a million years did they imagine that relationship coming together so soon. They had dreams for me too. Mom wanted me to pursue music. Which is what I was going to be able to do when I got an invitation to audition for a gospel vocal group. Seemed like my trip to Nashville with Traci and then our trip to Colorado were paying off. Mom was very disappointed when I declined the invite.

"Mom, I want to marry Brandon. I want to have a family. More than anything, *that* is what I really want. Whatever I experience in my life, I want to experience with him."

My dream for a family had started long before then in the ICU of the burn center. My desire for a family began the minute I realized the possibility I may never have what most people never think about *not* having. When I was a little girl playing with baby dolls, I never thought about not having my own baby one day. Not until I was seven. When I was draping Grandma's dining room lace curtains over my face, pretending I was walking down the aisle to get married, I never thought I wouldn't get married. Not until I was seven.

Yes. Absolutely, I was incredibly young. But I felt I had waited years for this gift I never knew I would receive. Of all the dreams I could dream, none was as alive and vibrant as the ones Brandon inspired in me. I didn't feel I was compromising. I didn't feel like I was settling or sacrificing. I knew with every ounce of my being that my fullest dreams would be realized through my life with him.

The same lady who prayed over me for my husband in the baptismal was the same one to ask Mom why she didn't want me to marry him.

Prayer Warrior Woman asked, "Do you not like him, Susan?"

"Of course, I like him," Mom corrected. "He's a precious boy."

"Do you not like his family?"

"No. No. I like them. They seem like great people."

"Then why do you not want her to marry him?"

"It's not that I don't want her to marry him. I just don't want her to marry him *right now*. People don't do that at this age in our family. I want her to go to college. I want her to sing."

Prayer Warrior Woman gently, respectfully and compassionately concluded, "So God's timing is not your timing."

It was a light bulb moment for Mom. It gave her insight into what God was working together in my life, leading to a knock on my bathroom door one morning. I opened it. Mom and I hadn't spoken much about anything since Brandon and I shared our engagement news. Which wasn't normal for Mom and me in the least. We talked about everything. So much that my friends frequently complained, "Don't tell Heather or she'll tell her mom." Mom and I had this beautiful, strong connection. But the brakes were slammed on when I derailed the visions she had for my life.

"When your dad and I get back from Israel, we will start planning your wedding," she informed.

It was January 1999. Brandon and I had set our date for June, and hardly anything had been planned. Mom kept hoping we would postpone. I wasn't aware of her conversation with Prayer Warrior Woman. I was a little skeptical as to her sudden change in direction. I simply said, "Okay," and continued getting ready. After their two weeks away, she came home and began making preparations full force for our big day.

I wasn't the only one experiencing resistance during that time. Brandon received heavy objection on his end too. His dad visited him several times over his first semester at the junior college he attended, about an hour from home. His dad took him to dinner, trying to deter him from his decision. What college guy doesn't appreciate a nice dinner? Plus, Brandon always enjoyed the time with his dad. But eventually he said, "Dad, you can keep coming down here and taking me to dinner, but it's not going to change my mind. I'm going to marry Heather."

The entire world could have been against us, but our parents' protests were the hardest. We were practically babies. Teenagers. But God was for us. Who could be against us if *He* was for us? God's promise was the power we needed to pursue what we believed to be His best plan for our life. It was an unexpected journey, captured through the words we chose for our wedding invitation. *A glance, a smile, became a friendship, grew into love.* It was just a *glance* at that

Drillers baseball game, truly a simple *smile* outside my French class. Through casual conversations and time spent together, a *friendship* formed. Each moment providing for the next, growing into a gift of *love*.

The church was full at 2 p.m. on Saturday, June 19, 1999. It rained that morning, but the skies quickly gave way to clear, bright sunshine. Our friends and family gathered together for our special day.

My wedding was the wedding Mom never had. There were lots of flowers and candles, and I even obliged by choosing her favorite dress. Although it wasn't my favorite, her excitement and deep care regarding those special details overjoyed me. The dress was truly beautiful, something of sorts for a princess. The traditionally formal, cathedral length, white gown had a sweetheart neckline, an embellished bodice of lace and pearls and long fingertip sleeves. The basque waistline led to a full skirt. A train-length tulle veil flowed from a tiara of pearls adorning my head. White Skechers were on my feet under the gown. I didn't want to tear the tissue on my feet from pretty shoes. I wanted to enjoy the entire day and my honeymoon. The sneakers were comfy and kind of cute too.

The most important detail of the day was the groom. I had just turned eighteen in March and graduated high school in May, but I knew weddings were only for a day; grooms were for forever. And I couldn't wait to spend my forever with the groom waiting for me at the altar.

Dad had tears in his eyes as he walked me down the aisle, giving me away to my forever. Hope fulfilled. A dream come true. Prayers answered.

A happily ever after, even after tragedy.

22

Big Dreams

Our married life started off in a converted barn sitting on the other side of Grandma's house. Mom and Dad were on one side of the wrap-around driveway; we were on the other. Grandma was perfectly content with her house right in the middle.

Initially, Brandon and I planned to move to Stillwater to attend Oklahoma State University (OSU). But living there, we wouldn't be working at jobs providing benefits. Like health insurance. Health insurance ranked up there with the importance of food, electricity and water. I was still having surgeries. And although we believed my heart repair was in good condition, we couldn't risk *not* having coverage in case something happened. So we stayed home right next door to my family.

Dad put me to work doing a job he had been training me for since the second grade. I grew up knowing the ins and outs of his business. Anyone who had a relationship with Dad had a relationship to his business. It was that personal to him. Mom was already working for him. She quit her job in the accounting department at Saint Francis after Dad's heart attack and quadruple bypass surgery in 1995. His heart condition was no surprise to the cardiologist: "The five risk factors we look for are family history, obesity, stress, smoking, and drinking." Dad met all five.

Even though his lifestyle was presently much different than it had been, the past caught up to Dad. He had congestive heart failure and cardiomyopathy; he was a diabetic and quick-tempered. Those qualities made it difficult at times to work for him. Often it seemed nothing was ever good enough for Dad and that he couldn't be satisfied. Which in part was true. However, it came from an internal drive for constant growth and improvement. He wasn't easy to work with, but understanding where he came from and the high expectations he held for himself made it manageable.

The team consisted of Mom, Dad, a lady he hired named Vicki and me. We kept the ropes swinging. We sold auto, home and life insurance; operated a monthly bookkeeping business providing a weekly payroll service to clients; assisted with licensing for setting up new businesses; and prepared annual tax returns, both corporate and personal. I gained a range of valuable experience, from providing customer service to working with governmental agencies. Plus, I enjoyed the perks of long lunches, which Dad typically treated us to; a company-paid reward trip to Vegas for our office; and I had health insurance!

Brandon continued cutting steel for a brief time before going to work for his dad, who was kicking off a remodeling and home-building business, sparking our desire to either build or buy our own place.

Grandma was a smart woman. Although she was very quiet, rarely sharing her opinion, she had a way of planting ideas.

Brandon and I had found a house in Coweta we knew would be the perfect fit for us. It was in a new housing addition, so we could either buy a lot and build one or purchase one of the already built spec homes.

We were in the discussions when Grandma said, "I could give you some land if you would want to build a house here." Well, by that point we understood we could build more house if we already had the land. We didn't take too long considering it before we took Grandma up on her offer.

• • • • • •

That first year of marriage was quite exciting. So many changes continued to unfold. Brandon and I both took some classes at the community college in Tulsa. There was no doubt I was simply going through the motions. Made quite apparent by my history grade second semester. It was a C. My young-laid-back-easy-going husband was not happy. At all.

"You made a C?" Brandon questioned.

"Yes," I confirmed. It was right there on the paper we got in the mail. No need to really ask a question. But he was upset.

"Why?" he interrogated.

I aimed to offer an explanation. "I don't know. It was boring."

"I get it," he said. "But a C? Even if you don't like it, it's easy. I mean it's history. It never changes!"

This was coming from a guy who had engineering on his radar. Engineering—a field requiring nothing but numbers and formulas and figuring out what does and does not change.

Needless to say, I didn't have much direction. My assumption that I'd follow in Aunt Donna's footsteps wasn't enough to inspire me to even study for a general education class. Brandon and I were paying for school, and we didn't have money to waste on classes we didn't care about taking. So we decided I'd quit until I had more direction. Brandon knew what he wanted. He wanted to be an engineer. He wanted to build a house. And he wanted to be a dad. Consolidating those goals extended the process, but the outcome was worth the time invested to get there.

• • • • • •

There's something about wanting what we think we can't have.

I wanted an attractive husband who loved God and loved me. While I wanted to believe it was possible, the reality was I was a seven-year-old girl when I started thinking I couldn't have a relationship like that. I also wanted to have children. But that too I thought I couldn't have. There had certainly been questions about my future ability to conceive. The stress my body sustained. The high doses of medication I absorbed. Had the trauma affected my fertility? No one knew for sure.

With hopeful optimism, Brandon and I decided to pursue our journey toward a family. We considered the possibility of it being a long journey, bracing our hearts for patience. To our surprise, we were able to announce we were expecting on Brandon's twentieth birthday! We had our house plans in hand and a baby on the way. Life couldn't get any more magical.

We were about eight weeks into the pregnancy when we met with our obstetrician to review the health history information obtained at a previous appointment. The consultation took place not in an exam room but in her office. Brandon and I sat across the desk as she explained the risk involved. Something along the lines of a woman's blood volume doubling during pregnancy, presenting possible complications due to the condition of my repaired aorta. We didn't quite understand what she was saying.

The obstetrician proceeded to discuss the restrictions of scar tissue and how that may influence not just the pregnancy but delivery. Still yet, we weren't following where she was leading. Not until she clearly explained I could die trying to have the baby, and it would be in our best interest to consider terminating the pregnancy. If we did not choose to do so, then she was sending us to a perinatologist who specialized in high-risk pregnancies.

Confused. Numb. Scared.

Those were just some of the emotions we left that appointment carrying. How could this be? Had we been irresponsible? It was certainly presented that way, despite the fact I had consulted with my primary care physician before we even started trying to get pregnant. My doctor and I discussed potential issues with my heart. She had ordered an electrocardiogram, also known as an EKG or an ECG. I didn't understand what that test had revealed. Moreover, I didn't understand what that test *didn't* reveal. Our appointment with the obstetrician informed me that an EKG didn't establish anything of importance. She said it only reported the electrical activity in my heart. She would have needed to see an image of the area that had been repaired behind my heart, which would involve a test requiring conscious sedation, not advisable during pregnancy.

It was terrifying. And it didn't make sense.

How? How could God give me a gift I might die trying to have? How could He bring me through everything I had experienced to abandon me here?

The following Sunday I stepped out from my seat and moved toward the front of the church. There may not always be miracles or healing at the altar, but there is most certainly always encouragement. I knelt down, soon feeling a hand upon my back, hearing a familiar voice praying for me. I looked up to see a woman who had generously invested in my life. "Shonna," I began. Tears flowed as I relayed the report of our doctor's appointment. "I can't believe God gave me this baby to die having. I just can't believe that." Shonna agreed with me in prayer, and I returned to my seat with assurance for what the future held.

One of my power tools was Philippians 4:6–7: "Don't worry about anything; instead, pray about everything. Tell God what you need, and thank him for all he has done. Then you will experience God's peace, which exceeds anything we can understand. His peace will guard your hearts and minds as you live in Christ Jesus."[1]

I didn't understand everything we were facing. I certainly didn't understand why we had to face such concerning issues. But telling the Lord what I needed, remembering where He had brought me from, created a supernatural peace about where I was going. We were facing the process with hope, peace and joy, being reminded of Proverbs 1:33, "But whoever listens to Me will dwell secure and will be at ease, without dread of disaster;"[2] and Romans 15:13, "May the God of hope fill you with all joy and peace in believing, so that by the power of the Holy Spirit you may abound in hope."[3]

Our miracle arrived on March 4, 2001, at 11:24 p.m. Because of preeclampsia, we were induced into labor five weeks before our due date. It took four days for active labor to start, and delivery required vacuum and forceps assistance. After nine hours of labor and two and a half hours pushing, we finally got to meet our five-pound, nine-ounce, eighteen-inch baby. Friends and family prayed over the months of pregnancy for her. I had prayed over much of my life for her.

My big dream-come-true was wrapped up in my tiny, beautiful Brooklyn Nicole.

● ● ● ● ● ● ●

The rest of everything I was meant to be was born with Brooklyn. She completed a part of me I never knew was incomplete, not until it had been filled. It was as if the rest of my soul came alive when she took her first breath. I felt like I had waited a lifetime for the gift of her life to touch my world. We savored the fairy tale we felt we were living.

Shortly after Brooklyn's first birthday, we began discussing if we were ready for our second baby. Our house was finished. We were all moved in and settled. We had prepared four bedrooms—for the one little life we held in our arms, and for the hope of the three we carried in our hearts. It felt time to proceed with the plan of filling those rooms.

First, we got my heart cleared. A cardiologist performed a transesophageal echocardiogram (TEE), obtaining images from behind my heart where my aorta had been repaired from the transection. I was a little freaked out about the procedure, having to swallow a probe. Of course, I was consciously sedated; however, being put out completely would have been my preference. It ended up being quite uneventful. I didn't remember anything until Brandon and I pulled into a drive-through for burgers on the way home. He informed me I repeatedly asked only one question. The only question I was there to answer: "Can I have more children?" The test determined, indeed, I could have more children. The cardiologist informed Brandon the Dacron velour graft looked to be in excellent condition, and I could have ten more babies if I wanted to.

The months continued passing with no big news, but just before Brooklyn's second birthday, we scored a positive pregnancy test. Our second miracle was on the way, and we couldn't wait to share the news. A good friend of ours created a special announcement, assembling a video of Brooklyn's first two years put to song. Those projects aren't as big a deal in today's technology, but it took a lot of work back in 2003. At the end of the video, Brandon, Brooklyn and I sat on our couch, sharing the news, "God did it again! Our new baby will be here sometime in October!" Brooklyn's little addition of "Surprise!" was the perfect touch.

Our dreams were coming true. However, even fairy tales have heartaches. I started cramping and spotting soon after our big announcement. Our obstetrician saw me immediately. He prescribed bed rest and high doses of hormone therapy. Brandon's mom was home with Brooklyn and me the day it progressed. She held my hair as I began throwing up, staying near to me as I miscarried our pregnancy.

Why?

The question revolves throughout seasons of our life.

I had a cyst on one of my ovaries—the reason it had taken some time to get pregnant. Our obstetrician explained to us that the ovaries produce progesterone until the placenta is developed enough to take on the role. The cyst had collapsed my ovary, reducing the necessary hormones to maintain the pregnancy. There it was. We had an answer. But it wasn't enough.

Our house had never felt so big to me as it did when walking in the door after our doctor's office visit. It felt huge because it was empty. Emptiness feels massive. Even in the smallest space, what is void feels vast.

I started to doubt if we would have the big family I had desired, dreamed of, longed for. I imagined those rooms we built for babies remaining empty. Never being filled. I tried focusing on what to be grateful for, my precious healthy little girl. I aimed to settle my mind with the fact she was more than I ever thought I would have.

Comments contributed to the pain. "There was probably something wrong with it," I was told. As if I only wanted my baby if it were perfect. Others minimized it like the baby wasn't real, saying, "Well, it's a good thing you weren't that far along yet." Naturally, I felt offended. So I prayed, "Lord, please help me see their good intentions. Surely they don't mean to hurt me. Please help me see their heart, and please quiet their comments." The experience grew me, giving me insight of what to pray for others going through difficulty. "Lord, please protect them from people's good intentions," I would pray. The problem is people feel they need to say something, when sometimes just "I'm so sorry" meets the need.

My friend Katie wasn't much of a talker, yet she ministered to me most effectively during that time. She wasn't married. She didn't have children. But she allowed God to use her to reach into my heartache. A heartache she didn't have to know for herself to love me through. "Heather, I've been wanting to read this book. Would you want to read it at the same time and visit about it?" Katie knew I needed the book, *The Purpose Driven Life* by Rick Warren. Warren writes,

> Genuine friendship is built on disclosure. What may appear as *audacity* God views as *authenticity*. God listens to the passionate words of His friends; He is bored with predictable, pious clichés. To be God's friend you must be honest to God, sharing your true feeling, not what you think you ought to feel or say. It is likely that you need to confess some hidden

anger and resentment at God for certain areas of your life where you have felt cheated or disappointed. Until we mature enough to understand that God uses *everything* for good in our lives, we harbor resentment toward God over our appearance, background, unanswered prayers, past hurts, and other things we would change if we were God.[4]

I needed to ask the Lord my questions. Bottling them up and hiding them would never have allowed the Lord to flood my thoughts and guide me in the direction I needed to go. Which is always closer to Him. God knew my heart and could handle my questions. So I started asking them.

"Why? Why did I have to experience the loss of a pregnancy? Haven't I lost enough in life? Isn't there some quota of grief we have to meet in life? Haven't I met mine at this point? Shouldn't everything be happy from here on out for me?"

I felt myself coming closer to God and Him to me through every question. "The Lord is near to the brokenhearted and saves the crushed in spirit."[5]

I felt Him holding me through each tear I shed, as if His heart were breaking with mine. "You keep track of all my sorrows. You have collected all my tears in your bottle. You have recorded each one in your book."[6]

And I felt strengthened, reminded of my hope in Him through all the pains and imperfections of this life. "Yet I still dare to hope when I remember this: The faithful love of the Lord never ends! His mercies never cease. Great is his faithfulness; his mercies begin afresh each morning. I say to myself, 'The Lord is my inheritance; therefore, I will hope in him!'"[7]

We planted a tree for our baby in our front yard. A beautiful red maple, also called an Autumn Glory, the memory of our little one we have yet to meet in eternity.

• • • • • • •

Our promises of tomorrow were wrapped up in a precious package weighing seven pounds, measuring nineteen inches in length on our eve of Christmas Eve 2003.

Jaron Michael arrived at 7:26 p.m. on that December 23rd night. His Hebrew name (pronounced as if rhyming with Aaron or Sharon) means, "He will sing or cry out." However, he was hardly doing either upon his birth. He was whisked away to a special care nursery where we anticipated he would need just a little help. Brandon followed. My room eventually cleared out, and I waited alone to hold my new baby when he returned.

The door opened slowly as two nurses pushed an isolette, or incubator, into my hospital room. My baby was inside. I was puzzled. They informed me he was having difficulty breathing and was being admitted to the neonatal intensive care unit (NICU). "I need to hold him," I stated matter-of-factly. The young nurses looked nervous. They exchanged glances as one spoke up. "Um, we were told to come by the mother's room and then proceed straight to the NICU."

"Well, I need to hold him," I restated.

"I'm so sorry," one said. "You can see him later when you come to the unit." Like that was supposed to be consoling.

Growing and delivering a baby can morph a mom into expressing a completely different personality. Especially when her baby is taken away from her. Despite the epidural I received, I proceeded to get out of the bed to go after them. Thankfully, Mom walked in the room at just the right time. There I was grabbing on to the bed railing, bodily fluids falling *out* as my hospital gown was falling *off.*

"What are you doing?" Mom yelled.

"They are taking him," I exclaimed as I began crying.

Jaron was admitted to the NICU for respiratory distress syndrome. His lack of respiratory effort required him to be intubated and placed on mechanical ventilation.

I felt completely responsible, thinking if I had done a better job, then Jaron would have been fine. His had been another challenging delivery. Our doctor admitted me to begin induction the day before. All efforts were given toward avoiding a caesarean section. Not only would it be major abdominal surgery, but cutting my scarred abdomen would have required a skin graft to heal. Considering the difficulty we had delivering Brooklyn, coupled with the estimation of Jaron's size, our doctor gave his best to deliver him vaginally. Again, it involved vacuum and forceps assistance.

We had never experienced a NICU before Jaron's birth. Additionally, we had never experienced having our hearts in two places at the same time. It was Christmas. We felt we needed to be with Brooklyn but didn't want to leave Jaron. Brandon and I came home, going through the motions of the holiday for our little girl. After Christmas morning, we returned to the hospital to sit by our baby boy's bedside. The unit was open with several babies together in one room. It didn't take much observation to realize how much we had to be thankful for.

While it was the most unnatural feeling having my baby taken away from me, my perspective changed seeing babies who possibly may never be returned to their mother's arms. Although we couldn't hold Jaron, we knew it was only temporary. In the meantime, we sat with him as much as we were allowed. By Christmas evening, a nurse came over, informing us they were going to be able to extubate him.

"You're going to take the tube out?" I questioned for clarity.

"Yes," she confirmed, "but you don't have to hurry. We can do it after your visit."

"Can you remove it now if we step out?"

"Yes."

"Can we come back in and see him if we step out for you to do that?" I probed.

"Sure," she said.

We did exactly that. When we returned, I heard the sweetest sound resonating the inspiring meaning of Jaron's name. My Christmas came with hearing a cry—Jaron's precious cry.

23

A Plan Stirring

Nothing in my life would ever compare to the privilege of being entrusted with the precious lives of our children. The honor of becoming a parent was the greatest gift to my world. It was like the hands of God wrapped up and placed the most unique, one-of-a-kind, specially created, perfect packages in our hands. And the fact that I was able to carry them and deliver them to this world was a gift I didn't take for granted.

While it wasn't the most tactful way to say it, I frequently expressed my awe and wonder to Brandon. "I feel so holy. I mean *I* just assisted *God* in creation!" What I meant was God used me as a vessel to bring these precious people into the world, these little lives He had a plan and purpose for from the moment He began knitting them together in my womb.[1] The experience of their perfectly flawless-skinned bodies coming out of my scarred one established a value and beauty I had never known of my body.

There was nothing I could ever do that would be of more value in my life than being a mom to my babies. My dreams were completely fulfilled. I had a husband who loved and cherished me. I had two healthy babies, and we anticipated the arrival of more. What more could I need?

The answer is *nothing*. I didn't need anything more. However, I knew there was something else.

Jaron was only about eight weeks old. I kept saying, "God wants me to do something that I'm not doing right now." Over and over again I shared the hunch with Brandon, my parents, my friends, my church family. Pretty much anyone who would listen heard me say, "God wants me to do something that I'm not doing right now."

I received a lot of encouragement. Mostly in the words, "Heather, you're a mom. There's no greater calling than being a parent." These are the times I'm so grateful for my independent relationship with the Lord. No matter how things look or sound, God knows our hearts. I'd reply, "Yes, yes. I know. But *still*, I'm supposed to be doing something that I'm not doing right now." I wasn't dismissing or minimizing the importance of parenting; I was just seeking direction. It didn't have anything to do with me being satisfied or content. I had all I ever wanted. However, I knew there were plans and purposes for me to fulfill in addition to being a mom.

For some strange reason, I thought maybe becoming a nurse was part of what I was supposed to do. I got online and began exploring the route to a nursing education. Brandon was attending OSU, still working toward his engineering degree. He felt if I was going to pursue a bachelor's degree in nursing, then I needed to attend OSU. It seemed as though OSU's orange color ran through his veins. "They don't have a bachelor's program, Brandon. If I went to school, I think I should get a bachelor's degree, so I'd need to go to OU." He rolled his eyes at the possibility of me attending OSU's rival. There were some other options, but for some reason, I felt the University of Oklahoma would be my only one.

Whatever possibilities I considered were shut down when I mentioned it to Dad.

"Dad, I feel like God is calling me to be a nurse."

"Well, why would He do that?" Dad questioned. "You can't take your kids to work when you're a nurse."

He had a great point. During the busy times of the year, I'd take Brooklyn and Jaron to the office with me. Mom watched them two days a week, but sometimes I needed more time to get everything done. Over tax season, I'd put them to bed and go back and work with Mom and Dad until two or three in the morning. It could be a really demanding schedule; however, there was flexibility in making it all work. That wouldn't be happening with a career in nursing. So I put the papers of information I had printed out regarding the OU College of Nursing in my desk. Why on earth I didn't throw them away, I didn't know. Instead, they were tucked away. Almost like I couldn't let go of the possibility.

What I didn't let go of was my dream for more children.

Through my pregnancy with Brooklyn, my scarred skin stretched out slowly in accommodating my growing belly. However, my body had *been there, done that* by the time Jaron was in the picture. I didn't gain any more weight than I had with Brooklyn, but I got bigger faster. Brandon came home several evenings to find me nearly in tears. I'd fan the palms of my hands in front of my abdomen, saying, "I just can't stretch any more today." The tissue was so incredibly tight. It was like rubber bands pulled to their breaking point. I knew if I was going to be able to withstand the pregnancy and delivery of two more babies, then some interventions would be required.

I scheduled an appointment with a local plastic surgeon within my network of insurance coverage. I was hopeful for some help in releasing the tight tissue on my side, my abdomen, my groin and my thighs. It was humiliating going in for yet another doctor's appointment, removing my clothes to be poked and prodded in the areas of concern. What made it worse was the negative report I received. He just didn't think much could be done about it. I began to cry during the consultation. I apologized for being so emotional and asked what he would do if it were his wife. He said, "One thing I tell my boys is that I can fix a lot of things, but burns are just not one of them."

Not one to give up easily, I emailed Dr. Park, who was living in another state, for a more specific recommendation. I found myself in the office of Dr. Robert Kirk. He casually declared hope for improving the places where I had problems.

In April of 2005, Dr. Kirk released some tissue in my right axilla, the fancy medical word for armpit. Over that summer, he slowly chipped away at the list of concerned areas I had. One particular area I felt might be a bit vain. During a visit, I told him I didn't like how the scar on the side of my face extended straight down into my neck. It appeared I didn't have a jawbone. I despised pictures of me from that angle, and yet, of course, most of my wedding pictures had been snapped capturing my right side. Dr. Kirk looked at my face and said, "Yes, you have a nice jawline." Amusingly, I received it as the most unexpected compliment.

In late July he inserted a tissue expander in my neck. I visited his office for injections into the balloon-like container under my skin. It gradually grew bigger and bigger with each injection, finally looking like a large mass growing out of my neck. I had a scarf in every color and pattern imaginable, tying them decoratively in attempt to conceal the growth. The results were well worth the process, even though it further dulled sensation to my right face and ear. I no longer avoided photos of my right side. Dr. Kirk gave me a beautiful jawline. It will forever be scarred, but it looks more in shape to what I was genetically designed to be.

Throughout the course of surgeries in the spring and summer of 2005 was the ever-present thought: *I'm supposed to be doing something I'm not doing right now.* I prayed, "Lord, please! Just tell me what it is so I can do it! This not knowing is so difficult!" By late July, I happened to be reading a book containing an appropriately timed message. It pointed to the importance of preparation, teaching how God prepared different people in the Bible before revealing His purposes to them. Joseph was prepared in Potiphar's house and in prison before being used to save the people of Egypt. David was prepared in a pasture, shepherding sheep before God used him as King of Israel. But the greatest example was the one Jesus provided. Jesus left the glories of Heaven and came to earth, knowing His purpose and yet still allowed God, His Father, to prepare Him for the work He already knew He would do.

I could not neglect the importance of preparation. There was such peace I received from realizing the season I was in. God was stirring *something* in my heart, but He had me in a place, *preparing* me for what He would reveal in His time.

On August 22, 2005, I went in for the last of the six surgeries that we had started the April before. We certainly saved the biggest for last. Since skin grafts required an inpatient stay, I pushed to do them all at once. I felt homesick being away from the kids. One hospital stay from one intense surgery seemed better than being in and out of the hospital all summer.

Dr. Kirk released the scar tissue on my right side, extending from my abdomen around my back. He also released both sides of my groin, and two areas on the inside of each thigh. Skin grafts were taken from my back and placed in each of the released areas.

The surgery was scheduled on the same day Brandon started his fall semester. He had chipped away class by class, getting closer and closer to his dream of an engineering degree. His goal was my goal. Marriage was like that for us. It felt just as much a part of me, so I insisted he go to class. Mom and Dad came to stay with me that evening after my surgery.

I wanted Dad to be close to me, so I asked him to sit on my bed, which provided for quite the laugh. Burn patients are routinely placed on air mattresses after skin grafts, and those beds are programmed to the patient's weight in order to keep the mattress inflated. When Dad sat on the end of the bed beside my left foot, he began sinking as the mattress slowly deflated, at which time my bladder started feeling very full. "Dad, I feel like I have to pee so bad." Come to find out, he hadn't just deflated the mattress, but he had also occluded the Foley catheter, obstructing urine flow. Through belts of laughter, we decided it'd probably be best for him to pull up a chair close by.

My family was highly skilled in the art of conversation. Sitting around visiting was something we did often. It seemed a simple start to some common chitchat when I randomly inquired, "Dad, you've never told me about when you were saved. What is your story of accepting Jesus into your heart?"

He proceeded to tell me about how many times the gospel had been presented to him. He shared his questions about how it all worked, how his choices, his past, his present and the all-encompassing picture of his life fit into a salvation package. His hang-ups included a combination of unworthiness with an unwillingness to give up his way for God's way. Nevertheless, it was a confrontation he couldn't avoid.

God's love chased Dad everywhere he went. Hopping in and out of bars. God's love chased him. Hopping in and out of bed with women. God's love chased him. God's Word said nothing could separate His love from us. "No power in the sky above or in the earth below—indeed, nothing in all creation will ever be able to separate us from the love of God that is revealed in Christ Jesus our Lord."[2] Nothing.

On a routine business trip, Dad grabbed a six-pack of beer and some Church's Fried Chicken for his evening alone in a hotel room. He turned on the television. A preacher was sharing a message that had been deposited in Dad's heart time and time again. It was a message he sat in the pews hearing Pastor Beller preach many times over. The seeds that were lovingly planted, and compassionately watered, sprung to life in a hotel room with a six-pack of beer and some Church's Fried Chicken. Dad got on his knees and received the forgiveness Jesus provided on the cross. Dad confessed his need for a Savior and relinquished being lord of his own life, for the Lord who gave His own life.

It was the most beautiful story of redemption. One I couldn't believe I had never asked to hear in my twenty-four years. For certain, it was instantly one I would cherish for the rest of my life.

• • • • • • •

There's a lot of pressure naming a baby. I felt the pressure for sure. During one of our pregnancies, I read a top twenty-five list about the best things couples experience when having a baby. Naming a baby made the list. I couldn't disagree more. I was like, "Lord, where is my angel to say, 'Heather, you are with child and your child's name shall be . . .?'" I mean, what if my babies didn't like their name? They'd be stuck with it their entire life! The responsibility didn't feel fun at all. I just hoped they'd love the name they had no say whatsoever in getting.

I always liked my name. Heather Renee. Heather was quite popular in the seventies and early eighties. Several girls in my class had the same name. The meaning comes from the beautiful, native, flowering plant found in the moorlands of Europe. And character traits of the name include "inspirational, highly intuitive, spiritual teacher, extremely bright, uplifting, truth-seeker."[3] There's so much a person carries in their name. Mine was given to me in tribute to Dad's Aunt Heather, a sister to Grandma Cochrane. I was nearly a teenager before I met her and loved my name even more once I knew the person I was named after.

While I understood the importance of a name, I didn't realize the power in one name until August 29, 2005, when there were no words to speak but only a name.

Pastor Gary had just been to visit and pray with Brandon and me in my hospital room of the burn unit. I had been there a bit longer than anticipated as one of the skin grafts wasn't taking and furthermore was infected. Brandon walked out with Pastor Gary and came back in to find me on the phone with Mom. She was staying with Brooklyn and Jaron at our house. We discussed the devastation of Hurricane Katrina hitting New Orleans. It was heartbreaking as we watched the coverage unfold on our televisions.

While we were visiting, Brandon got a call on his cell phone. Strangely enough, he stepped out of the room. I was off the phone by the time he came back in just moments later. But even more strange was that Pastor Gary was with him. I was confused as to why he'd be back. He had just left.

The door was to my right. I knew the room well. It just so happened to be the same room I was in seventeen years earlier when I moved out of the ICU to the progressive part of the burn unit. This place was like my second home.

Brandon came directly to my right side. Pastor Gary came to my left and sat down. Brandon knelt beside me. He grasped my right hand and spoke words I couldn't completely understand.

"Heather, I'm so sorry." I didn't understand what was happening. Brandon paused only a moment before continuing, "Your dad has died."

There were no words.

As I emptied myself of every tear I could shed, Pastor Gary whispered over and over, "Jesus." There just weren't any other words. But there was His name. The sweetest name I know: the name of peace, comfort and strength; the name that conquered death and the grave; the name that gives hope in the face of loss, the hope of eternity, and the promise of no more goodbyes.

Dad started that morning doing what he normally did: working. Just eighteen months before he had sold his insurance business and moved the tax and accounting service to the pool house in their backyard. His health had been deteriorating. There had been some close calls where we thought we'd lose him, but not in August of 2005. He looked better than he had looked in a while. And he was just getting ready to go in for a pacemaker the next month.

He was sitting at my desk, talking to a client that Monday morning. The client just happened to be the Prayer Warrior Woman from our church who had prayed for my husband with me when I was sixteen. Of all the people for him to be on the phone with, Prayer Warrior Woman shared with us the people he was talking about when he passed from this life into eternity. He was talking about us. His family.

Part of me felt numb in those moments. Nevertheless, I knew a few things. I knew God gave me the greatest gift of hearing my dad's testimony just one week to the day before he was called home. That was the very last time I saw my dad. And while, at first, I felt it was cruel to be in the same burn unit to be told my dad had died, as I had been seventeen years earlier when I was told my brother had died, I soon discovered the blessing in such painful similarities.

Bobbie took me back to the tank room for bandage changes. She knew Dad. She had known him for seventeen years, since I had first been a patient as a seven-year-old little girl. As Bobbie proceeded with my care, she reminisced about Dad. With every sweet memory she shared, I felt goodness wrap around my heart. I was back in the same place I was when being told Jon had died, but I was back in the same place, wrapped in the presence of love, comfort and compassion.

Furthermore, I knew while we mourned, Heaven rejoiced. In October 2004, Dad bought me Max Lucado's latest book. It had become kind of a thing. Dad demonstrated his love through gifts. And he knew how much I received from Max Lucado's writings. So when a new book was released, he almost always got one for me. As was the same with *Come Thirsty*. However, I could have never imagined the words I eagerly shared with Dad from that book would be the words comforting us months later at his memorial service. "Heaven enjoys a maternity-ward reaction to funerals. Angels watch body burials the same way grandparents monitor delivery-room doors. 'He'll be coming through any minute!' They can't wait to see the new arrival. While we're driving hearses and wearing black, they're hanging pink and blue streamers and passing out cigars. We don't grieve when babies enter the world. The hosts of heaven don't weep when we leave it."[4]

I suddenly knew what the Lord had been stirring in my heart over the past year and a half. As our family gathered together in my hospital room of the burn unit that night, I realized God had been preparing me for that moment. I'm not sure anyone was even listening. At the time, the information was completely irrelevant, but I felt it profoundly in my being. Without much emotion or apparent conviction, I stated, "I'm going to go to nursing school." I didn't know when. I didn't know how. I just knew.

The next day I checked myself out of the hospital against medical advice. My leg was infected. Plus, I had a rejected skin graft. Despite the circumstance, Dr. Kirk was compassionately supportive of my decision. He just couldn't write discharge orders with things being as they were.

As Brandon drove us up our thousand-foot driveway, I looked out at the land I called home. I wasn't emotional. I was matter-of-fact.

"I don't want to live here anymore," I said. "I've been here my whole life. I've lived here when Jon died. Now I've lived here when Dad has died. I just don't want to live here anymore."

Sometimes it's painful to be where our roots are, because they serve as a reminder of our loss. Many things had changed, but moving away from the home we had wasn't going to be one of them. The path would be one we knew well: *get through the hard season, shift focus and allow God to reveal the goodness He holds on the other side of it.* Even though it was painful, staying where our roots ran deeply provided strength and comfort. We needed an abundance of it facing the changes before us.

Nothing was the same for Mom.

And it all hit her after Dad's memorial service when everyone left. The house was completely empty for the first time since the house had been built in 1978. It was an overwhelming emptiness. I wish I could have filled it somehow, but I couldn't. It was the first time I had ever seen Mom so grieved. Even with losing Jon, I had never before observed her so desperately depleted as I did after Dad died. In those moments, I realized that while losing a child was unimaginable, they had each other to face it. Even in a marriage that was tattered, torn and hanging by threads, they still had one another to grieve. But now Mom, for the first time in her entire life, lived alone. She would crawl into an empty bed in a quiet room with no one to hold her.

Life had a way of offering distractions. Almost like we couldn't fully accommodate the grief on our doorstep. We had a business to keep going.

We buried Dad on a Friday and were in the office tending to urgent needs by Saturday. Mom and I were in full force again the following Tuesday—eight days after Dad passed. Clients would call asking, "Can I speak to Mike?" "I'm so sorry," we'd start. "He passed away last Monday." His clients were devastated. Some didn't even know he had had heart issues as Dad never ever slipped a complaint. His motto was "You can't hurt steel." And he certainly tried to be strong as steel. Mom and I found ourselves offering comfort to our clients, being comforted by the fact that Dad's loss was felt by so many who cared.

It was terrifying trying to keep the office running. So many times, I sat at his desk putting items into general ledgers, thinking things like, *Okay, how do I include this client's truck as depreciation?* Several times I instinctively reached for the phone to call Dad. But he wasn't there. Never again could I ask him a question. Not one. He was gone.

Mom encouraged, or maybe rather demanded, from her desk. The minute I'd utter, "I don't know how to do this," she'd fire back, "Just keep looking at it, Heather. You'll figure it out!" Each evening I'd tell Brandon, "I don't know how God is going to do it, but I just know He *will* because He knows we *can't.*" The experiences of my past established my hope in the present. I interpreted the situation in light of what God had already worked on our behalf. My words declared, "If God could do *that*, then He can do *this*." Isaiah 41:10 says, "Fear not, for I am with you; be not dismayed, for I am your God; I will strengthen you, I will help you, I will uphold you with my righteous right hand."[5]

I truly had a supernatural peace. Which is saying a lot in consideration of my type-A, always-have-a-plan, control-freak nature. And sure enough, as His Word says, He did help us. He did uphold us, and He upheld Dad's business until a buyer came our way.

Mom signed the papers in November of 2005 for the buyer to take over after the New Year. We had incredible joy, as well as relief, knowing the business Dad had worked so hard to build would continue on with the dreams of a new accountant.

Christmas was bittersweet. The celebrations weren't the same without Dad's larger-than-life personality. But Christmas came with a precious package of hope. Another baby to name was on the way!

24

Flawed Fairy Tales

Our Christmas present pregnancy turned out as ideally as it could get. By comparison.

Unlike my previous experiences, morning sickness only plagued my first trimester instead of nearly the entire pregnancy. The surgeries removing scar tissue and providing skin grafts proved to be helpful in allowing for a more pleasant process of my expanding abdomen. And we made it closer to our due date than ever before.

Our obstetrician admitted us to the hospital the evening of August 14, 2006, to begin induction. Before each of our babies' deliveries, I received prophylactic doses of antibiotic therapy because of my aortic repair. After the three doses had been administered, my doctor came in, as he had in our prior experiences, to break my water and place internal scalp monitors on the baby's head, which offered the most precise reflection of the baby's heart rate throughout the process. As labor progressed, I required some oxygen on into the delivery.

Something hit me during the pushing process. Dad had been gone just nearly a year. And suddenly I became overcome with emotion that he wasn't out in the waiting room to meet this new baby of mine. I began crying, expressing my grief as the oxygen mask was strapped over my face and the bag's re-breather portion was crunched up between my chin and chest. Despite all the responsibilities of the labor and delivery nurse, she compassionately handed me tissues for my tears through her sympathetic condolences.

It was another challenging two-hour delivery requiring vacuum and forceps assistance, but at 8:40 in the morning, on August 15th, we welcomed our second son, Caden Robert. He was perfectly on time—six pounds, eight ounces and twenty inches long. The joy his big sister and big brother had in meeting him soothed the sadness I had for my loved ones who never would.

Caden was my third baby. Meaning some things just didn't intimidate or bother me like with Brooklyn and Jaron. Surprisingly, the breastfeeding topic bothered me more.

It had been an issue right from the start. When Brooklyn was born, we were asked, "Breast or bottle?" I detected pious judgment when I answered, "Bottle." Same experience with Jaron's birth, only his was even *worse* considering he was a NICU baby. I was informed, "Breast is best," as if I were holding out on giving my baby what was deemed to be best. I found myself explaining my situation each time. "Well, I would, but I was burned when I was little. My entire chest was burned, so I don't have any equipment to breastfeed. It's just not an option." Brandon tried to reassure me that I didn't owe anyone an explanation. But I didn't want conclusions drawn about how much I loved my baby based on whether I *chose* to breastfeed or not.

Each birth the nurses proceeded to instruct me on the importance of wearing a supportive bra and cover the risks of becoming engorged. Our doctor seemed to follow the same routine speech for discharge after Brooklyn's birth. I reminded him, "I don't have any breasts, so I don't think that will be an issue."

Always one to teach, he told me, "Breast tissue develops along two 'milk lines' that start at the armpit and extend to the groin." I surprisingly replied, "Really?" It was new information to me. He comically clarified, "Yeah, well, I mean, it doesn't mean you'll grow a nipple on your arm and start breastfeeding, but at least you have an idea of how it works."

I found the information applicable shortly after Jaron's birth. While I was sitting beside his isolette in the NICU, I reached down to place my book back in my bag. As I leaned forward, my shirt brushed up against my left forearm. My shirt was wet! I couldn't believe it. During my pregnancies, I had to wear a bra insert just for my right side because my fake left boob amazingly got a bit larger, but nothing drastic. Nothing indicating the possibility I was capable of milk production. I couldn't even believe I was secreting breast milk! It leaked at the five o'clock area of the left breast through a tiny crevice of scar tissue. Realizing the fact of the new circumstance felt a little late for Jaron's birth, but I felt it may be of help for future babies. Like when Caden came along.

Honestly, the situation made me feel obligated to try. Although I had no clue how it might be obtained, I felt it was my duty as a mother to explore the possibility. I wish someone had given me permission to pass. If someone would have said something like: *Providing breast milk doesn't make you a better mom. It doesn't indicate how much you love your baby. In fact, your baby will still bond with you. Your baby still has great chances of growing healthy and strong. And your baby could even grow up to be an honor roll student.* No one said that. So, by suggestion of the lactation nurse, I found myself trying to pump milk out of the scarred crevice of my skin. I couldn't use a flange. There wasn't enough tissue to fill the compartment. Therefore, I placed the connector piece next to my skin to pump. It was sore, but I persisted. The skin broke down quickly. And I did too.

A tender beauty glows from a mama feeding her baby. John and Stasi Eldredge wrote about such beauty in their book, *Captivating*: "Beauty nourishes. It is a kind of food our souls crave. A woman's breast is among the loveliest of all God's works, and it is with her breast that she nourishes a baby—a stunning picture of the way in which Beauty itself nourishes us."[1] The unsuccessful process of making food for my baby reignited my confrontation with beauty. I felt completely deficient. Like my body didn't even meet the standard for being a woman.

My inability to nourish my baby partnered with the glaciers of emotion already inside me. I felt different. This was my third baby, and I knew I didn't feel the same as I did with the others. I felt incredibly sensitive. As if I were a delicate surface being scrubbed by a scouring pad. I expressed my concerns to Brandon.

"I don't feel right. I've been depressed before. I know the difference between sadness and depression. It's not just a bad day or a rough season. I'm telling you, I think I'm depressed and I need help."

What's the last thing a mom does for herself? It's get help. I didn't really even know how. My world was taking care of my kids. How did taking care of myself fit into that? And where would the money come from? We had pretty much budgeted out every single penny to get Brandon through school. In August of 2005, we decided he would quit working to pursue school full time. It felt like he had been working toward his degree forever. We didn't feel we'd ever get there taking one and two classes at a time. Our decision came in light of the fact I had a great job with health insurance. That was until Dad's unexpected death and us selling the business—taking with it my job and benefits. By the time Caden was born, we were tight on a budget until Brandon graduated in the spring of 2007. Nowhere in that plan was the cost for treating postpartum depression.

So we suffered. One night I threw all Brandon's clothes out of the closet, screaming at him that I felt crazy and needed help. He didn't know how to help me. Because, come to find out, he was in desperate need of help himself.

• • • • • • •

One night I was having difficulty finding some documents on our home computer. In my troubleshooting to find them, I found file names that would make any wife's heart fall to her intestines. *This could not be. How in the world did they get on our computer?*

I called Brandon who was always at school. The precious little miracles God gave to us were all tucked in bed. I informed him of my activity during the evening of trying to locate some documents. I told him of the ones I found. He insisted he had no idea how they got on our computer. I pressed in, knowing without a doubt my ears were receiving lies.

Dishonesty. Disappointment. Deception. Again.

Yes. Again. This was a place we had visited before.

Five years earlier in 2002, Brandon felt the overwhelming weight of an addiction he had battled since he was a child. At ten years old, he found pornographic material under a disguised label on a VHS tape. Having an understanding of the content in the images, he understood this tape was meant to be hidden and the arousings he felt had to be secret. He returned many times over through his young childhood and teenage years to view that which he knew was wrong but never had the strength to resist. What my husband kept hidden as a child and a teenager, he kept hidden as a young husband and new father. He wanted to stop but never could. So he chose to tell me about it.

I felt betrayed. I felt like I had been lied to. I felt foolish believing a young man could look upon the heart and not the flesh, because my flesh was scarred from a third-degree burn injury.

My desire to believe for such a man felt like a fairy tale. It certainly wasn't something I had observed firsthand. Quite the opposite actually. I came from a long line of infidelity. My dad had been unfaithful to my mom. Grandpa had been unfaithful to Grandma before their divorce. Grandma Cochrane had been unfaithful to her husband before he died. Two of my aunts both had unfaithful husbands. Infidelity was thick on both sides of my family. If those perfectly skinned, beautiful people suffered the insecurity of not being enough, then why in the world did I think my scarred-skinned body would have it any differently?

It was a subject I was slapped with before we even walked down the aisle. Someone questioned Brandon if he really could be proud being married to me, if he would be fulfilled with my scarred body.

Never would I have imagined those questions having any relevance in our marriage. But all of a sudden, they seemed to. Even though Brandon had this hang-up before I ever came into his life, I automatically felt it was my fault.

My beauty was lost on that dirt road; there is nothing attractive about my body, nothing special or exciting to offer. If I had what a man needed to be fulfilled sexually, this would have never happened. We really would be the strong Christian couple we were striving for, but since I've never had, nor will ever have, the feminine body of an inviting woman, I need to let my husband go to find a woman he can be fulfilled with sexually.

Brandon adamantly assured me he wanted me and that his addiction had nothing to do with his satisfaction or fulfillment in our physical relationship. He expressed his desperation for deliverance and healing from this bondage.

It made sense to me. That's why he told me, right?

We got books to read. We buckled down in prayer together. We made accountability arrangements. We were determined to overcome.

But apparently we hadn't, because there we were in 2007 facing the same darkness all over again. My internal battle of inadequacy automatically rebooted with the discovery of those files.

Nothing is true. Nothing in our relationship has ever been true. Brandon doesn't love me. He has never thought I was beautiful. He has never been fulfilled with me. He's just a nice guy who got caught up in a young relationship. He needs more to his life, but he now has kids with me and he doesn't know how to end it. There's too much he's invested into this relationship. He can't afford to start somewhere else right now, so pornography fulfills the needs in him that I could never meet.

Standing in the hallway between our bedroom and back door, Brandon knelt down, bowing over, holding my feet, declaring his love for me. I wanted to shake him off like dust on my sandals. I wanted him to leave. I didn't want to forgive him. I didn't trust him. I just couldn't imagine the thought of living with this kind of insecurity.

So much of me wanted to move on with my life with my three little precious people. But one memory continually returned to my mind. It was when we were engaged, so young without a lot of external encouragement. I was babysitting for a young mom in our church. Before I left she shared with me what someone had once told her: "Marriage isn't finding someone you can live with. It's finding someone you can't live without." I didn't want to live without Brandon, but I didn't really want to live with him either. I was just too hurt.

Although tempted to return to the self-destructive coping methods of an eating disorder, I turned to God, to His Word, to personal moments of worship, bringing the bitter disappointment, the broken emotion, and the raw wounds to His healing hands.

I said to Brandon, "I don't want to be married to you, but I know that whatever God wants to do in *my* life, He can only accomplish through our marriage."

I knew what I looked like in the mirror. But I had spent a good amount of my life fighting. Fighting the vent to breathe when mechanically ventilated. Fighting the pain as bandages were ripped off my raw body. Fighting to bear weight on my legs that had minimal muscle left. Fighting to walk. Fighting to climb stairs. Those years as a teenager, fighting an eating disorder. Fighting to find peace, security and joy again. And I was going to fight this fight too. No matter the outcome, I knew the Lord had my heart.

Steven Furtick said it like this in his book *Crash the Chatterbox*: "Whatever may be happening to me right now cannot disfigure God's view of me. In fact, the things that may be happening to me will only serve to drive my stakes down deeper. The less I can depend on circumstances to define my identity, the more I must look to the Lord to reinforce His thoughts concerning me and to impress them into my heart until I respond as if it's a second nature: I know who I am."[2]

It was a long process. We didn't even sleep in the same room for quite some time. However, the identity of our marriage was being redefined as we drove our stakes down deeper. We did things differently than before. We broke the secrecy and reached out for help.

Brandon had such admiration for our small group leader, Larry. Although Brandon didn't want to jeopardize Larry's opinion of him, Brandon knew he needed to humble himself and get the accountability and counseling he needed.

In reflection, Brandon said, "Pornography is like having your hands cuffed together, and then walking in a jail, being shackled to the wall, someone closing the bars, locking them and yet still thinking you can get out of it on your own. Reality is: you can't. You need someone to unlock the door and release the chains."

Brandon Meadows never gave up. And he became stronger through the transforming process of overcoming. He became *more* by way of confronting the emptiest places of his heart. More humble. More compassionate. More sensitive. Willing to abandon himself in order to speak hope into families hurting in similar ways. And he became more of a father, more of a husband, fully free to walk in who God designed him to be.

Our family reaped the blessing through the pain. Galatians 6:9 says, "Let us not become weary in doing good, for at the proper time we will reap a harvest if we do not give up."[3]

God had great plans on the other side of not giving up—some immediate, some distant.

On May 5, 2007, Brandon walked the stage in the Gallagher-Iba Arena on the campus of Oklahoma State University and received his bachelor of science in mechanical engineering. The doors to his life's dream had already started opening. He landed an ideal job launching his career.

I shed tears that day—tears of gratitude for where we had been and tears of anticipation for what was in store. Our goals were incorporated. His were mine and mine were his.

And now it was my turn to take aim at that vision of a nursing degree.

25

Gaining Focus

Shortly after Brandon and I married, we identified some kinks to smooth out.

Like how to fight.

Our first fight took place on day fifteen of our wedded bliss. We were staying in a hotel out of state for a Fourth of July family reunion. I went into the bathroom and remained there crying for a good amount of time, thinking, *They were right! Obviously, we shouldn't have gotten married. It's already over!* When I thought I didn't have any tears left to cry, I opened the bathroom door, made my way across the pitch-dark hotel room, and crawled into bed, hugging the edge of the mattress to avoid any contact with Brandon.

It appeared he wasn't bothered at all and had fallen right to sleep. Only he hadn't. He was very much awake. His arm wrapped around me, and he said those words we learned were so important in premarital counseling. "Heather, I need you."

I immediately began to cry again and said, "I need you too."

Having the first fight out of the way was good. Countless more followed, but our blueprint was to keep it fair, keep focused that we were on the same team and *always* need one another. It didn't always look tidy and clean. Sometimes things got superheated. But we circled back to one another through our set structure in dealing with problems.

Another issue was my inclination toward fear. Every time Brandon left the house for work, I'd imagine a variety of accidents. I was so scared he would die. But he was compassionate to my concerns and offered as much reassurance as he knew how. Apparently though, he didn't thoroughly understand my battle with fear. He found out one night after trying to scare me.

He hunkered down outside our kitchen window, shined a bright light in and made an atrocious sound like some wild boar. Unfortunately for him, he succeeded in scaring me. I sprang into a run toward our back bedroom. My heart was still racing when he came in the door, doubled over in laughter. I didn't think it was funny. Not at all. I was fuming. I've heard something said before that fear externalized is anger. Seems accurate in the way I responded that night. "Brandon Meadows! I don't like to be scared!" I yelled, hitting him. "Don't you *ever* do that to me *again*! It pisses me off!" And he didn't. Never. When it came to fight or flight, he learned I was a fighter.

Perhaps the largest concession he had to make involved the kitchen. Brandon was accustomed to some good cooking. He grew up on his mom's delicious meals. From fried okra and homemade bread to fancy desserts. She served them all.

Then there was me.

Food and I had had somewhat of a volatile relationship—certainly a love-hate dynamic. Nevertheless, I was determined to learn the ways of cooking for my new husband. Brandon was incredibly sensitive to my challenges and supportive of my efforts. He always said if a dish didn't turn out too tasty, we'd just put cheese on it. Something we certainly had to do a time or two. But I set lofty goals, sometimes getting in over my head. Exactly where I was with this chicken I needed to make. A whole chicken. The kind Grandma and I used to catch for chicken and dumplings. Those years had passed, and I was nearly dry heaving just taking the hen out of the packaging. So I summoned for help and she came to my rescue. But I knew it was something I *had* to conquer. I couldn't be calling Grandma each time I had a chicken dish. Although, she would have most certainly come.

The next time I prepared a recipe requiring a whole chicken, I shifted my frame of mind. Instead of dinner, I envisioned saving a life. *I'm a surgeon. I'm saving someone's life. I'm a surgeon. I'm saving someone's life.* I repeated it over and over until my queasiness in cooking chicken subsided.

Seems crazy to think my stomach was so sensitive to something so normal, considering my experience with a burn injury. I had known disgusting sights and smells just from my own body. There was a lot I learned throughout the journey. It's why so many of my nurses, doctors and physical therapists, at some point or another, spoke a future in health care over my life. I shunned the idea. Never did I imagine I'd be in one of their roles. Taking *care* of a patient, rather than *being* the patient! It took time, but that's exactly where my experiences were leading me.

• • • • • • •

School wasn't simply part of life's next stage, or some rite of passage for Brandon and me. It wasn't hard earned solely by us alone. It was hard earned by the commitment and sacrifices of one another and our kids. We weren't traditional students. It was intimidating to think we'd be the weirdos of the group. But thankfully that didn't deter us, because come to find out, there were a lot of people pursuing their education whose lives looked more like ours than we'd have thought.

I started taking classes the fall of 2007, the first semester after Brandon graduated. I finally pulled out those papers I had thrown in the desk drawer more than two years earlier. While I wasn't ready for OU yet, I did contact them to advise me on prerequisite classes for their nursing program. If Brandon and I had learned anything, it was to verify whether a class would transfer from one school to another before taking it. It's hard on an already tight budget to find out the class the community college said would transfer wouldn't actually transfer. So we first confirmed with the school that would be receiving the credit.

The advisors at OU were incredibly understanding and helpful with mapping out my community college classes before I enrolled in them. It felt like I had a boatload of prerequisites to take, because I did. The goal seemed nearly unreachable. Forever away. Nevertheless, I enrolled in one online class after another, slowly knocking them out at night after I put my babies to bed.

By the summer of 2009, I was down to my last three prerequisites. And expecting our fourth baby!

I was taking microbiology over the summer. I had mapped it out where I'd only have microbiology in the summer, anatomy in the fall, and physiology in the spring before starting the nursing program—one class each semester in consideration of having our new baby.

Our due date was mid-August. It'd work out perfectly to finish my summer class, have the baby, then start my class for the fall.

Only it didn't work out that way.

Thankfully, I had this unction to finish our main class project early. Probably because of everything I had on my radar. The assignment involved a lengthy paper and a PowerPoint presentation.

My friend Amber, who had been my maid of honor ten years earlier, was getting married the next month. Right after the baby was due. I was her matron of honor, and wedding festivities were already well underway. Her couple's shower was the evening of July 11th. I finished my project that morning and felt guilty because I just didn't want to go for the shower. Making the one-way, two-hour drive seemed dreadful. But I couldn't imagine not being there for her. So Brandon and I headed out, stopping by Target to grab a gift.

He dropped me off and pulled over to a nearby gas station to fuel up.

I walked over to print out the gift registry. The papers printed out in a neat pile. I picked them up to explore my options of what to purchase. But I couldn't read what it said. I could see the blue paper. I could tell it had words on it, but I couldn't make out what they were. For some reason, that alone didn't alarm me. I was still focused on what to get for a gift. I figured since it was a couple's shower, a game would be fitting. As I meandered through the store, trying to find the games, I came across an employee.

"Excuse me," I said. "Could you tell me where your board games are?"

I realized while I was talking to him that something was off. I couldn't see his entire face. Only his right eye and right cheek. The rest was blacked out.

Still, I didn't consider it to be a big problem. I just thought, *I hope he doesn't think I'm weird*, assuming my inability to make appropriate eye contact was obvious to him. He motioned his hand toward the direction I needed to go.

I made it over to the games, but I couldn't read the titles. I didn't know what to do. Not about me—about the gift. Taboo was written large enough, and the package was familiar enough I was able to identify it. *That's a good group game. I'll get it.* I picked it up and headed over to grab a card. Only I couldn't read what they said either. So I got a small blank gift card, then some tape and wrapping paper, and done. I headed to the register.

Brandon was waiting for me right outside the door. I got in the car and he asked, "So what did ya get?" I pulled some little sandals for Caden out of the bag. I started telling Brandon that I saw them while looking for the shower gift and just couldn't pass them up. Only that's not what I said.

"Monkey. Banana. Apple," I heard myself say.

Brandon gave a little courtesy chuckle but looked at me with a face as if to say, *That wasn't really funny.* I knew what I meant to say but had no idea why I ended up saying what I did. So I tried again and repeated another blurb of unintelligible garble. As I heard the words come out of my mouth, I stared blankly at Brandon. Tears slowly began streaming down my cheeks. I had no clue why I couldn't talk. I knew what I meant to say. I just couldn't say it.

Brandon quickly pulled the car off into another strip center parking lot. "I'm taking you to the urgent care," he stated. Since I couldn't communicate the words I wanted to, I just shook my head. I continued adamantly shaking my head no!

"There's something wrong!" Brandon exclaimed.

My thoughts were that whatever was wrong wouldn't be helped at the urgent care.

"I-c-e C-r-e-a-m." It took everything I had within me to focus on forming those words. I thought maybe my blood sugar was low. Even though I had never had issues before with blood sugar, I figured if I could get some ice cream in me, I'd be fine.

Brandon pulled into Braum's drive-through. He asked what I wanted, but I couldn't tell him. By that point, I couldn't form any words.

"Would you like chocolate almond with marshmallow topping?" he asked.

I shook my head yes, thinking how grateful I was he knew me well enough to know what I wanted when I couldn't communicate. After I ate the ice cream, I needed to go to the restroom. My speech returned so it seemed everything would be fine. I insisted we proceed to the wedding shower.

After my third request to stop for the restroom, Brandon asked, "You need to go *again?*"

"Yes," I said. Fanning the palms of my hands in front of my baby bump, I said, "I just keep having…" I couldn't find the word.

In a concerned tone, Brandon offered, "Contractions?"

"Is that the word?" I asked.

It sounded like it might be the word. But it didn't quite sound right to me. Apparently, I wasn't quite right. Brandon called our obstetrician and proceeded directly to the hospital.

By the time we got there, I felt absolutely fine. For real. It didn't appear I had any alarming symptoms. Nevertheless, the nurse took us into a hospital room, laid a gown on the bed and said, "Please leave a urine sample in the restroom." She walked out.

I looked at Brandon. "She thinks I'm staying," I said, irritated.

We had five weeks left until our due date. I knew if our baby was to come, it'd be a straight shot to the NICU. I had been there before and didn't have any plans of returning. I was determined to go home. Even when they came in to place my IV, I stayed in my clothes, convinced my obstetrician would let me go.

I was wrong.

This was our fourth delivery with him. He had delivered Brooklyn, Jaron and Caden. We had a strong relationship. I begged, pleaded and bargained with him. "I'll go on bed rest. I won't get up for anything but the bathroom."

"Listen," he started. "You have to stay, sweetie." *Sweetie?* He never called me sweetie, but now he was talking to me in this tone of a father deeply concerned about his daughter. It certainly got my attention. He continued, "Your blood pressure is still high, and I don't even know *what* it was when you couldn't see anything in Target. We can't take the risk of you seizing. You and the baby could die if we don't keep you here."

The tears returned, flowing down my face again.

The process of getting antibiotics for my heart commenced, along with my first experience of receiving magnesium sulfate. The mag was administered for my high blood pressure, which is also a medication used when needing to stop labor. But here we were trying to *induce* labor!

On top of that, for the first time ever, they started my epidural before I was even having pain. The goal was to minimize anything that would elevate my blood pressure, which pain is known to do. Unfortunately, the epidural didn't carry me through delivery. My fourth baby provided me the full feeling of a childbirth experience. However, the delivery was consistent with how the others had been: a prolonged process including the assistance of vacuum and forceps. Concern continued into the postpartum period as I was treated with an injection of Hemabate to stop hemorrhaging. It was the most difficult delivery we experienced. Brandon was stressed with a high sense of danger. The experience made for what would be our last delivery—fulfilling our dream for four.

That first night we were admitted, I laid awake praying until morning. Not that I wouldn't have to deliver early, but that the Lord would help me be okay when they took my baby away from me to the NICU.

He answered that prayer.

At 6:32 in the morning on Monday, July 13, 2009, Gavin Lee was born. He was our smallest baby, weighing five pounds, four ounces. He was eighteen and a half inches long. And he headed to the NICU for a short five-day visit.

Our patient experiences in the NICU from Jaron's stay to Gavin's were a night and day difference. Even though we were at the same hospital, it was apparent more had changed than just the newly redesigned state-of-the-art unit. The staff had implemented an overhaul of their commitment to patient-centered care.

By the time Gavin was born, the hospital had individual private rooms for babies, meaning parents didn't have to leave. It provided the option of rooming in with their baby over the duration of the stay. Furthermore, when it came time for medication to be administered, I didn't have to ask, "What is that you're giving my baby?" The question had been offensive to the nurse when Jaron was in the hospital. She snapped back at me, "Aminophylline." It was so condescending. As if I knew what aminophylline was. So I asked, "What is that?" She added, "It's just like caffeine to stimulate the baby to breathe." That was the short answer. I didn't know what I didn't know, but I knew she wasn't willing to provide any patient education.

Not so the story with Gavin. The staff came in the room at every shift change, introduced themselves and wrote their name on the whiteboard hanging on the wall. I was informed what our goals for Gavin were over the shift, like "He's still getting one liter of oxygen through the nasal cannula. We're going to see if he can come off that today." The staff explained to me that a *brady* was bradycardia, meaning an episode when Gavin's heart rate dropped below the normal limit; *tachy* was their short way of referring to tachycardia when his heart rate went above the normal limit; and a *desat*, their condensed word for desaturation, meant his oxygen level dipped down lower than desired.

Most importantly, I felt welcomed to be with my baby. When Jaron was born, the NICU was open, with several babies in one room. But I still wanted to be with him. I felt like such an irritation to the staff as they shuffled around my chair to work. For sure it made me feel bad, but not bad enough to leave my baby. That wasn't even an issue when Gavin was in the NICU.

The remodeled unit with private rooms was an incredible blessing. And the staff not only supported my desire to stay as long as Gavin was there, but they involved me in whatever care I could provide to him. It's the hardest thing having someone tell a mom what she *can* and *cannot* do with her own baby. Their encouragement for including me built an immediate bond with those I felt I could trust.

Those basic courtesies made for a completely different experience. And I wondered if maybe, just maybe, there might be a future place for me in NICU nursing.

26

Acceptance

I started my fall semester of anatomy after my eventful finish to microbiology. I went in with complete focus on the University of Oklahoma's College of Nursing. Although I still had two classes left to complete, anatomy would be the last one I'd take before applying to OU's program. I needed a strong grade. I had heard "Oh, you can't do the OU nursing program with kids" one too many times. Along with comments like "OU only takes fifty students at their Tulsa campus, so the average GPA to get in is really high." It would've been great to apply a nickel from every naysayer to my college bill!

Needless to say, I had to do my best to increase my chances of being accepted. I wasn't there to make friends. And yet I did.

The very first day of class, a girl took a seat on my right at the lab table. I introduced myself. She introduced herself. And come to find out, we not only had the same name but the same goal. OU!

I never thought I needed a friend. But what a gift it was to have one while facing the process. We encouraged each other through the challenges of completing classes while having kids at home. We shared the tedious task of applying to the program. And we exchanged anxieties over the waiting period to find out if we were accepted.

The time following my application was filled with a range of emotion. I started to question if I should have applied to some other programs. How crazy was it that I had come all this way to place all my eggs in one basket? I expressed my doubts to Brandon. He questioned me with words my own mouth had spoken.

"Didn't you say you felt God was calling you to go to OU?"

"Yes," I replied.

"Well, don't you trust Him that He'll open that door?"

I didn't know how to respond. Brandon was right. I needed to chill out and trust. "For thus said the Lord God, the Holy One of Israel, 'In returning and rest you shall be saved; in quietness and in trust shall be your strength.'"[1]

My letter came in April of 2010. I wanted to wait for Brandon to get home before opening it. Mom could hardly take the anticipation.

"I'm just gonna go on home, Heather," she said. "You can call and let me know what it says."

"You don't think I got in, do you?" I accused.

In Mom's comically high-strung manner, she said, "Well, I don't know! What if you didn't?"

"Thanks for the encouragement, Mom!" I teasingly shot back.

Once Brandon arrived, we all gathered together on the floor of our living room. I thought it'd be special to have Brooklyn read the letter. She had just turned nine and was a big part of this moment for me. Mom hardly maintained the patience to wait for Brooklyn to read it.

I opened the envelope. Removed the letter. Handed it to Brooklyn.

She unfolded the letter and started, "Heather R. Meadows, 375..."

Realizing she was starting at the very top portion of the letter where the address was listed, I said, "No, no, no, just skip down."

Brooklyn studied the letter for what seemed like an eternity, but in actuality was just a couple seconds. She proceeded, "Dear Ms. Meadows: We are pleased to inform you . . ." That's all I heard! We erupted with cheers, falling into a pile of hugs on the floor. Of course, I started crying, feeling the awe of being accepted. That one letter changed the course of my life.

My friend Heather was accepted in the program as well. It was a journey we'd get to continue together. We stepped onto the campus one day over the summer to buy our books, get our student identification badges and order our scrubs. While trying on sizes, Heather said, "These don't look like scrubs to me, Heth." (She rarely called me Heather, consistently shortening the pronunciation to *Heth*.) "They look like a uniform God has entrusted us to wear for His calling." I would never look at scrubs the same again. It was a wardrobe I sensed God Himself was honoring me to wear.

Even though we felt elated, the possibility of failure was heavy. However, every detail that unfolded before us didn't seem coincidental but appeared as if it were completely orchestrated. Down to being in the right place for a most timely talk. Heather and I passed by one of the nursing instructors after exploring the student-nursing lounge. A small program meant familiar faces. This instructor hadn't seen us before, so she sparked up a conversation. We were transparent in sharing our uncertainties regarding our ability to successfully complete the program. The instructor asked, "Do you know what happens to coal when it's placed under extreme pressure? It becomes a beautiful diamond. Remember that, girls. When the pressure feels too much, remember that you'll be a beautiful diamond when you finish."

She was certainly right about the pressure. I was so scared of failing. Math and science were never my strong subjects. And yet here I was pursuing a bachelor's degree . . . in science! What if I couldn't do it? Mom had agreed to watch the kids for me. Gavin was just thirteen months old. Brandon's mom enlisted to take Brooklyn and Jaron to school every day, and Aunt Donna pitched in offering to take Caden to his preschool. Oh yes. And then there was the pricey financial investment my husband was so willing to make. The second bachelor's degree in our house we'd be paying for.

The thought of letting so many people down was nearly overwhelming at times. So I prayed. I prayed always. On my drive to school I prayed. On my drive to clinical I prayed. On my drive home I prayed. I prayed before every test, before every quiz, on bathroom breaks, and walking between classes. God's peace reassured me. I felt Him speak to my heart, "Heather, I haven't brought you this far to drop you off on your own now. I'm still here. I'm still with you. Trust Me."

Any doubt I had was counteracted with how specifically things pieced together. The Lord wanted me at OU to connect with people, opening doors He had planned for me long before. "Lord, you are my God; I will exalt you and praise your name, for in perfect faithfulness you have done wonderful things, things planned long ago."[2]

Such things unfolded before me during my 3:00–11:00 clinical at Hillcrest Medical Center. The exact hospital I had been a patient many times over since my burn injury.

I had the privilege of taking care of an elderly man who was going for a hernia repair the next day. However, his hernia repair was scheduled to take place earlier in the day, before I would be back for my next shift. I really wanted to go to surgery with him. I asked my instructor if I could go early, even though it'd be before she would get there. "You'll have to call and ask surgery if it's okay," she stated.

I was at the school early the next morning to work the health fair, registering people for a local run. Our clinical group had a poster presentation with information regarding barefoot runners. Appropriate for the audience. The health fair began, and I slipped out briefly to call the hospital. They gave approval for me to observe the surgery. I checked with my instructor about cutting out a smidge early from the health fair to make the surgery. She agreed.

It was surreal taking the elevator down to level one and walking through those doors. I had been through them so many times before. But this was the first time I wouldn't be the one having surgery. I was given some surgical scrubs to change into, then directed into a surgical suite where I was told to find a corner and remain unnoticed because the surgeon didn't like students. I did just that.

Moments later, a man walked in the operating room and right up to me.

"Are you the student?" he asked.

"Yes, I am."

"Do you want to see something you'll never see again in your life?" he challenged.

"I certainly do," I answered.

We proceeded over to the computer where he pulled up an X-ray image. "This," he said, "is an Amyand's hernia, meaning the appendix is trapped within an inguinal hernia." He wrote the name on a note card and handed it to me. The opportunity to be there for the surgery was made even more valuable by the fact that only about 1 percent of all hernias contain portions of the appendix.[3]

"So, do you want to scrub in?"

I couldn't believe what I heard. This is the guy who didn't like students?

"What does that entail?" I responded.

"Well, come on. I'll show you!"

As we scrubbed our arms and hands he noticed my scars. "How did you get the burns?"

"I was in a motorcycle accident when I was seven. My brother and I hit a truck head-on. He was killed and I was burned. Third degree. Eighty-seven percent. I also had a tear to my descending aorta."

"Did Norberg take care of you?"

"He did!" I confirmed. "And Dr. Park."

"I remember you," he stated.

The moment was briefly somber as we progressed over to put on sterile gowns and gloves. The surgeon invited me right up next to him, instructing me to place my hands on the surgical field. The patient had respiratory insufficiency, so they didn't intubate him and put him on mechanical ventilation for the surgery. He wasn't completely out of it. Every now and again he aroused a bit, and they'd hit him with more sedation. Furthermore, he had quite a large abdomen. When the surgeon started cauterizing the fat, I started feeling lightheaded. Kind of queasy like the chicken used to do to me.

Suddenly I remembered I hadn't eaten all day, but it was too late now. I attempted a mind-over-matter challenge, telling myself what my clinical instructor would say: "Never let anyone take away your opportunity to learn." *Pull it together. Don't throw this opportunity out the window.* Leaving my hands where I was told to place them on the surgical field of the patient's abdomen, I stiffened my arms, stepped back and slowly dropped my head down between them.

Someone wrapped their arms around my waist. The team started asking, "What's her name? Do you remember her name?" Nursing students don't usually have names, I learned. I was simply known as *The Student.* Hearing their voices and trying my best to hold it together, my voice rose up informing, "Heaaatherrr." The arms around my waist gently pulled me back off the surgical field and placed me in a chair. Unfortunately, the surgical assistant who grabbed me had to repeat the entire scrubbing-in process getting a new gown and gloves before returning to his responsibilities.

Amazingly, the surgeon invited me in on his next case. I must have looked shocked because he amusingly clarified, "I'm not going to let you scrub in, but you're welcome to watch." It was such a nice offer. He added, "It's a skin graft for a fellow who got burned by a carburetor. You might want to see it."

I watched the surgery with somewhat of an out-of-body feeling. It almost didn't seem real. There was a lot of blood, but it didn't bother me at all. Apparently, the smell of cauterizing fat does. I watched as they obtained the skin graft, sent it through the machine poking holes in it to expand the coverage of surface area, and attached it to his skin with staples. I kept thinking, *Man. I feel so sorry for how much pain you're going to feel when you wake up.*

The entire experience was thrilling to share with my clinical group that evening. And hysterical. But the even bigger shocker came a couple months later when a marketing agent from the hospital contacted me. The surgeon had suggested me for an upcoming marketing campaign. I was overwhelmed they chose to use my story in an interview for a television commercial and a photo shoot for billboards and print ads. They labeled the material with one powerful phrase: "87% Burned. 100% Alive."

I wish Dad could have seen it. The description was a label he spoke over me many years before. Countless times, I heard people in the medical field, in the stories from newspapers and television, and in the community, refer to me as a burn victim. Naturally, I concluded that's what I was. Dad heard me say it one day. Probably around the time I was ten or eleven.

"That's something," he commented.

Unsure of what he was talking about, I asked, "What?"

"That you see yourself as a burn victim."

I was a little confused where he was going, but I knew it was somewhere, so I stared at him and waited for the rest of his thought.

"I would have thought you'd see yourself as a survivor. Victims die, but survivors live."

Dad gave me a new identity in that moment. I didn't fully understand it at the time, but he planted a new concept in me. One that would continue growing throughout my life, until one day, I would grasp the victory, power and strength that come from being a survivor. Seeing my face on a billboard with that very message reflected the significance of having my parent put such a label on me first. Looking at the sign, I realized how long it took to believe it for myself, but at some point along the way, I did!

My scars are evidence. Not of a deformity, but of a fighter. Not of pain and loss, but of strength and survival. The scars will remain on my body. Forever. I was a little girl with burn scars. A bride with burn scars. A new mom with burn scars. And one day, I'll be a grandma with burn scars. My body will, at some point, be placed in a grave with burn scars.

And throughout my days, people will continue to stare. Forever. They'll continue to notice me. Never will I blend in. Whether they ask or not, the *what-happened-to-her* looks will still show on their faces. However, I can determine what they see when they see me. Because I know full and well, they *will* see me. I can look at it as an opportunity instead of a misfortune, possibly sharing the story of hope found after tragedy.

So many years I prayed for God to take my scars away. But instead, He uses them in ways I would have never thought or imagined. What I saw as ugly, He had a way of spinning into something good for others to see. Even for me to see.

Nursing school opened not only opportunities, but also my eyes. My awareness of God's specific plans for my life grew. The marketing campaign was just one. Considering all the programs I could've applied to, I only applied to OU. Of all the clinical groups, to be in the specific one I was, to take care of the one particular patient going in for surgery, to meet the one surgeon opening the door to sharing my story for the hospital that had taken care of me—each step connecting to the other was mind blowing!

It was also overwhelming. Through my studies, I continually gained a deeper understanding of the miracle of my recovery. My instructor in pharmacology talked about the importance of keeping mechanically ventilated patients sedated: "When sedation wears off, they will arouse, see the lights off, hear the nurses talking and sense they are all alone." I could hardly contain my emotions. It was a memory shoved so far back in my mind but came crashing over me as I instantly remembered exactly what that was like.

When the subject of peritonitis was covered, I felt a fog come over me. "I had peritonitis," I said to my instructor during our short break. The statement fell off my lips with confusion that I could have survived peritonitis on top of a third-degree burn and a transection to my descending thoracic aorta. And then there was *that*. The heart injury. From what I was learning, I didn't think it was possible I could've had the injury I was told I had. So I retrieved my medical records to look for myself. Surely I didn't understand what I was reading, so I took the operative report to my instructor. She confirmed, "You're reading it correctly. There's no reason you should have ever made it to the hospital. It's certainly a miracle you lived."

On May 8, 2012, I graduated with my bachelor's of science in nursing—with distinction. The fact I could graduate with honors was a wink from God. I was the little girl who missed so much school I had to have a tutor. Although I never fell behind or had to be held back a grade level, I struggled to keep up. Kids called me "dumb" and "stupid" and "slow" when they found out I was tutored. There was my own perception of being weak in math and science. Then there were all the comments of doubt in whether I could be successful in a demanding program with four kids—one who was only a baby.

Graduating with honors wasn't about getting to wear a special stole and cords, although that was really neat. For me it was more about Romans 8:28, the Scripture I stood on facing each challenge of the calling I felt before me: "And we know that God causes everything to work together for the good of those who love God and are called according to his purpose for them."[4] I knew God had called me to nursing school. I could see how everything in my life had led me there. So when I questioned my ability, or lack thereof, I reminded myself He would work it all together for good. And He did. Down to every single detail. Including those attending my graduation festivities.

Lois came. She was the one nurse who seemed to understand my needs when I was a little girl unable to talk on the ventilator. The one who had to administer a blood transfusion without a cross match the night of the accident. The one who stood over my bed, demonstrating patient advocacy by arguing with my doctor on my behalf. She had moved to Florida but came and stayed for a week to commemorate the accomplishment.

My nurse Kelly came too. And so did Vicki. Vicki, who took care of me countless days but ever so often reflected on the day when a blood clot was emergently removed at my bedside.

I would have the privilege of taking care of future patients because these nurses had taken care of me. They celebrated the beauty of the long journey—watching as I received my nursing pin in the traditional ceremony followed by my walk across the graduation stage.

It was more than becoming a nursing school graduate. It was a time for displaying that heartache, difficulty and pain had a bigger and better role in my life. Everything God created me to be walked across that stage, illustrating His use of every preceding experience in molding and preparing me for *that* moment and each one to come thereafter.

27

Stewarding the Story

New stories continue to be written in my life. Some of them happy. Some not so much. But the threads of hope weave each one together, pulling in even the darkest of places to create an exquisite tapestry of God's magnificent love and supernatural ability.

I began my ministry of nursing right after graduating—getting to work in the same hospital where I received all my physical therapy to learn to walk again after the accident. It was the hospital where I had some deep roots: the one where Mom worked in accounting, Aunt Margie worked in business services, Grandma Cochrane worked as the clinical secretary of the cardiac care unit, and the one Barry worked in for a time. Saint Francis. It made for another full-circle detail.

Considering the various areas to work, I felt drawn to neonatal nursing for the opportunity to do for other babies what I had wanted to do for my own. Desiring to be the nurse for another as so many had been for me. Believing that while I couldn't possibly remember every patient, every patient *could* possibly remember me. Establishing my goal to be the nurse patients remembered for bringing goodness into their moments of need.

My ministry of writing coincided with the commencement of my nursing career. One of my instructors had agreed to help me in preparing for a leadership trip to Washington, DC, right before graduation. For some reason or another she said, "Heather, you should start a blog."

"A blog?" I responded. "Why would I start a blog? I don't cook. I don't do photography."

"But you write," she said.

"Who would want to read what I write?" I couldn't imagine my words being of benefit to the world.

"Just pray about it," she nudged. "Pray over the summer and see what you write."

She had to say, "Pray about it." 'Cause I did. And guess what? I wrote!

Grandma passed away over the summer, right before I started my job in the NICU. I was so happy for Grandma. I knew there was a beautiful eternity for her on the other side of this life that had rendered her confused and aggravated from Alzheimer's. But gracious. It was so hard to say goodbye to her.

So I did what I knew to do. I prayed. And I wrote.

I wrote about finding inspiration, joy, strength and encouragement from the most mundane to the most painful places of life.

By the fall, my former-instructor-turned-friend, Rhonda Lawes, came to my house and set up a blog. Amazingly, people started reading it. It opened the door for more speaking invitations. Steve and Michele had encouraged me in that direction, providing opportunities for me shortly after Brooklyn was born. I had served as a speaker for a handful of events, but the blog opened up more. People were able to read my messages, get an idea of what I was all about and determine if I'd be a fit for what they needed.

Through time, I realized some were having difficulty finding us online. The website address was long, and this thought kept returning: *simplify*. Visiting with people revealed they were searching for our website by my name. It seemed changing the website to my name would be the simple fix. But I had a lot of hesitation. "I don't want to send the message that this is all about me," I said to Brandon.

The same approach to starting the blog was the same approach in consideration of renaming the blog. I prayed.

I couldn't understand why, but I felt it was important. So Brandon and I got online to register *heathermeadows.com*. Only it was already taken. Someone already had it registered. It wasn't a website, just a registered domain. Therefore, we thought whoever had it registered would sell it to us. We had a little bit of money we could use, so we contacted a broker to see about purchasing it.

Time passed. No word.

More time passed. Still. No word.

The broker told us the owner wasn't responding, so we should increase our offer. We did.

Still. No word.

We made another offer but didn't have any response from that one either. Until finally, after four months, the broker sent an email saying the owner wanted ten thousand dollars for the domain name. Ten thousand dollars!

Obviously, *that* was a big negative. Nothing could've more affirmatively said we weren't supposed to have the name. I was dumbfounded. Not that we weren't going to get the website, but why I ever felt we were supposed to. I felt I had missed God's leading completely. Which made me question if it was really His will for me to even be writing and speaking at all.

The one component of peace I had in life was feeling secure in being guided by His desires for me. It may sound melodramatic, but that email caused me to question if indeed, this was all about me or if I truly was doing what God was calling me to do. I just want to be right *where* He wants me to be, *when* He wants me to be there. Therefore, I continued to pray, asking Him to examine my heart and my intentions.

I felt this rise up in my heart. *Heather, you want the website to share this story, so share the story.*

It felt absolutely crazy, but I did just that. I wrote a letter to the owner, telling my story and how we wanted to use the website in sharing it. I emailed the letter to our broker on a Monday morning. And I continued to pray the Scripture I had stood on throughout the process, "'Not by might nor by power, but by my Spirit,' says the Lord Almighty."[1]

I prayed, "It's not by *my* might, Lord. I can't make this happen. If it does, it has to be by *You*. If it is Your will, move upon the heart of the owner by Your Spirit."

I opened my email the following Thursday. To my amazement, there was a message from the owner. It read, "I wanted to make sure you are truly the person buying the domain. You have a very inspiring story; your strength is nearly unimaginable. If you are truly looking to use this domain to start a new chapter on your journey, let me know and we will work something out!"

The owner informed me he thought he was negotiating with a realty company in the Pacific Northwest leading to the steep cost. Once he knew otherwise, he no longer wanted to sell the domain to me at all; but rather *give* it to me for a promise! We agreed to come speak at their church in exchange for the domain name. We traveled to Massachusetts to share our story and meet Joel and Lori, a couple who gave us not only a website, but also a beautiful new friendship.

In his book *The Grave Robber,* Mark Batterson writes, "By definition, a God-ordained dream will always be beyond your ability and beyond your resources. But that is how God gets the glory."[2] Ten thousand dollars was certainly beyond our resources. In addition to the Lord growing us in obedience and trust through the experience, He also removed my identity from my name. When I see *heathermeadows.com*, I see Him! It was only by His might, His power, His Spirit. I'm so grateful we didn't quit short of the opportunity to see Him so creatively bring it all together. And in such a way that was beyond what I could have thought or imagined.

• • • • • • •

The website continues to be a big tool in sharing the messages beating out from my life's heart. When I think, *It doesn't matter; no one is depending on my post this week*, I hear the still small voice of the One who first called saying, "It matters to Me." God blesses the little things. He rejoices over the faithfulness demonstrated through small beginnings.[3] Regardless of the magnitude or insignificance of what I have to offer, He uses every piece for His plans and purposes, giving value to each one of my days.

So I write. I speak. I live.

I live for not one, but for two. Not just for me, but for Jon too.

I encounter each day with a sense of responsibility. Trading the survivor's guilt for the opportunity to make the most of life for both of us. For all those years, I just wanted to be with him. For all those years, I wish I could've had the choice whether or not to live as a sole survivor from our journey on the dirt road that day. For all those years, I longed to leave this life and join him in eternity, asking, "Why didn't I die too?"

Today, I'm so thankful I didn't. I'm so grateful the water of grief never extinguished the fire in my fight. Never missing out on all the goodness in store for the other side of our tragedy. I've concluded throughout my days that we miss the joy of new seasons when we continue grieving the old ones.

So I don't just live. I live happy.

I continue living on the land Grandma and Grandpa Creekmore bought back in 1951, in the home Brandon and I built for our family fifty years later in 2001, raising our children, the fifth generation to live on this land—this land that is our heritage and our roots. I live as a neighbor to my mom like she did to her mom. She's not right across the driveway, but she's a hop, skip and jump away. I live driving back and forth on the road where Jon and I had our accident as I conduct a common-life routine of chauffeuring kiddos to activities.

Encountering the area throughout normal everyday life has defused the heaviness of what happened there. Just like when I see the scars I carry on my body, when I pass the location, I don't think *victim*; I think *survivor*. I'm a survivor, still surviving through the ongoing experiences of periodic operations, tallying up over one hundred at this point. Dad kept a running count of procedures and operations until he reached the triple-digit mark. Being a survivor isn't something I did; it's something I continue doing.

I live with fun. I live with enjoyment.

And even though it's not popular, I live believing in fairy tales. Sometimes it's a belief that's fought for. Walt Disney had to. When it came time for distributing *Snow White and the Seven Dwarfs*, executives told Disney to play down the fairy-tale angle because audiences didn't buy fairy tales. They wanted to market it as a romance between the Prince and Snow White, simply calling it *Snow White*. But Disney fought for his fairy tale, saying, "No, it's *Snow White and the Seven Dwarfs*." He continued, "It's a fairy tale. It's what I put a million and a half into, and that's the way it's going to be sold."[4]

Fairy tales aren't cheap. They cost a lot. Sometimes they look like a dead brother, a burned little girl, a grieved family and scarred skin. As much as I admire the stories Walt Disney worked so diligently and so persistently to give us, God writes even better fairy tales on the pages of our life. We just have to give Him the pages to work with. Just like Disney fought for his fairy tale, God is fighting for ours. He sent His one and only Son to die on a cross to give hope for eternity and for today.

I live as a steward. Stewarding the story, this beautiful story of triumph over tragedy, peace over anxiety, light after darkness, happiness over hurt, healing after pain, courage over fear, joy after grief, beauty from ashes, hope after brokenness, strength over weakness.

I live with a confident optimism in spite of life's heartaches. Helen Keller said it best: "Optimism is the faith that leads to achievement."[5] Triumph is attained from the combination of hope and confidence.

I'm confident no matter what I face, I won't face it alone. I never have. God's presence never left me. From the moment my body burned on a dirt road to the uncertainties of four high-risk pregnancies, He was there. He never left me. And He never will. His past faithfulness gives me future confidence.

That fire produced more than it consumed.

First, the trial of fire created the components of a genuine faith—a faith that says I can be joyful regardless of how good or bad my circumstances may be. "In this you rejoice, though now for a little while, if necessary, you have been grieved by various trials, so that the tested genuineness of your faith—more precious than gold that perishes though it is tested by fire—may be found to result in praise and glory and honor at the revelation of Jesus Christ."[6]

Second, the suffering of fire developed strong endurance, character and hope in me. Nothing was wasted. I was made into more, even when it seemed I'd live as less. "Not only that, but we rejoice in our sufferings, knowing that suffering produces endurance, and endurance produces character, and character produces hope, and hope does not put us to shame, because God's love has been poured into our hearts through the Holy Spirit who has been given to us."[7]

Finally, the fire established my resolve that no matter what I faced, *nothing* would outmatch the power of the One who walked me through it. "When you pass through the waters, I will be with you; and through the rivers, they shall not overwhelm you; when you walk through fire you shall not be burned, and the flame shall not consume you."[8] That's right. Whether it be the flame of death, or injury, insecurity, disappointment, shortcoming, doubt, fear, grief or despair, the flame will not consume me!

The fire didn't disprove God's faithfulness. It proved it. He has been faithful *beyond* the fire.

Who would have ever imagined tragedy could be transformed into something good?

It's possible . . . if put in the right hands.

Catch It and Put It In Your Heart

I have this thing I do with my kids when we leave one another. Usually it's when we're dropping off for school or when they're heading out the door to work or practice. I blow them a kiss and say, "I love you." They raise their arm in the air, and with an open palm grasp the invisible kiss in their hand. With a closed fist, as to not drop their newly caught kiss, they move their hand to their chest, placing it over their heart. An "I love you too" comes back my way with a kiss for my heart too. When we first started our routine of affection, I'd say, "Catch it and put it in your heart." I don't have to say it anymore, but sometimes I do for old times' sake.

God does that for us. He sends us love to catch and put in our heart. I pray this book has illustrated that type of message for you. Did you connect with the components of this story? Maybe not with a life-threatening injury but the identification of a soul-threatening injury—the one where all hope seems lost, and only pain and darkness accompany the details of the day. Allow me to ask, would you have ever imagined tragedy could be transformed into something good? God could imagine it. He is in the business of transforming tragedy.

If you would like to invite Him into your journey to begin the transforming work in your life, simply pray this prayer:

> *Lord Jesus, I invite You into my life to be my Lord and Savior. I ask for You to take full control of every area in my life, from the worst mistakes to the deepest hurts. I ask You to forgive me of my sin. I believe You died on the cross for my forgiveness and You rose again. I believe You will return one day for me. For such time, I give You all my days to work all things together in Your good, pleasing and perfect will.*

John 3:16: "For this is how God loved the world: He gave his one and only Son, so that everyone who believes in him will not perish but have eternal life."[1]

Romans 3:23: "For everyone has sinned; we all fall short of God's glorious standard."[2]

Psalm 32:8: "The Lord says, 'I will guide you along the best pathway for your life. I will advise you and watch over you.'"[3]

Isaiah 46:3–4: "I have cared for you since you were born. Yes, I carried you before you were born. I will be your God throughout your lifetime—until your hair is white with age. I made you, and I will care for you. I will carry you along and save you."[4]

There is a lot that may not make too much sense. It's hard to wrap our minds around the magnificent supernatural work of God. His ways are so much higher. There are many more things I'd love to share with you, but the pages of this book have to come to a close. Please, find a church family to connect with if you haven't already. You may have to visit a few to explore where your family is, but just know God has a church family set apart for you where you can grow in Him and serve His people. Your life will be transformed in ways you never imagined possible.

Visit
**heathermeadows.com/
bookpics**
to see photos
from the
powerful moments
captured
throughout this
inspiring story.

A BLESSED JOURNEY BY

HeatherMeadows.com

Acknowledgments

I've heard writers compare writing a book to having a baby, and I've thought: *Really? Having a baby? I don't know about that. I've had four. I'm sure writing a book is laborious, but I don't know that it's like having a baby.*

Well, let me say, I've learned a few things through this process and one of those is that writing a book is very much like having a baby. There was a place within me where the words grew long before I ever began typing them into a manuscript. Then there was a delivery team who came alongside me to bring it from manuscript to book. It is my hope for those individuals to know how valuable their contributions were to this project and to what I pray is accomplished in the lives of readers through it.

Many thanks to...

...my copy editor, Kim Foster. You connected with and cared for this book polishing it into the best version we could offer. Thank you for holding my hand and teaching me the publishing ropes in the process.

...Robin Bethel for the proofread and Kevin Mullani with Tru Publishing for seeing it across the finish line to print.

...my beta readers for providing, not only the first set of eyes on this manuscript but the many prayers over it.

...my high school English teacher, Donna Elliott for offering the final proofread, providing the most fitting touch while creating one of those full-circle life moments.

...everyone who made the cover photo come together—Josh with K&N Motorcycles for providing the motorcycle in the photo; Amber McCollough for always knowing just what to do with my hair, in addition to being one great stylist, you're also one incredible neighbor; and to Mallory Billups for always bringing heart along with your incredible photography skills to capture a message in one image.

...my friend, Sara Mankin for your unwavering vision and constant commitment toward every graphic design project over the last six years; from blogging, speaker menus, brochures, magnets, pens and bookmarks to now the cover and interior designs of this book. I know this was part of the Lord's plan when He connected us back during those crazy years of nursing school. He so creatively blessed my life with your creativity!

...our online-home advertisers for your financial support in laying the groundwork for this project and launching it out to readers, including Marshall with Byler Media who designed and built our website with a link to powerful images from this journey.

...Jason Ruby, Gary Fears, Katherine Malloy, Krista, Barry, Aunt Donna and Mom for meeting with me to recount the difficult details of that tragic day. Your interviews provided essential pieces for sharing this story powerfully.

...Roy and Kathy at Hersman-Nichols Funeral Home, Saundra at Porter First Baptist and Danette at Rogers State University for your time to provide records and information relevant to the construction of this book.

...my sweet black lab, Ruby Sue, who sat by my side as I cried composing the words from the most difficult to the most joyful pieces of this story. Every person should know the love, support and comfort of a precious pet.

...Mom, for your supernatural faith and ever-present optimism. Thank you for being the type of explorer who searches for light even in darkness. Our world needs more individuals passionate to find such a discovery.

...Brooklyn, Jaron, Caden and Gavin for the unlimited inspiration you bring to my life. You are the highlights of every story. You completed my world and I'm more passionate for it, because of each of you.

...Brandon, for seeing this book and what it could accomplish long before it was part of our scenery. Thank you for pushing me even when it was out of sight. You have an ability to see what so many of us miss. I'll be forever grateful you sighted something in me to share for whatever we may find across our horizon.

...You, Lord—thank You for nudging me to see beyond myself and catch a glimpse of how You desired to use this journey in the lives of others. I pray I have been a good steward of this story You entrusted me to carry. I'm so honored to write it for You.

Notes

Chapter 1

1. OKC: The Boom, the Bust and the Bomb, directed by Mick Cornett, aired June 13, 2016 (Oklahoma City, OK: Oklahoma Educational Television Authority). Reprinted by permission.
2. Servicemen's Readjustment Act of 1944, also known as the GI Bill, https://www.ourdocuments.gov/doc.php?flash=true&doc=76.
3. Paul B. Hatley, "Oklahoma Military Academy," The Encyclopedia of Oklahoma History and Culture, accessed July 10, 2018, http://www.okhistory.org/publications/enc/entry.php?entry=OK064.

Chapter 4

1. Sharon Lewis et al., Medical-Surgical Nursing, 7th ed. (Saint Louis, MO: Mosby Elsevier, 2007), 488.
2. Frederic Martini, Michael Timmons, and Robert Tallitsch, Human Anatomy, 6th ed. (Glenview, IL: Pearson Benjamin Cummings, 2009), 555–6. Reprinted by permission.
3. The University of Rochester Medical Center, s.v. "Blood Type and Crossmatch," accessed April 17, 2018, https://www.urmc.rochester.edu/encyclopedia/content.aspx?contenttypeid=167&contentid=blood_type_crossmatch.
4. National Library of Public Medicine, s.v. "Transfusion Reaction—Hemolytic," accessed April 17, 2018, https://medlineplus.gov/ency/article/001303.htm.
5. Lewis et al., Medical-Surgical Nursing, 491.
6. Lewis et al., Medical-Surgical Nursing, 1650.
7. Lewis et al., Medical-Surgical Nursing, 1618.

Chapter 5

1. Hebrews 11:1 (NIV).

Chapter 6

1. Online Etymology Dictionary, s.v. "Indian summer," accessed January 25, 2018, https://www.etymonline.com/word/Indian%20summer.
2. Fran Cox, Dare to Be Different, Porter School 1988 Yearbook, Porter School (Marceline, MO: Walsworth Publishing, 1988).

Chapter 7

1. Mayo Clinic, s.v. "Peritonitis," accessed July 3, 2018, https://www.mayoclinic.org/diseases-conditions/peritonitis/symptoms-causes/syc-20376247.
2. "Pseudomonas aeruginosa in Healthcare Settings," Centers for Disease Control and Prevention, accessed July 3, 2018, https://www.cdc.gov/hai/organisms/pseudomonas.html.

Chapter 9

1. Audra Clark, Jonathan Imran, Tarik Madni, and Steven Wolf, "Nutrition and Metabolism in Burn Patients," Burns and Trauma 5, no. 11 (April 2017), https://burnstrauma.biomedcentral.com/articles/10.1186/s41038-017-0076-x.

Chapter 10

1. Jason Ankeny, "About James Horner," Apple Music Preview, accessed February 14, 2018, https://itunes.apple.com/us/album/an-american-tail-original-motion-picture-soundtrack/596506504.
2. Linda Ronstadt and James Ingram, "Somewhere Out There" (from An

American Tail), James Ingram Chart History, Billboard, accessed February 14, 2018, https://www.billboard.com/music/james-ingram/chart-history/hot-100/song/332383.

Chapter 11

1. Laurie Winslow, "CMC to Relocate Services," Tulsa World, January 7, 2000, http://www.tulsaworld.com/archives/cmc-to-relocate-services/article_d790669a-b75a5ba0-ba59-6979c536f36e.html.

2. "You Give Love a Bad Name," by Desmond Child, Jon Bon Jovi, and Richie Sam bora, Slippery When Wet, Bon Jovi, 1986, Spotify.

3. E. B. White, Charlotte's Web (New York, NY: Harper & Row, 1952), 37.

Chapter 12

1. Krystine I. Batcho, "What Your Oldest Memories Reveal about You," Psychology Today, April 4, 2015, https://www.psychologytoday.com/blog/longing-nostalgia/201504/what-your-oldest-memories-reveal-about-you. Reprinted by per mission.

2. Mark Batterson, If: Trading Your If Only Regrets for God's What If Possibilities (Grand Rapids, MI: Baker Books, 2015), 28–9.

3. Janet Jackson, vocalist, "Escapade," by Janet Jackson, Jimmy Jam, and Terry Lewis, on Janet Jackson's Rhythm Nation 1817, A&M Records, 1990, Spotify, https://open.spotify.com/track/5HAvICkfe50DUjv8ghwTrz?si=IqREsxjVQ_iGDLPYiu-lw.

4. Jerry Webber, Positively Oklahoma, aired November 1988, on KJRH Channel 2 News, Tulsa, Oklahoma, https://www.youtube.com/watch?v=UUJaYmdB2M.

Chapter 13

1. "Long Term Treatment for Burns," Burn-Recovery.org, accessed March 6, 2018, http://www.burn-recovery.org/long-term-treatment.htm.

Chapter 15

1. Alexander G. Reeves and Rand S. Swenson, "Pain," chap. 19 in Disorders of the Nervous System, site ed. Rand Swenson (Hanover, NH: Dartmouth Medical School, 2008), accessed March 15, 2018, https://www.dartmouth.edu/~dons/part_2/chap ter_19.html.

2. Rachel Nall, "Hyperalgesia: What You Need to Know," Medical News Today, Au gust 6, 2017, https://www.medicalnewstoday.com/articles/318791.php.

3. "Facial Feed-Back Hypothesis," Psychology.iresearchnet.com, accessed March 14, 2018, http://psychology.iresearchnet.com/social-psychology/emotions/facial-feedback-hypothesis/.

4. Buck Ross, "Nonverbal Behavior and the Theory of Emotion: The Facial Feedback Hypothesis," Journal of Personality and Social Psychology 38, no. 5 (June 1980): 813.

5. Bob Benson and Phil Johnson, "Give Them All to Jesus," Hymnary.org (originally published in Praise! Our Songs and Hymns by Singspiration Music, 1979), copyright 1975 by Dimension Music, accessed March 17, 2018, https://hymnary.org/text/are_you_tired_of_chasing_pretty_rainbows.

6. Benson and Johnson, Give Them All.

Chapter 16

1. Neil Morris, "A Clean Bill of Health: The Physiological and Psychological Effects of Bathing," Visually, published by Better Bathrooms, accessed March 18, 2018, https://visual.ly/community/Infographics/health/clean-bill-health-physio logical-and-psychological-effects-bathing.

2. Albert Einstein, "Quotable Quotes," Goodreads, accessed July 27, 2018, https://

www.goodreads.com/quotes/82878-i-must-be-willing-to-give-up-what-i-am.

Chapter 17
1. Bob Goff, Love Does: Discover a Secretly Incredible Life in an Ordinary World (Nashville, TN: Nelson Books, 2012), 57. Reprinted by permission.
2. Genesis 3:1 (ESV).
3. Genesis 3:4–5 (ESV).

Chapter 18
1. C. S. Lewis, The Problem of Pain (New York, NY: Harper One, 1940 & 1996), 91.

Chapter 19
1. Larry Osborne, Thriving in Babylon: Why Hope, Humility, and Wisdom Matter in a Godless Culture (Colorado Springs, CO: David C. Cook, 2015), 62.
2. John 9:1–5 (ESV).
3. 2 Corinthians 4:17–18 (NIV).

Chapter 20
1. Proverbs 3:5–6 (NKJV).
2. Gretchen Carlson, Getting Real (New York, NY: Penguin Books, 2015), 57. Re printed by permission.

Chapter 21
1. Lisa Bevere, Lioness Arising: Wake Up and Change Your World (Colorado Springs, CO: WaterBrook Press, 2010), 92. Reprinted by permission.
2. Romans 8:31 (ESV).

Chapter 22
1. Philippians 4:6–7 (NLT).
2. Proverbs 1:33 (ESV).
3. Romans 15:13 (ESV).
4. Rick Warren, The Purpose Driven Life (Grand Rapids, MI: Zondervan, 2002), 94. Reprinted by permission.
5. Psalm 34:18 (ESV).
6. Psalm 56:8 (NLT).
7. Lamentations 3:21–24 (NLT).

Chapter 23
1. Read Psalm 139:13.
2. Romans 8:39, NLT.
3. Oh Baby! Names, sv. "Heather," accessed April 4, 2018, http://www.ohbabynames.com/meaning/name/heather/744#W0f599VKjIU.
4. Max Lucado, Come Thirsty: No Heart Too Dry for His Touch (Nashville, TN: W Publishing Group, 2004), 41. Reprinted by permission.
5. Isaiah 41:10, ESV.

Chapter 24
1. John Eldredge and Stasi Eldredge, Captivating: Unveiling the Mystery of a Woman's Soul (Nashville, TN: Thomas Nelson, 2010), 39. Reprinted by permission.
2. Steven Furtick, Crash the Chatterbox: Hearing God's Voice above All Others (Colo rado Springs, CO: Multnomah Books, 2014), 46. Reprinted by permission.
3. Galatians 6:9 (NIV).

Chapter 26
1. Isaiah 30:15 (ESV).
2. Isaiah 25:1 (NIV).
3. Galyna Ivashchuk et al., "Amyand's Hernia: A Review," Medical Science Monitor

20 (2014): 140–6, https://www.ncbi.nlm.nih.gov/pmc/articles/PMC3915004/.

4. Romans 8:28 (NLT).

Chapter 27

1. Zechariah 4:6 (NIV).
2. Mark Batterson, The Grave Robber: How Jesus Can Make Your Impossible Possible (Grand Rapids, MI: Baker Books, 2014), 141.
3. Read Zechariah 4:10 and Luke 16:10.
4. Bob Thomas, Walt Disney: An American Original (Glendale, CA: The Walt Disney Company, 1994), 141.
5. Helen Keller, Optimism: An Essay by Helen Keller (Memphis, TN: Bottom of the Hill Publishing, 1903 & 2011), 40.
6. I Peter 1:6–7 (ESV).
7. Romans 5:3–5 (ESV).
8. Isaiah 43:2 (ESV).

Catch It and Put It in Your Heart

1. John 3:16 (NLT).
2. Romans 3:23 (NLT).
3. Psalm 32:8 (NLT).
4. Isaiah 4:3–4 (NLT).